BRIGHT EYES, APE CITY

EXAMINING THE PLANET OF THE APES MYTHOS

BRIGHT EYES, APE CITY

EXAMINING THE PLANET OF THE APES MYTHOS

EDITED BY

RICH HANDLEY
JOSEPH F. BERENATO

SEQUART ORGANIZATION   EDWARDSVILLE, ILLINOIS

Bright Eyes, Ape City: Examining the Planet of the Apes Mythos
edited by Rich Handley and Joseph F. Berenato

Cover art by Patricio Carbajal. Cover design by Joseph F. Berenato and Julian Darius. Book design by Julian Darius. Interior art is © their respective owners.

Published by Sequart Organization. Edited by Rich Handley and Joseph F. Berenato.

For more information about other titles in this series, visit Sequart.org/books.

Contents

Bitter Rind, Succulent Fruit: An Introduction

by Rich Handley

Sometimes, being a fan requires a healthy measure of tolerance. (Wearing a shiny new pair of rose-colored glasses doesn't hurt, either.) Nothing, not even our favorite hobbies, can completely satisfy us at all times. The thrilling, thought-provoking highs are often offset by the forehead-smacking, face-palming lows, and only a willingness to take the bad with the good enables us to sustain our fandom. And, yet, sustain it we do. We're fans. It's our nature.

No matter what franchise you find delectable, it's sometimes necessary to suffer the bitter rind to reach the sweet, succulent fruit within. If you're a *Star Trek* fan, it's easy to devour masterpieces like "The City on the Edge of Forever," "Yesterday's *Enterprise*," "Far Beyond the Stars," and *Star Trek II: The Wrath of Khan*. But to get to those, you need to sift through missteps like "And the Children Shall Lead," "Code of Honor," "Threshold," and "These Are the Voyages." And if you're into *Star Wars*, loving *A New Hope* and *The Empire Strikes Back* is far easier than embracing *The Star Wars Holiday Special* and the *Ewoks* cartoons.

Planet of the Apes fans have had to digest our fair share of bitter rind as well. As addictive as the classic films, live-action television show, and current movies are (basically, anything starring Roddy McDowall or a lookalike, or Andy Serkis, is well worth watching), there are other *Apes* tales that are admittedly less appetizing. Anyone who has ever read Marvel UK's "Apeslayer" storyline, with its Fabio-haired hero and Martian gorilla overlords; or marathoned the animated series, *Return to the Planet of the Apes*, with its giant screeching eel-bird, repetitive backgrounds, and subpar voice acting; or sat through Tim Burton's 2001 "reimagining," with its sleep-acting Mark Wahlberg and nonsensical conclusion, knows this all too well. Each of these tales actually contains fun moments among the dreck, especially the cartoon... but *Planet of the Apes'* answer to *The Wrath of Khan*, they certainly are not.

Roddy McDowall, the ape of a thousand (or at least three) faces.

When it comes to the apes, there are many good stories out there, but a number of weak ones as well. It's the *great* stories along the way that keep the latter from dampening our enthusiasm for the franchise. Somehow, the very existence of *Escape from the Planet of the Apes*, *Conquest of the Planet of the Apes*, and *Dawn of the Planet of the Apes* makes up for a dozen Fabio-esque Apeslayers, ear-splitting eel-bird screeches, and comatose Mark Wahlbergs.

Well, mostly.

Each author assembled for this anthology has taken a look at some aspect of the *Planet of the Apes* saga, from his or her own unique perspective. The first volume (2015's *The Sacred Scrolls: Comics on the Planet of the Apes*) dissected every comic book set in the *Apes* universe, from the 1960s up to press-time. For this second volume, we tasked the writers (some returning, some new) with examining the films themselves, as well as both TV series, the novels, the stage show and rodeo (yes, there were an *Apes* stage show and rodeo), the music, politics, parodies, precursors, real-world ape behavior, and more.

This, of course, meant *someone* had to discuss the 2001 reimagining, a film widely panned by viewers and critics ever since its theatrical release. The movie, for many fans, remains *Planet of the Apes'* bitterest rind. Needless to say, when the authors were invited to pitch essay topics, no one volunteered to tackle Burton's film (though several might have gladly tackled Burton himself). And so it fell to me to return to the director's controversial entry in *Apes* lore. I can hear you all groaning from here.

The thing is, though… I was fine with that. In fact, I looked forward to it.

You see, I'm a fan who tends to root for the under-ape. To me, even bitter *Planet of the Apes* rind is still fruit to be devoured. While not all apes are created equal (no sane person, for instance, would claim that the original Charlton Heston film is on par with the apes' comic-book crossover with *Alien Nation*'s Tenctonese), I've never met an ape I didn't like. I've met several I didn't love, and a few that made me want to have myself lobotomized like Landon, but I can find something to enjoy about every *Apes* tale published, filmed, or broadcast… even Apeslayer, even crossovers, even a drunk-sounding cartoon voiceover actor droning the line "Billll? Jeffff? Novaaaa!" and, yes, even Tim Burton's much-maligned franchise reboot.

For me, writing and reading about the less-popular corners of simian lore is not a chore – it's all part of the fun. It's the same reason *Star Trek* fans get a kick out of the absurd episode "Spock's Brain." It's why *Star Wars* enthusiasts vainly hope that Lucasfilm will someday announce an official Blu-ray release of the *Holiday Special*, complete with deleted scenes. It's why many *Stargate* collectors have the DVD of the truly horrid *Stargate Infinity* cartoon on their shelves, even if they can rarely bring themselves to watch it. And it's why 007 aficionados hold out hope of *James Bond Jr.* being packaged as a complete TV series on Blu-ray.

In short, it's why editing this book and its predecessor has been a labor of love.

In *The Sacred Scrolls*, I revisited the oft-overlooked *Apes* comics from Malibu Graphics. I enjoy those Malibu tales more than most, and so I was able to discuss not only the series' flaws, but also what it got right. As it happens, that's also how I feel about the Burton reboot. (I know, I know. Heresy. Call Doctor Zaius.) It's the worst of the eight (soon to be nine) films, sure, with many writing, directing, and acting problems. But for my money, it's not the *complete* disaster it's often made out to be. Alongside its long list of negatives are aspects worthy of praise – not the least of which is the casting of such talented actors as Tim Roth, Helena Bonham Carter, Paul Giamatti, Michael Clarke Duncan, Cary-Hiroyuki Tagawa, David Warner, and Glenn Shadix.

Tim Burton's reimagining was neither the *Apes* film we deserved, nor the *Apes* film we needed, nor the *Apes* film we wanted, nor... actually, I'm not sure where I was going with all that, but when I think "Burton," I think "Batman." Never mind.

In any case, given the retrospective reviews I've read of late, it appears I am not alone. Fifteen years have passed since the film hit theaters, and the anger and disappointment have had time to subside. Some folks are now re-appraising the reimagining, and are finding that time has been somewhat kind to it – despite its problems, the movie doesn't suck as badly as they recall. There's suckage, some of it major, which explains the headache I had after spending so many hours pondering Mark Wahlberg's totem pole-like performance. But it doesn't *entirely* suck. Plus, without the film, we'd never have been treated to the surprisingly superior comic books and novels that spun off from that reboot. When there's no rind, there's also no fruit.

The other authors' essays (you know... the ones focused on areas of the franchise that people actually *do* like) turned out fantastic, and I couldn't be happier to have them in this follow-up to *The Sacred Scrolls*. I'm especially grateful to award-winning novelist, *Star Trek* writer, and tribble creator David Gerrold, who penned the novelization of *Battle for the Planet of the Apes* and appeared in the film as a chimp-faced extra, for contributing the book's

Tim Roth as Thade and Helena Bonham Carter as Ari, doing their best impressions as fans on the night of the Tim Burton film's premiere.

foreword. As you can imagine, adding a good and wise ape of David's caliber to the lineup was no tribble at all.

I am delighted to have worked with writers Dave Ballard, Corinna Bechko, Stephen R. Bissette, Ian Brill, Joseph Dilworth, Matthew J Elliott, Robert Greenberger, Edward Gross, Zaki Hasan, Jim Johnson, Neil Moxham, Steven J. Roby, John Roche, Paul Simpson, and Dayton Ward, who have provided us with such rich content to present to you, the readers. This isn't just a collection of "Gee, ain't *Apes* swell?" love letters. The writers serve up both the bitter rind *and* the succulent fruit,[1] offering much to chew on. The opinions expressed in their essays might not necessarily mirror my own (though most do), but I have immensely enjoyed reading them, both as an editor and as a fellow fan, and I'm confident you will, too.

Bright Eyes, Ape City features a beautiful cover by my friend Pat Carbajal, who also illustrated *The Sacred Scrolls* and other *Apes* books I've worked on in the past.[2] I'm grateful to my co-editor on both volumes, Joe Berenato, as well as

---

[1] Hopefully not bananas... Zira loathes those.
[2] *Timeline of the Planet of the Apes: The Definitive Chronology* and *Lexicon of the Planet of the Apes: The Comprehensive Encyclopedia*, both for Hasslein Books

to my pals at Sequart, Lawgivers Julian Darius and Mike Phillips, for allowing us to lease out a corner of Ape City on their property.

Finally, I offer a big hug to my wife Jill — the gorilla my dreams — and our children, Emily and Joshua, who often put up with my sequestering myself for hours so I can write about a planet where apes evolved from men. It's a madhouse, but I'd never want to live on it without them.

Incidentally, keep an eye out for *Planet of the Apes: Tales from the Forbidden Zone*, an officially licensed short fiction anthology that I co-edited and contributed to, along with *Sacred Scrolls* contributor Jim Beard. I'm immensely proud of that book as well, which features short stories from an astounding lineup of talented authors, including Dan Abnett, Kevin J. Anderson, Nancy Collins, Greg Cox, Drew Gaska, Robert Greenberger, Greg Keyes, Paul Kupperberg, Jonathan Maberry, Bob Mayer, John Jackson Miller, Will Murray, Jim Sams, Ty Templeton, and Dayton Ward.

The stories tie in not only to the five classic films, but also to both the live-action and animated TV shows, which is especially exciting. This is unprecedented in *Apes* history, and I can't wait for you to read it.[3]

In the meantime, I hope you enjoy your stay in Ape City, Bright Eyes.

---

[3] You can read more about the project at my blog: "Prose of the Apes: Guiding the Planet on Its Next Titanic Adventures."
http://hassleinbooks.blogspot.com/2015/10/prose-of-apes-guiding-planet-on-its.html.

Tales from the Forbidden Zone, now available from editor Rich Handley and *Sacred Scrolls* contributor Jim Beard.

Unity from the Planet of the Apes: An Introduction

by Joseph F. Berenato

The 2012 New York Comic Con changed my life forever.

I attended it for three reasons: to hang out with my buddy Jim Beard, to get my copy of *Gotham City 14 Miles* signed by Adam West and Burt Ward,[1] and to meet up with Rich Handley from Hasslein Books for the first time.

Hasslein Books was originally founded in 2008 to publish Rich's *Timeline of the Planet of the Apes: The Definitive Chronology*, followed by 2010's *Lexicon of the Planet of the Apes: The Comprehensive Encyclopedia*.[2] Both works cemented Rich as an undeniable expert on *Planet of the Apes*, and have rightly given him a bit of a reputation as an absolute madman when it comes to attention to detail (see, for example, his work in *A Matter of Time: The Back to the Future Lexicon*, or *Watching Time: The Unauthorized Watchmen Chronology*. And just *try* to find something he missed. I dare you).

---

[1] Both *did* sign my book, with varying lasting results. Burt Ward spent twenty minutes trying to sell me on the virtues of his homemade dog food – really. The talk with Adam West ultimately led me to pursue an entirely new career, which you can read about here: https://atomicwanderers.wordpress.com/2013/09/12/the-statement-of-purpose-that-got-me-into-grad-school/.

[2] The company has since gone on to publish several other timelines and encyclopedias, each as exhaustively comprehensive as these two.

Jim and I had been in talks with Rich about a possible project. Since Rich is from New York and Jim and I would both be in the city, a meet-up seemed like a logical choice. Plus, we also wanted to have a few drinks and hang out and talk nerd stuff for a while.

And we did just that. For hours, we talked about *Star Trek*, *Star Wars*, Batman, James Bond, *Ghostbusters*, and, of course, *Planet of the Apes*. By night's end, drinks were consumed, appetizers were eaten, geekery was celebrated, and – most germane to this introduction –new friendships were forged.

Not long thereafter, Rich contributed to my first book[3] and apparently had so much fun that he invited me along to co-edit a book he was pitching. That has turned into a very rewarding partnership between the two of us, and the book you are now holding is the fourth product of that joint venture.[4]

If you've read our previous volume regarding *Planet of the Apes*, you may recall that I wasn't a lifelong fan of the franchise, like my esteemed co-editor is (or perhaps like you yourself are). But thanks to a movie marathon in 1998, I'm an avowed lover of apes these days.[5] It doesn't matter if it's the original films (yes, even *Battle*) or the two most recent ones (I've tried, I really have, to watch the 2001 remake, and I think I've cumulatively watched the entire thing, but have no desire to do so again, if for no other reason than the inexplicable casting of Michael Jackson,[6] thank you very much); if they're on television, I watch them. If nothing's on TV, it's either *Star Trek* or *Apes*.

What amazes me is how many other people feel that way about the franchise. It's been my experience that people often literally wear their fandoms on their sleeves – walk through any crowd, and you can pick out *Star Wars* or *Star Trek* or *Spider-Man* or even *Gilmore Girls* fans by the shirt they're wearing. You don't see that so much with *Planet of the Apes*. Oh, we're out

---

[3] *New Life and New Civilizations: Exploring Star Trek Comics* (Sequart, 2014).
[4] Jim and Rich have also forged their own alliance; the fruit of that partnership – *Planet of the Apes: Tales from the Forbidden Zone* – is now available from Titan Books..
[5] Read my intro to *The Sacred Scrolls* for the full skinny on the subject.
[6] Yes, yes. I know it wasn't *really* Michael Jackson. But the make-up job on Helena Bonham Carter was awfully close, don't you think? No disrespect intended to Michael Jackson – I love his work as much, if not more than, the next guy – but his appearance near the end of his days made him look rather extraterrestrial. Even *he* knew it; how else do you explain his cameo as an alien in *Men in Black II*?

there, to be sure, but – much like Caesar – we don't often go announcing ourselves in a room full of humans, unless they're in on it already.

Nor, really, do we keep it a secret. We're not Doctor Zaius, trying to suppress knowledge of the Forbidden Zone. If someone brings *Apes* up, we're all too eager to share our love for it, no matter our station or present company. Recently, I've had some rather rewarding conversations – independently generated, days apart – with both the judicial officer and the now-retired president of the college where I teach, regarding *Planet of the Apes*, our mutual love of the movies, and the unique view that the films present.

That view is one of the many things presented in this volume, which seeks to examine the entire mythos, from 1968 to the upcoming *War for the Planet of the Apes*. The only things not covered herein are the comic books – see Sequart's previous volume for those, and look to BOOM! Studios for the next two *Apes* crossovers, one with Tarzan and one with Green Lantern[7] – and the fiction anthology edited by Rich and Jim, now available wherever books are sold. Everything else, however, is fair game, from the flicks to the cartoon to some *Apes*-inspired… um… well, damn dirty movies briefly covered in this tome's last essay (so you've been warned far in advance about its content).

Rich and I have been very fortunate to be able to work with the writers on all of our books, and those who have come together because of their love of *Apes* for this volume are no exception. Dave Ballard, Corinna Bechko, Stephen R. Bissette, Ian Brill, Joseph Dilworth, Matthew J Elliott, Robert Greenberger, Edward Gross, Zaki Hasan, Jim Johnson, Neil Moxham, Steven J. Roby, John Roche, Paul Simpson, and Dayton Ward have each and all turned in fantastic examinations of their specific realms of the franchise.

Patricio Carbajal has solidly delivered another inspired cover for the book, and Sequart honchos Julian Darius and Mike Phillips have earned our gratitude once more for indulging our crazy notions and allowing us to put them to paper under their banner.

And none of this would have been possible if it weren't for a meet-and-geek after NYCC '12, which happened because Rich wrote some books about *Planet of the Apes*. That franchise brought so many of us together, and changed our lives in unexpected ways.

---

[7] I have mixed feelings about continuing to have different franchises cross over onto the planet of the apes, but *damn* if this doesn't look like fun.

Four covers for the *Planet of the Apes/Green Lantern* crossover. Plausible or not, don't they make you want to get your stinkin' paws on them?

So thanks to Jim Beard for introducing me to Rich Handley. Thanks to Rich for inviting me into what has been a hell of a partnership. Thanks to Nancy Porfido and Doctor Peter Mora for showing me that *Apes* fans are *everywhere*.

Thanks to you, dear reader, for continuing to find our works worth your money.

And thanks most of all to my wife Robyn, the Zira to my Cornelius. I thank the Lawgiver every day for her.

My Life as a Chimpanzee: A Foreword

by David Gerrold

So there was this fellow who owned a disco in New York. It was called The Electric Circus and it was momentarily famous. In 1968, it was the place where *it was happening* in the East Village. So this fellow made some money – enough that he got the idea that he should become a movie mogul.

He went into a bookstore and asked the clerk, "What are the kids buying?"

The clerk gave him J.R.R. Tolkien's *Lord of the Rings* and Robert A. Heinlein's *Stranger in a Strange Land.*

This fellow could not get the film rights to *Lord of the Rings.* But he did get the rights to *Stranger in a Strange Land.*

And shortly thereafter, my agent called to ask me if I had ever heard of the book, and if I wanted to write a screen treatment for *Stranger in a Strange Land.* Of course, I said yes. I'd only read the novel five times since its original publication in 1961, but I wouldn't mind reading it again.

So my agent put me on the phone with this fellow, this wannabe mogul. I shared my enthusiasm for the book and… he started giving me notes.

"It's gotta have a spaceship in it. *Planet of the Apes* has a spaceship. We gotta have a spaceship."

"Okay," I said. "We can start with the trip back from Mars, with Valentine Michael Smith aboard the spaceship. No problem."

"And..." he continued, "don't use Heinlein's dialogue. My girlfriend doesn't like Heinlein's dialogue."

It went downhill from there.

Okay, I was just a beginner at the time. I'd sold one script to a science-fiction show on TV, and I'd done an uncredited rewrite for a subsequent script, so technically, I was a professional. But... that one conversation killed my enthusiasm.

Actually, there was no chance that I was ever going to write the script. I knew the game. What he wanted was something to go shopping with. If he could get a studio to invest in the picture, they'd hire a *real* writer. Uh-huh.

But it was a paycheck and when you're still a beginner, you don't turn down work that pays the bills – and there was always the chance that I'd impress someone enough that I could springboard into a better opportunity.

So finally, I decided to write it the way I felt it should be written.

To be fair, I didn't do a very good job of it. As much as I tried to boil the story down to a cinematic structure, *Stranger in a Strange Land* was a book very much of its time – and it defied easy translation to the screen.

Subsequently, the rights to the novel passed on to another owner and another and another, at least 30 times at last count, until it died in development hell, and because there was now so much baggage attached to it, it had become unproduceable. (By "baggage," I mean financial obligations to previous owners.) I have no idea who owns the rights these days.

But what does any of this have to do with *Planet of the Apes*?

Well, aside from the fact that *Planet of the Apes* had a spaceship in it, this fellow broke one of the primary rules of film: NO SPOILERS.

He asked me, "Have you seen *Planet of the Apes* yet?"

I admitted I hadn't – I intended to, but it was only playing in Beverly Hills, so far.

Sidebar: In those days, before the first multiplex was built, a movie opened at a single prestigious theater – like Grauman's Chinese – and played there for a few weeks, or even for a few months, at premium ticket prices. Then it would move to the first-run theaters in various neighborhoods for a couple of weeks, then the second-run theaters, and so on, until finally it arrived in West Elbow, Idaho, as an exhausted, worn-out, spliced, scratchy, dirty print. From there, the print would either be discarded, stored someplace, or sold to a fanatic collector.

So, I said, no, I hadn't seen *Planet of the Apes* yet. And after he told me there was a spaceship in it, which was why *Stranger in a Strange Land* had to have a spaceship, he said, "In the end, Charlton Heston finds the ruins of the Statue of Liberty and realizes he's still on Earth."

Uh –

Thanks.

What I didn't say was, "Gee, thanks, asshole, for spoiling the big reveal. Next, you'll tell me that Rosebud was the sled and all I have to do to get back to Kansas is click my heels together three times and say, 'There's no place like home.'"

No, I didn't say that.

But a few days later, I did drive into Beverly Hills – that theater is no longer there – to catch an afternoon screening of *Planet of the Apes*.

Despite the spoiler, the picture still worked. In fact – at the risk of starting an internet flame war, I still regard it as the best of all the *Apes* pictures.

Why?

Because the script was written by Rod Serling.[1] And it was brilliant. It was a parable, an allegory, a moral fable – and a warning. The story was perfectly structured, the characters were intense, and the dialogue crackled. "Take your stinking paws off me, you damn dirty ape!" I don't know about you, but I applauded when Charlton Heston growled that line. I still do. Every time.

That first visit to the planet of the apes was like a two-hour episode of *The Twilight Zone*, only better. It was in color, widescreen, and stereophonic sound, with a stunning score by Jerry Goldsmith. And the ape makeup?! It was incredible!

Looking back at the film today, I believe it still works. It's still a powerful story. It's about religion's fear of science. It's about dogmatic tyranny refusing to acknowledge the evidence. And, ultimately, it's not just about orangutans and chimpanzees and gorillas – it's about the naked apes called humans and the stupid things we do to each other.

Of course, there were sequels, generally enjoyable – but because there's not a lot of future in dystopic visions, the sequels had to focus on the adventure of individual survival.

---

[1] *Editors' note:* An early draft of the movie was written by Serling. The version that ended up in theaters, however, was heavily rewritten by Michael Wilson.

Pierre Boulle's original novel, *Planet of the Apes*, was published in France in 1963. An English translation showed up in the United States shortly thereafter. But the idea of a planet where apes were in charge was not exactly new.[2]

DC Comics published *Mystery in Space* and *Strange Adventures* comics throughout the 1950s – and *Strange Adventures* had at least a half-dozen stories in which apes ruled humans, including one in which humans were kept in a zoo.[3]

Issue #45 of *Strange Adventures* featured "The Gorilla World" as its cover story. Several gorilla doctors examine a half-naked man strapped to a table, and one with a stethoscope says, "Incredible! This puny creature is the *missing link* between ape and animal!"

Issue #64 had as its cover story "Gorillas in Space!" – in which space-suited gorillas gloat about beating humans into orbit. Issue #69, meanwhile, had a cover story titled "The Gorilla Conquest of Earth!"

Issue #14 of *My Greatest Adventure* published as its cover story "I Was a Prisoner in a Human Zoo!" This tale featured humans performing in a circus for the amusement of gorillas.

Strange Adventures #108 published "The Human Pet of Gorilla Land!" The cover shows a human in a cage being admired by a Kong-sized gorilla family, and the gorilla child wants the human for a pet.

Apparently, editors at DC believed that covers with gorillas sold better. Also dinosaurs, fire, motorcycles, crying heroes, and the color purple. At least one critic[4] has wondered what that says about our collective psyche.

Is it possible that Pierre Boulle saw some of those American comic books and was inspired to write *Planet of the Apes*? Perhaps. Or perhaps, some ideas are just so obvious they're the low-hanging fruit of creativity.

Anyway…

By 1973, the franchise was finally sputtering toward exhaustion. The last film in the series was *Battle for the Planet of the Apes*. Someone at 20th Century Fox thought the movie would benefit from a novelization. Award Books had the contract; they were in the same building as *Galaxy Science Fiction*, only one

---

[2] See the essay in this volume by Stephen R. Bissette.

[3] Cronin, Brian. "I Can't Cover What I Am – 'Is That a Gorilla on the Cover? I MUST HAVE IT!'" Comic Book Resources, 15 Nov. 2014: http://goodcomics.comicbookresources.com/2014/11/15/i-cant-cover-what-i-am-is-that-a-gorilla-on-the-cover-i-must-have-it/.

[4] "Drancron," a reader who posted a follow-up comment to Cronin's online article

floor down. They called upstairs and asked Judy-Lynn Del Rey (then the magazine's associate editor) if she could recommend a writer who understood science fiction and scriptwriting. She recommended me.

The problem? They needed a manuscript within two weeks.

Actually, not a problem. I type fast.

They needed 60,000 words – that's 5,000 words a day for twelve days. Not impossible. The script for the film was 110 pages. I needed to flesh out each page, expanding one page of script into three pages of prose.

It was an interesting challenge, and it turned out to be a lot of fun. Along the way, I tossed in a few in-jokes and one salacious visualization regarding the size of the villain's missile.

When I turned in the manuscript, one of the executives at Fox remarked, "This is a better book than this movie deserves." High praise, I guess.

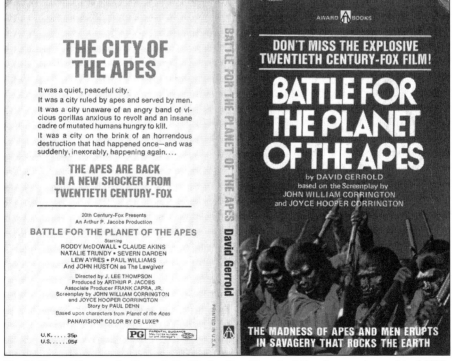

David Gerrold's novelization of *Battle for the Planet of the Apes*, released in 1973, was, according to one executive, a better book than the movie deserved.

There wasn't a lot of money involved, so I asked if I could be an extra ape in the movie, still filming. They agreed, and I ended up at the Fox ranch out in

Malibu (where *M*A*S*H* was also filmed) for a day of action scenes. I'm in one wide-angle shot in which a school bus breaks through a barrier. That's it.

Getting into the ape makeup was an arduous and painstaking process. I wore the Caesar-double makeup – the same appliances Roddy McDowall wore, but the shape of the wearer's face changed the look of the makeup. Those who worked on the shoot quickly learned how to recognize individual actors, stunt men, and extras, despite the ape appliances they wore.

I arrived for an early call, and a remarkably talented makeup artist named Werner Keppler spent three hours making a monkey out of me. Seated in the chair next to mine was McDowall. But he was asleep, so I never had a chance to chat with him.

Apparently, that was his daily routine: come in, sit down, fall asleep, and wake up three hours later as a chimp. And apparently, he found the whole process very depressing. I can understand that.

After I was appropriately costumed, one of the stunt men showed me how to lope along like a chimpanzee – a skill that is easily learned and never forgotten. I can still do it, but not in public.

There is a profound psychological impact that occurs when you wear the ape makeup – when you look down at yourself, or when you look into a mirror, you become what you see. You fall into character and stay there – it's a seductive bit of role-play, like Halloween for real – so much so that when the makeup is finally removed, you experience the same disconnect in reverse. "Oh, I'm human again...? What a disappointment." It's more fun being an ape.

I did notice one interesting thing on the set: at lunch time, the humans ate with the humans, the orangutans ate with the orangutans, the gorillas ate with the gorillas, and the chimpanzees ate with the chimpanzees. Whether it was unconscious or not, it seemed a strangely natural segregation. Maybe we were all staying in character...?

It's very difficult to eat in the ape makeup, by the way. You have to either take off the lower jaw-piece (and have the makeup man put it back on after lunch) or learn how to push the fork deep past the two foam appliances into your actual mouth.

A few months later, at the 1973 Equicon in Los Angeles, we arranged to have Werner Keppler come to the convention and put me back into the ape makeup as a demonstration – and that evening, I emceed the masquerade as an ape. I asked Werner how long it took to remove the makeup and he replied, in a thick Germanic accent, "Ven I put it on, it *stays* on!"

And, yes, it did.

After the masquerade, a friend and I went up to the bar on the top floor of the hotel. The bartender said, "We don't serve monkeys in here."

Werner Keppler transformed David Gerrold from human to chimpanzee, both for his cameo in *Battle* and for a sci-fi convention demonstration.

Indignantly, I said, in my best Cornelius accent, "I am not a monkey. I am a chimpanzee."

He said, "Oh, that's different. What'll you have?"

I said, "I'll have a banana daiquiri."

I'll stop now.

The other contributors to this book will have more important things to say. Go read their words. Enjoy.

Welcome to the Monkey Planet

by Robert Greenberger

Student. Engineer. Soldier. Spy.

Man's inhumanity to man and society's growing dependence on machinery became two of the larger themes that informed Pierre Boulle's novels and stories. The French writer liked to explore how these conflicts developed, tracing the origins to their outcomes. When he set out to be a writer, after harrowing experiences during World War II, he never imagined he would be best remembered for just one novel – one he considered a lesser work, but one that has endured, being retold for new generations in ever increasingly sophisticated ways.

Born on 20 February 1912, Pierre Francois Marie-Louis Boulle used his myriad careers to soak up the atmosphere of his native France and the countries he visited to prepare him for his most satisfying career, that of writer. While he wrote more than 30 novels and collections of short stories, he is primarily remembered, depending upon the audience, for one of two works: *Bridge Over the River Kwai* or *Planet of the Apes*, each a vastly different commentary on society and mankind. Both have endured thanks to their mesmerizing and memorable film adaptations, bringing his ideas to vivid life. Boulle (rhymes with "pool") never thought *Apes* to be a particularly strong work, yet he saw his social satire spawn an industry and cult following that has ensured his immortality in the annals of science fiction.

French novelist Pierre Boulle, whose career spanned more than 40 years, is perhaps best known to modern audiences for *The Bridge Over the River Kwai* and, of course, *Planet of the Apes*.

Pierre Boulle wrote *Planet of the Apes* at a time when the world was gripped in the Cold War, with France caught between the Soviet Union and the United States. Concerned with the direction of modern society, he speculated what life might be like had a different species gained dominance. He was also likely still dealing with his harrowing experiences as a prisoner during World War II, when he witnessed some of the worst aspects of humanity. It was those experiences that propelled him to be a writer and create his first great work.

Boulle was raised as a happy child in Avignon, attending Lycée d'Avignon and at the Faculté de Sciences, in Paris. His upbringing was fairly typical, as he enjoyed reading and cited Jonathan Swift, H.G. Wells, Robert Louis Stevenson, and Voltaire among his favorite authors. He consumed movies, both domestic and foreign, and was a fan of American fantastic fare.

Boulle went on to study electrical engineering at the École Supérieure d'Électricité, also in Paris. Upon graduation, he worked as an engineer for just two years before giving it up and leaving France for Kuala Lumpur. There, he ran a rubber plantation for about a year before enlisting in the French army, assigned to a unit in Indochina. Once France fell to Nazi troops in June 1940, Boulle joined the Free French, a Gaullist resistance group. As he changed allegiances, he also changed careers from soldier to spy, assuming the alias of Peter John Rule, a Mauritius-born Englishman.

A part of Force 136, Boulle was trained at a place called The Convent. In his first memoir, *The Sources of the River Kwai*, he discussed his training in which "serious gentlemen taught us the art of blowing up a bridge, attaching explosives to the side of a ship, derailing a train, as well as that of dispatching to the next world – as silently as possible – a night-time guard."

"Pierre Boulle was profoundly Anglophile," Jean Loriot, head of the Association of Friends of Pierre Boulle, told the BBC[1]. Loriot happens to also be the husband of Boulle's niece Françoise. "In the Far East he worked alongside English people. He was impregnated by English culture. He admired the English greatly. And when he came to write he made many of his heroes English." The faux-Englishman then worked to organize resistance to the Japanese invaders in China, Burma, and Indochina.

Boulle's good deeds did not go unpunished. He was aboard a raft, floating down the Mekong River headed for Hanoi, when the Vichy French finally captured him near Lai Châu in 1943. For actions that were deemed crimes against the Axis, he was court-martialed in Hanoi and sentenced to a life of hard labor. With the war beginning to wind down a year later, it was arranged for him to escape his Saigon prison. With him were scraps of paper on which he had been writing notes about his experiences – the formative pieces of his next career as an author.

Once free, Boulle allied himself with British Special Operations Executive in Calcutta (now Kolkata). He eventually returned to his rubber plantation, where he began rejecting Catholicism in favor of agnosticism, and started writing stories, some of which remained buried for decades. In 1949, with the war ended, Boulle returned to France with the rank of captain. Once again on home soil, he was decorated with the Croix de Guerre and the Médaille de la Résistance. Boulle was also made an Officier de la Légion d'nonneur, and then settled down, embarking on his writing career. He later recalled, "One night I had a revelation of a certain truth – that I had to be a writer."[2]

---

[1] Schofield, Hugh. "The French spy who wrote *The Planet of the Apes*." BBC, 4 Aug. 2014: http://www.bbc.com/news/magazine-28610124. Unless otherwise stated, all further statements from Loriot stem from this article.

[2] http://www.independent.co.uk/news/people/obituary-pierre-boulle-1391376.html

Using a second-hand Underwood typewriter, the newly minted author wrote in a small, rented room in Montparnasse. His first published novel was 1950's *William Conrad*, which told of a German spy on a mission to Britain. Boulle honored one of his favorite authors, Joseph Conrad, with the character name. It was a small commercial success, and was later adapted in America as an episode of *Playhouse 90*.

After the book was completed, Boulle left the hotel to move in with his widowed sister, Madeleine Perrusset, and help raise her daughter Françoise. There had been plans to formally adopt her, but it never happened.

Boulle's third novel, *Le Pont de la rivière Kwaï*, or *The Bridge Over the River Kwai*, was published in 1952 and brought him his first real taste of fame. Receiving nearly universal acclaim, the book was translated into 22 languages and sold six million copies in the United States alone, earning the writer the Prix Sainte-Beuve. The bestseller was optioned by Hollywood, where director David Lean adapted it into a feature film starring Alec Guinness and William Holden. The story told how Japanese prisoners were ordered to build a 258-mile railway spanning a bridge that became an Allied target. Nearly 120,000 men died during its construction, and Boulle created composite characters for some major figures in the story.

Boulle was interested not only in telling the story of what happened, but in exploring the clash of cultures. As the novel opens, he wrote, "Maybe the unbridgeable gulf that some see separating the western and the oriental souls are nothing more than a mirage? [...] Maybe the need to 'save face' was, in this war, as vital, as imperative, for the British as it was for the Japanese."

Boulle maintained close contact with his fellow soldiers and prisoners throughout his life, but that did not protect him from outrage aimed his way from those who felt his fictional leader, Lieutenant Colonel Nicholson (portrayed on film by Guinness), betrayed the memory of the real Allied senior officer, Philip Toosey, by depicting Nicholson as collaborating with the enemy.

The author did not speak English but agreed to lend his name as the movie's official screenwriter, since the actual writing was done by Carl Foreman and Michael Wilson, who suffered under the infamous Hollywood Blacklist. During the House Un-American Activities Committee (HUAC) hearings that decade, Senator Joe McCarthy sought out Communists and Red sympathizers, demanding that those testifying before the committee name names or suffer the consequences. Foreman and Wilson were among those who refused to do that and, at the time, the political might in Washington, D.C., proved stronger than the will of Hollywood moguls. The screenplay won the Academy Award, but their names were not properly added to the official credits until 1984.

According to Jean Loriot, there is a "remorseless logic to his stories. In fact, he wrote the concluding page first and then worked backwards to construct the way to that conclusion."

Boulle once said, "A novel is built around an abstract idea, on the logic of the absurd. Only after having got the thing precisely plotted do I add my own memories and experiences, and research documents. One cannot write a good novel if it is not given the support of one master-idea."[3] It also gave him a platform for moralizing about mankind's ills, which is often found in his works.

Boulle went on to write seven more novels before a fateful trip to the zoo. "I believe it was triggered by a visit to the zoo where I watched the gorillas," he told journalist Jean Claude Morlot in 1972. "I was impressed by their human-like expressions. It led me to dwell upon and imagine relationships between humans and apes."[4]

By then, Boulle had been reading the works of Ray Bradbury, H.P. Lovecraft, and Isaac Asimov, so he was familiar with science fiction. Three of his other works also bordered on science fiction. *Contes de l'absurde* (*Tales of the Absurd*, 1953), *E=mc²* (a short story collection, 1957), and *Le jardin de Kanashima* (*Garden on the Moon*, 1964) all addressed man's growing dependence upon machine technology. The latter work focused on the former Nazis' role in the Soviet-American space race, adding in Japan's burning desire to best both. Despite having read and liked science fiction, Boulle rejected the label and called these works social fantasy.

Inspired, in part, by Jonathan Swift's social satire in *Gulliver's Travels*, Boulle went on to spend about six months imagining a society with apes as Earth's predominant species. The finished novel was released in 1963 as *La Planète des Singes*. His frequent translator Xan Fielding turned it into English, and the novel arrived in America as *Planet of the Apes*, a hardcover through Vanguard Press. Signet/New American Library released the paperback the following year, while, that January, British readers were treated to the imaginative *Monkey Planet* from Secker & Warburg. The title switched to the more familiar *Planet of the*

---

[3] http://www.independent.co.uk/news/people/obituary-pierre-boulle-1391376.html
[4] http://www.breitbart.com/big-hollywood/2011/09/04/remembering-planet-of-the-apes-1968/

A first-edition copy of *La Planète des Singes*, originally published in 1963.

Apes in August 1973 to cash in on the film series. Abridged versions were also published in *Saga: The Magazine for Men* (May 1964) and *Bizarre Mystery Magazine* (November 1965).[5] Contemporary publications gave it positive reviews, acknowledging its commentary and visual imaginativeness.

The novel is written in epistolary form. A couple of honeymooners, Jinn and Phyllis, are cruising through space when they encounter a bottle containing an amazing message written sometime in the past by journalist Ulysse Mérou:

In the year 2500, the reporter accompanies Professor Antelle and physician Arthur Levain on a journey to the star Betelgeuse. As their ship nears the speed of light during the two-year voyage, time dilation means years pass on Earth. As the ship enters the solar system, they find a habitable planet that they dub Soror. Accompanied by their pet monkey Hector, the trio take a shuttle to the surface, where they find the water drinkable and the fruit edible.

Just then, a nude, golden-skinned version of Dejah Thoris – that is, a woman whom they name "Nova" – finds them. Hector frightens her for some reason and she manages to kill the chimp. The men study her and realize she is mute and not especially intelligent, but clearly human. Her tribe arrives, deem the newcomers' clothing and transportation bad things, and destroy both.

Soon thereafter, the astronauts and tribe alike are besieged by police officers – but, to Ulysse's horror, they are intelligent apes in clearly recognizable human clothing. Levain is slain during the fight and the others are captured and taken to a prison. Entering the community, Ulysse is stunned to see the familiar trappings of Earth, from storefronts to traffic lights. The apes smoke tobacco, drink alcohol, and have a societal structure very much mirroring mankind's. This means there are social classes with clearly indicated groupings: warlike gorilla soldiers, political orangutan administrators, and liberal chimpanzees, who are the culture's intellectuals. Humans are the animals on this world, hunted or experimented on, or kept as pets.

Ulysse is clearly attracted to Nova, so they are caged together. During the next few months, he witnesses the Pavlovian conditioning being conducted and the scholarly note-taking going on. He also begins to understand the simian tongue and, unlike the native humans, learns how to speak to his captors. This catches the attention of Zira, a female scientist, who forms a bond with him. In

---

[5] In addition, writer-artist Zórád Ernö adapted Boulle's novel for a Hungarian publisher in 1981, under the title *A Majmok Bolygója*. More recently, BBC Radio 4's *Book at Bedtime Series* presented the novel as an audio, read by Michael Maloney.

time, they bring in her fiancé, an archaeologist named Cornelius. The pair exchange information about their respective cultures, and Ulysse is eventually prepared to address Doctor Zaius and the governing body.

So amazed are they with Ulysse that he becomes a media darling and is immediately granted freedom, clothing, and a place to live, rapidly becoming the focal point of social conversation. During all of this, Cornelius has been working on a dig, and when he deems the time right, the chimp brings the journalist on a field trip to help interpret what they have uncovered. It is clearly the remains of a human city and, in time, they realize that the humans had experimented on the apes until the caged creatures rose up and overthrew their captors. With mankind crushed, the apes took predominance over the world, with humans reduced to the savages they are today.

Back in the city, Ulysse realizes Nova is carrying his child and has been secreted away for study up to the time of birth. Zira smuggles him in to her and he names his son Sirius. The hybrid grows rapidly and is already speaking at the age of three months, a fact Zira wants to hide from Zaius. There's little doubt that something has to be done, so they hatch a plot to replace the human test subjects for a spaceflight designed to access the Earth ship still in orbit. Since all humans look alike to the apes, Ulysse, Nova, and Sirius manage to gain access to the starship. They rocket back to Earth and return, landing at France's Orly airport. The passengers then discover that, during the intervening centuries, humans have been replaced by apes on Ulysse's world as well.

At the end of the novel, Jinn and Phyllis complete reading the manuscript but don't believe it. "... Phyllis, after dismissing a last shred of doubt with an energetic shake of her velvety ears," Boulle writes, "took out her compact and, in view of their return to port, touched up her dear little chimpanzee muzzle."

The critics were taken with the imaginative tale, complete with its unexpected ending, but recognized his commentary, likening it not only to Swift but also Aldus Huxley's *Brave New World* and Karel Čapek's *R.U.R. (Rossum's Universal Robots)*. Boulle told *Cinefantastique* in 1972, "It is a story, and science fiction is only the pretext. I wouldn't even know how to define SF... I think it's the genre where you can deal with and imagine unhuman characters, but in my book my apes are men, there is no doubt."[6]

---

[6] http://pota.goatley.com/magazines/cinefantastique-summer-1972.pdf

Stephen Baxter, one of the great contemporary science fiction authors, gushed in *SFX* magazine[7]:

> The novel's society of intelligent apes is gentler than that of the movie. But the horrific elements of Ulysse's ordeal are all here: we see humans hunted for sport, kept in zoos, and used in laboratories for the benefit of ape-kind. And familiar characters appear: crusty, skeptical Dr. Zaius, and the scientist girl-chimp Zira with whom Ulysse forms a platonic attraction (ahem again – actually, in the novel there is definitely a physical undertone to their flirting).

> The book is more compassionate and ironic than the movie – and the more affecting for it. Brian Aldiss has compared the book to other meet-the-animals classics, including George Orwell's *Animal Farm* and H.G. Wells's *The Island of Dr. Moreau*. To my mind the most telling comparison is with Jonathan Swift's *Gulliver's Travels*. Like Gulliver among the clever-horse Houyhnhnms, Ulysse identifies with the smarter species, and rejects his own brutish kind.

Boulle definitely touched on issues of racism, not just ape versus man, but the social stratification of the simian species. It's interesting to note that others read far more into it. Blai Guarné, an assistant professor of anthropology at Barcelona's Pompeu Fabra University, delivered an academic paper in 2008 titled "On Monkeys and Japanese: Mimicry and Anastrophe in Orientalist Representation."[8] Given Boulle's experiences in the Pacific Rim, Guarné felt the depiction of the apes might be a sly commentary on his former captors.

> This inferiority has its representational punctum in the simian mystification of the colonized. With profound historical implications (W. D. Jordan, 1968), the image of the monkey constituted a fertile metaphor for both justifying the colonial enterprise and denying its consequences.

> The society described by Boulle confronts us with a totalitarian system, where a profound sense of honor and a deep respect for hierarchy and traditional values run parallel to the unease about identity that arises from the encounter with human civilization. Contrary to the film adaptation directed by Franklin J. Schaffner (1967), Boulle describes an ultra-futuristic civilization where simians dress like humans, drive motor vehicles and live in skyscrapers. Boulle's works enjoyed publishing success in a world, which, still persuaded by the positive nature of Western/Eastern classification, expectantly observed the Japanese miracle. The recovery of a country historically shaken by "modernity" that now relocate the desire to achieve political equality with the West, projecting itself into a technological future as an economic equal or superior.

---

[7] http://static.gamesradar.com/images/sfx/SFX169planetoftheapes.pdf
[8] http://www.uoc.edu/digithum/10/dt/eng/guarne.pdf

Almost a decade before the *La Planète des Singes* was published, Boulle had come to the public attention with a novel that reflected his experience as an Allied prisoner during the war against Japan. Entitled *Le Pont de la rivière Kwaï* (1952), Boulle would capture his memories as a combatant in China, Burma, and Indochina through the moral experience of the captivity of a group of British soldiers condemned to forced labor in a Japanese POW camp. What would eventually become his most famous work, situated the reader in a position of unease when confronted with their own brutality in the escape from the Other – faced with the abyss of discovering that the absolute difference with this Other is simply one of the multiple expressions of a shared reality.

If we consider *La Planète des Singes* in the light of the biography of its author – French colonist in Southeast Asia and combatant against the Japanese – the dystopia that he proposes is revealed as the backdrop on which are projected both the terrors of the colonial experience40 and the anxiety for a colonized who overcomes the colonizer with their own weapons. In this sense, Ulysse Mérou, the protagonist of the story, bitterly agrees.

When with the benefit of hindsight we link *La Planète des Singes* to the works of Loti, a strange tension is established in the Western tradition of narrating Japan as a paradoxical and inverse civilization. A tradition in which its representation as cultural anastrophe finds in the image of the monkey a metaphor of polysemic nuances, both in the definition of "the Japanese" and in the characterization of "the Western".

While that may have been subconsciously there, Boulle never once suggested his war experiences influenced this particular book. The novel is actually slight, its science fuzzy, and the society depicted way too close to that of Earth to be plausible (certain episodes of *Star Trek* notwithstanding). There's a reason Boulle considers this an inferior work compared with his previous novels, and it's also why the movie made substantive changes. As a result, it is one of the rare cases in which the film is genuinely better than the book.

Arthur P. Jacobs had just made a splashy debut as a producer in 1964, so his studio, 20th Century-Fox, gave him *carte blanche* to propose his next projects. He pitched two: *Doctor Doolittle* and *Planet of the Apes*. As legend has it, Jacobs was in France in 1963 and literary agent Alain Bernheim suggested that the American might like Boulle's latest novel. He produced a copy of the manuscript, and Jacobs was so taken with the visually imaginative story that he tracked down Fox honcho Richard Zanuck in London and asked him to acquire the property. Based on the description alone, Zanuck agreed.

At some point in 1963, before Jacob's APJAC Productions got their hands on the novel, a smaller outfit, King Brothers Productions, had the novel adaptation rights, and they reached out to one of the strongest writers working in filmed entertainment at the time: Rod Serling. A native of Syracuse, New York, Serling went on to become one of the best-known writers for dramatic television during the live-action days of *Playhouse 90* and *Stage One*. He parlayed that success into creating his first series, *The Twilight Zone*, for CBS in 1959. With the series beginning to wind down, he was amenable to taking on the scripting chores in 1963, but not without a little arm-twisting. As Serling recounted for Marvel's *Planet of the Apes* magazine in 1974:

> I first became involved with *Planet of the Apes* about ten years ago. I was approached by an outfit called the King Brothers, who did mostly Indian-elephant pictures which were shot for about a $1.80 – because elephants didn't have a union, then! The King Brothers had a notion about doing the Pierre Boulle book as a nickel-and-dime picture. I was convinced that it could be done and at the time, as I recall, I did a whole treatment for them, a scene-by-scene breakdown of how we would lick the problem. They ultimately discarded it because of the ape population.[9]

Kim Hunter (seen here in full Zira make-up) and Rod Serling monkey around on the set of *Planet of the Apes*.

---

[9] Johnson, David. "Rod Serling Recalls." *Planet of the Apes* #1 (Marvel Comics, August 1974).

Jacobs finally gained the rights by April 1964 and wisely retained Serling, who was challenged by the novel's literary structure. Since this was a Hollywood production, he immediately changed the French astronauts to Americans and upped the ante by skipping the shuttle and crashing the spaceship itself into the newly discovered planet.

So began a lengthy pre-production process that saw the project bounce from studio to studio until it wound up back at Fox, while the leading-man part was first offered to both Marlon Brando and Paul Newman before Charlton Heston accepted the role.

Jacobs and J. Lee Thompson prepared a pitch memo in late 1963 that breathlessly described the property: "*The Planet of the Apes* is a rip-roaring horror story – a classic thriller utilizing the best elements of *King Kong*, *Frankenstein*, *Dr. Jekyll and Mr. Hyde*, *Things to Come*, *The Birds*, and other film classics."[10] Boulle was happy to earn extra income from the book's film rights, having previously enjoyed the American adaptation of *William Conrad* in 1958 and *La Face* in 1959.

Serling told Dale Winogura in 1972, "[The novel] is [extremely heavy] because as talented and creative a man as Boulle is, he does not have the deftness of a science fiction writer. Boulle's book was not a parody, but rather a prolonged allegory about morality, more than it was a stunning science fiction piece. But it contained with within its structure a walloping science fiction idea."[11] Given Serling's penchant for characters to make preaching monologues and Boulle's moralizing tone, they were philosophically a perfect match.

Serling continued to modify the story structure, going through draft after draft. After a great deal of scholarly study, writer Gordon C. Webb deciphered the many retellings of the film's development and determined conclusively, in *Creative Screenwriting Journal*, that the film's memorable twist ending was all Serling's.[12] Not that it didn't change throughout the drafts, beginning with a 15 May 1964 version in which astronaut John Thomas (the former Ulysse Mérou) and Nova find the doll that says "mama" and they manage to return to Earth, only to find it now dominated by apes. Throughout 1964, the drafts played with the final reveal, leaving them on the planet but making it clear it was a future

---

[10] Russo, Joe; Landsman, Larry; and Gross, Edward. *Planet of the Apes Revisited* (St. Martin's Griffin, August 2001).

[11] *Ibid.*

[12] Webb, Gordon C. "Thirty Years Later: Rod Serling's *Planet of the Apes.*" *Creative Screenwriting Journal* (July-August 1998).

version of Earth, not an alien world. It wasn't until the 6 January 1965 draft that the Statue of Liberty entered the story. At times, Thomas died and Nova passed the statue as she crossed the Forbidden Zone.

As Webb wrote, "Fans of *Twilight Zone* would recognize this sort of 'twist-ending' as a trademark of the series, for which Serling had personally written nearly 100 scripts by the time he began working on *Planet of the Apes*." The future Earth element was certainly familiar territory to Serling, who used a similar twist ending in the episode "I Shot an Arrow into the Air" during the show's first season.

Initially, Boulle was displeased with the use of the iconic Statue of Liberty. In his lengthy *Cinefantastique* interview, he told Morlot:

> I never thought it could be made into a film. It seemed to me too difficult, and there was the chance that it would appear ridiculous. When I first saw the film, nothing was ridiculous because it had been very well made.
>
> I feel that the author of a novel is the last person who should be asked for advice for turning it into a film. In comparison to the book, there were a lot of changes made. Some of them were disconcerting. The first part of the film was very good, and the makeup of the apes was particularly good, and, as I've said, that could have been ridiculous, but it wasn't. I disliked somewhat the ending that was used – the Statue of Liberty – which the critics seemed to like, but personally, I prefer my own.

"It is a big difference. In the film there is this sense of human responsibility. It is man that has led to the destruction of the planet," Clément Pieyre, who catalogued Boulle's manuscripts at the French National Library, told the BBC in 2014. "But the book is more a reflection on how all civilizations are doomed to die. There has been no human fault. It is just that the return to savagery will come about anyway. Everything perishes."[13]

Jacobs kept Boulle informed throughout the scripting process. Boulle told *Cinefantastique*, "I'm a poor judge. I knew they wanted to do it from the beginning. Arthur Jacobs had talked with me about it, and finally I said, 'Let's try it, then.' The critics seemed to approve of the change. They had the final scene in mind from the first day."

He experienced a similar issue with *Kwai*, as the novel ended with the prisoners doing their job *too* well and the bridge withstanding attack. The David Lean film, though, gave it the happier Hollywood ending, with the bridge being blown up.

---

[13] Schofield, Hugh. "The French spy who wrote *The Planet of the Apes*." BBC, 4 August 2014: http://www.bbc.com/news/magazine-28610124.

Michael Wilson, who had previously adapted *Kwai*, was brought in to "punch" up the script, adding some of the wincing dialogue that ape-ized human expressions. He also had to scale back Ape City from Serling's close approximation of Boulle's novel to the more primitive – and affordable – adobe aesthetic that was filmed. John T. Kelley was brought in for additional dialogue adjustments, though he remained uncredited. The final screen credits were shared by Serling and Wilson, who did not work together at all.

The movie opened to rave reviews and strong box office in February 1968. Stan Hough, a Fox executive, turned to Jacobs and asked if a sequel was possible. He mulled over whether or not it was feasible with associate producer Mort Abrahams, who had a kernel of an idea that interested Jacobs. The producer phoned Serling, who came up with his first ideas on 8 April, exactly two months after the film debuted. A day later, Fox was enthusiastic at the prospect of working on a sequel, and this was the first time involving Boulle was mentioned. The executives wanted his input, as long as his ideas "could not make the film prohibitive cost-wise."[14]

Boulle recounted, in his interview with *Cinefantastique*, "After the success of the original film, Arthur Jacobs requested that I do a sequel for him. They accepted the treatment that I worked on, but they made so many changes that very few of my ideas were left... I did read the script for *Beneath the Planet of the Apes,* but it doesn't interest me because it's no longer my work. It's something totally different."

In fact, by the time of that interview, in February 1972, Boulle had not seen the second or third films in the series, which less and less resembled his novel. Interestingly, he took elements from both the book and Serling's script and went to work.

According to Mort Abrahams, though, "When we made arrangements to do the sequel, [agent] Alain [Bernheim], who had apparently spoken to Boulle, said Boulle had an idea to make a sequel script and he sat down and wrote it. There was no commitment on our part. We didn't invite him, we didn't have a deal. As I recall, we didn't even pay him anything. He wanted to do it but it did not seem to work."[15]

---

[14] Russo, Joe; Landsman, Larry; and Gross, Edward. *Planet of the Apes Revisited* (St. Martin's Griffin, August 2001).
[15] *Ibid.*

Sometime that month, Boulle delivered his first written approach to the film, prompting Abrahams to recount:

> The preliminary outline was rather straightforward and simple, I do not mean to understate Pierre's creative work here, but merely to say that his approach to the story of the second film, while interesting and logical, did not seem to present any surprises. It would seem to be an imperative for the sequel that we have two visual surprises for the audience – a surprise hopefully of the intensity and novelty of the two contained in the original...
>
> Now, as I understand Pierre's original book, he was saying that the apes (or at least Dr. Zaius) know the history of mankind and that Man had destroyed the world – in short, he was saying to the audience 'What are we doing to ourselves?' His concept of the new film is more hopeful in tone since it says that the human race be can reeducated along less destructive lines; in short, that there is hope for men. Now I do not know what visual presentation this leads to at the end of the film, but whatever it is, it must fulfill the obligation of hope.

On 24 April, Serling proposed that Taylor find a pocket of civilized men and women, along with portions of a spaceship. By film's end, they would rebuild and launch the ship just ahead of attacking apes. Picking up directly from the novel, they would return to Earth to find the apes had already taken over. Jacobs appeared to like the idea but did not share it with Boulle, who was turning his outline into a first-draft screenplay.

Boulle's *Planet of the Men*, which he completed in the spring of 1968, tells of the next two decades of life on Earth as Taylor sets out to civilize mankind, teaching the younger generations, the future of mankind, how to speak, write, and think. When Taylor encounters a man spontaneously creating art, he knows things are headed in the right direction. Taylor and Nova raise Sirius, who is clearly being groomed to be the next leader. However, resentment is building along with jealousy, residing side by side with their race hatred for the apes and what had been done to them in the past.

Meanwhile, the ape side of the planet is having its own political upheaval regarding the decision of what to do with the humans, especially once the apes learn that mankind is now speaking and thinking, forming an actual threat to their way of life. Zaius, Zira, and Cornelius vie for the leadership, but the voting overwhelmingly re-elects the aging scientist. Plans are drawn up to wipe out the humans before they can attack first.

Zira and Cornelius sneak off to warn Taylor, but the humans capture the two apes and want them to pay for the experiments some still remember. After a lot of speeches, Taylor winds up shot dead and a bleak future is left hanging in the air. Meanwhile, Zaius and other apes are inexplicably losing their intelligence and the good doctor winds up a caged curiosity. It appears man may have won.

Boulle had never written a script before, and it shows. Jacobs outlined the basic structure for him, but the screenplay for *Planet of the Men* is rudimentary at best. It leapfrogs through time, starting moments after the first film, then skipping ahead a few months, then a few years, then a decade. While the tensions on both sides are nicely delineated, it is a very static story with none of the action that thrilled audiences in the first. Abrahams recalled:

> Neither Arthur or I were enchanted with it, but we were flattered by the idea that he sat down and wrote. I don't recall any of the details, the story itself simply didn't work. There was a lot of, as I recall, conversation. Not an electric story. It was more in narrative form. I think it would have made a relatively good novel. But for visual purposes, and as I explained we went for visual in the sequel, it didn't have the gimmick – it didn't have the visual possibilities. Just didn't have the excitement of the first piece.

Jacobs knew that Boulle's screenplay was unfilmable but shared the script with Serling, who was initially unsure what to do with it. In time, he offered a number of suggestions to tighten things and add in action, but never signed on to actually rewrite it. On 22 July, David Brown and Richard Zanuck both felt Boulle's screenplay lacked the impact they were hoping for. At the end of July, Jacobs wrote to Zanuck:

> Having carefully analyzed Boulle's and Serling's ideas and the comments from both you and David Brown, I've come to the conclusion about *Planet of the Men*: There is much that is valid and fresh in the Boulle material and Serling's ideas, but they have a basic weakness in their underlying concept since they depend too much strongly on a primitive military engagement between apes and humans. With all the combined thinking, the weaknesses can be strengthened.[16]

In August, Serling saved Jacobs some hard choices by announcing he was committed to another project and couldn't work further on the sequel until sometime in the future. That gave the producer the freedom to cast aside the Boulle script and turn to a fresh writer, Paul Dehn, who went on to craft what became *Beneath the Planet of the Apes*.

Boulle was never again intimately involved with the growing media franchise that stemmed from his novel. He rarely criticized the films or television shows, noting they were so far removed from his original story that

---

[16] *Ibid.*

they were something set apart in his mind. He saw the story "E=mc^2" filmed in America in 1985, and *Un métier de seigneur* was adapted in his native France in 1986. He never again tried to write a screenplay.

Boulle received the Grand Prize of the Société des gens de lettres for his contribution to French literature in 1976 – his last major award for service to his country. He continued to write and explore big ideas with more than a sprinkling of science fiction or fantasy elements, such as 1978's *Le Bon Léviathan*, focusing on a nuclear-powered petrol supertanker and terrified ecologists trying to save the oceans from irreversible disaster.

Then there's the 1988 novel *Le Professeur Mortimer*, which concerned itself with a cancer specialist and Miss Bridget, an animal rights activist (yes, named after Brigitte Bardot). War was still on his mind, though, as he used the Falklands War as the basis for *La Baleine des Malouines (The Whale of the Falklands)* in 1983. He continued to mine his previous experience, as seen in *And Le Malheur des uns (The Misfortune of Others)*, in which he used rubber from Malaysia as a key element in a story of commercial interests attempting to profit from and exploit the AIDS epidemic.

Boulle continued to produce novels and short stories, publishing his final work in 1992, just two years before his death at age 81. He never married after his one great love affair ended, just before the outbreak of World War II, with the woman returning to her husband in Malaya. The author's body was cremated, and his remains now reside in the family vault in the Saint-Veran, Avignon cemetery. Today, Boulle is only associated with *Apes*, and is largely a forgotten literary figure in his native land. As he was dying, he told his niece Françoise and her husband Loriot that he wanted to be remembered.

Françoise and Loriot discovered unpublished Boulle manuscripts five years after his death. As a result, there have been new works released during the past few years, including the novel *L'archéologue et le mystère de Néfertiti (The Archaeologist and the Mystery of Nefertiti)*, published in 2005, as well as *L'Enlèvement de l'Obélisque (The Missing Obelisk)*, a collection of previously unpublished short stories, unveiled in 2007. All of Boulle's manuscripts are currently housed at the National Library of France.

"I think part of the problem is that the French don't know how to categorize him," Pieyre told the BBC. "Some people think he's too 'Hollywood' because of the two films. But no. He was rooted in France."

Stephen Baxter nicely summed up Boulle's efforts in *SFX*: "For all their thoughtless cruelty, Boulle's species of smart apes live in reasonable harmony with each other, which is more than mankind has ever managed. As chimpanzee expert Jane Goodall once remarked: 'We've exterminated all the other branches of hominoid, and now we're doing the same thing to the only slightly more distant.' In an age when we're still hunting our closest cousins for bush meat, Boulle's classic story is as relevant as ever."

Love Conquerors All: Sci-Fi's Greatest – and Most Feminist – Couple

by Ian Brill

When I edited the *Planet of the Apes* comics at BOOM! Studios, I would often discuss how the franchise had the most cynical outlook of all major cinematic science-fiction worlds. *Star Wars* finds hope, new and old, in the Force. *Star Trek* has "where no one has gone before." And although the Doctor often becomes cynical about the human race, in the end he knows that we hairless apes are worth saving. But *Planet of the Apes*? This is a franchise that ends its first film with a toppled Statue of Liberty, and follows that up by destroying all of Earth in the second. Perhaps I was just calling it the most cynical sci-fi franchise because I was scared of declaring it nihilistic.

But the finales of the 1968 film and its first sequel, *Beneath the Planet of the Apes*, are just bumps in the road, albeit very bleak bumps down a very dark road. One of the best things about the *Apes* franchise is that you can watch *Beneath* with a friend (a very patient friend, one to whom you may later owe a favor) and tell her "We're not even halfway through the franchise." That's because even after that green and insignificant planet dies, one of the greatest couples in sci-fi history keeps going. Zira and Cornelius, along with their son Caesar, are why I no longer consider the franchise so cynical. In the face of ignorance from humans and apes alike, their love perseveres. The bond between Cornelius and Zira is so powerful it would reshape the planet itself.

If the love between two smart and feisty scientists can change the world, I can't go around calling this franchise cynical, now can I? Well, then, let me atone for the sin of miscategorization by exploring and celebrating a love story that ended before it began and, through its revolutionary progeny, became the most powerful force in existence.

Watch the first few minutes of the original *Planet of the Apes* and you'll forgive my transgression. Our main character, George Taylor, pilots a spaceship as an integral part of a major accomplishment by the United States and the human race as a whole. In front of him are the wonders of the heavens. His reaction? He ponders whether mankind in the future will "still make war against his brother… keep his neighbor's children starving." To those on Earth, the mission of Taylor and his crew may seem like a beacon of hope in troubled times. The Apollo project was something many hung onto as a sign of humanity's salvation, during a time when it seemed the world was on the eve of destruction. But Taylor seems wholly unimpressed by what he and his colleagues have accomplished.

When Taylor, Dodge, and Landon make their trek through the "new" planet they have discovered, Taylor truly lays into Landon for daring to have hopes and dreams. Frankly, one wonders how Taylor became a military leader with that attitude. Re-watching the film in preparation for writing this essay, I found it remarkable that he laughs at Landon when the latter planets an American flag in the ground. Remember, this film came out more than a year before astronaut Neil Armstrong did the same thing on the surface on the Moon! It's almost as though Taylor is laughing at major human accomplishments before they even happen.

Perhaps this is all built off of Taylor's loneliness, which he mentions before indicting his entire species. Later on, Taylor tells Nova, "Imagine me needing someone. Back on Earth, I never did." When I discovered this film as a moody teenager, Taylor's outlook resonated with me. But in my 30s, I now suspect that the colonel is covering up for something. Is he keeping others at arm's length as a sort of psychological protection? Given his military career and the era he came from, he likely saw battle, perhaps in multiple wars. Many men who returned from World War II and Korea found salvation in familial domesticity. Not Taylor. There's a great darkness behind those bright eyes, one that prevents others from getting close to him. And yet, a family does provide Taylor with salvation after all.

That family is Zira and Cornelius. What other sci-fi film franchise spends so much time anchored by a married couple? Han Solo and Leia Organa don't count, as they aren't married or truly a couple for most of the original *Star Wars* trilogy, and we learn, in *The Force Awakens*, that their love didn't last. Similarly, Will Riker and Deanna Troi don't marry until *Star Trek: Nemesis*, considered by many to be the nadir of the *Trek* film franchise. Movies even have a tough time with famous married couples from comic books. Reed Richards and Sue Storm are only married in one of the three *Fantastic Four* films (the less said about these, the better). Lois Lane and Clark Kent get married on television, but their relationship never reaches that point in the many film versions of the Superman character. One can only imagine film executives scratching their heads while reading Brian K. Vaughan's and Fiona Staples's *Saga*, which revolves around a husband and wife team from warring extraterrestrial races.

Do filmmakers feel that married couples are hard to relate to for audiences, which are too often thought to be teen and male (a short-sighted observation, but a sadly persistent one, alas)? It's only further ironic, happily so, that many view Zira and Cornelius as the humorous, welcoming characters to whom younger viewers can relate in this mostly G-rated franchise.

We know Zira and Cornelius are great because they are beloved by kid and adult audiences alike. For children, they are the funny apes who could be your friends, the ones you don't mind seeing on your shelf in the form of an action figure. For adults, it's a joy to see the plot of a sci-fi film pivot on characters who are past the oft-adolescent "hero's journey" and have spent so much of their lives together. Beyond just being married, they each have a career as a learned citizen. In the second film, they discuss the idea of becoming parents, which leads to the major storyline of the remaining movies. It's incredibly invigorating to see sci-fi film characters whose strength and agency come from domesticity, which is usually a factor against which such characters fight. For Taylor, it's this quaint couple who save his life.

In particular, Taylor's salvation comes from the two chimps' revolutionary love. Not that Zira and Cornelius would consider themselves revolutionaries (ironically enough, given where their lives and bloodline would go). But there is something defiant in their love. Taylor's trial is the pivotal scene of the film. The main players are gathered, and the major themes that the movie wants to explore are put forth. One of those themes is the role of faith in society. It's clear that Doctor Zaius and the other orangutans in power keep their status by treating ape faith and history as one and the same, and a proprietary element of their own. But notice how Zira and Cornelius hold each other's hands when Zira asks "Why is [Taylor] accused?"

It's clear, in that moment, that their love for each other trumps the faith in society with which they have grown up. Through this love, they are able to look past simian society's limitations and join the few voices for science and reason in this world. Doctor Honorius calls the couple "young cynics," but nothing could be further from the truth. Their actions and knowledge are empowered by their love for one another. They question society, and demanding answers from a faith-based culture is, in and of itself, a revolutionary act.

Cornelius and Zira, through their love, find the strength to ask why Taylor is accused at his trial in *Planet of the Apes*.

I've written about Zira and Cornelius as a couple, but I must make special note of Zira by herself. It was quite remarkable in 1968 for a sci-fi film to feature a female scientist so prominently. We see her work front and center, whereas we never actually see Cornelius at work in his field. The two are clearly equals. She is never afraid to argue with her husband, and the arguments are never portrayed as shrewish or shrill. Rather, they are the arguments of two mature scientists in love. In 1968, science fiction had just left behind the very male-dominated "creature" films of the 1950s. In those movies, female characters were usually there to be told what to do by men, to help make the male characters (and audience) feel superior, or to shriek in terror when man's science inevitably went horribly, horribly wrong.

In the 1960s, horizons expanded, but things hardly got better in terms of representing women as intelligent equals. Raquel Welch, in *Fantastic Voyage*, is merely another character's assistant and mostly serves as eye candy. I do enjoy Jane Fonda's *Barbarella*, and I am sure there are many great feminist readings of that film, but I think it's fair to say that science is not the first thing on any character's mind. In fact, one of the other unique aspects of Zira is that, by virtue of being an ape, she is not under the male moviegoer's gaze, which was very much the case for Welch and Fonda in their respective films. Zira is an intellectual, first and foremost. She is not ruled by cynical or regretful thoughts, like Taylor and Zaius are. Instead, she is quite happy in her career. Her journey in the *Apes* franchise is not one built on yearning for personal fulfillment (at least, not at first). Her defense of Taylor comes from a place of genuine scientific curiosity and compassion.

Before delving more deeply into *Beneath the Planet of the Apes*, I want to note the great culmination of the first film's major themes. Under Doctor Zauis's orders, Cornelius reads the 29th scroll, 6th verse, of the Sacred Scrolls, beginning with "Beware the beast, man..." You may know the words, but watch the scene again and notice how Charlton Heston has Taylor react. He does not seem angry as the Lawgiver's words indict man. Rather, he seems to have some familiarity with this sentiment. He should – they are not so different than how Taylor himself indicts man at the start of the film. The astronaut asks, "Does man...still make war against his brother?" The scroll seems to answer with "Yea, he will murder his brother to possess his brother's land."

Taylor's dark outlook and Zauis's faith are just different faces of the same coin. The true alternative is the hope espoused by Zira and Cornelius. It is the hope they find in each other, and in their nephew Lucius, who frees Taylor. We know the astronaut is lonely, and Zaius seems lonely as well, burdened with knowledge he can never share with society. But it is family and friendship that provide hope against fate. Taylor is even able to prove man's accomplishments with a little doll that utters a single word: "Mama."

In *Beneath*, Cornelius and Zira are kept to the sidelines (despite Kim Hunter receiving second billing). It makes the film feel weaker and, with all due respect to David Watson, the lack of Roddy McDowall is certainly felt. But there is one standout moment for Zira. The films do not explore gender dynamics as explicitly as they do other themes. But we see Zira undermine and take advantage of a sexist society in one of her few scenes in the movie, as she and Cornelius hide Brent and Nova. To cover up for her medical equipment being out, Zira claims that Cornelius hit her for arguing. Zauis takes this as a given, and does not seem at all surprised or upset about it. Only the product of a truly misogynistic society could believe that Cornelius would hit Zira and get away with it. Zira plays on the orangutan's assumptions and prejudices, which includes her being called "headstrong," in order to protect the humans.

When Zira is not on screen in *Beneath*, things go badly – apocalyptic, even. Without her or Cornelius standing up for reason, chaos erupts between apes, humans, and mutants in the film's finale. In fact, it's deliciously appropriate that the mutants use psychic illusions to ward off apes. This population has been under the illusions of a history censored by Zaius and other leaders. Indeed, only Zaius can see through the mutants' illusions, as though he were the only one granted the privilege to see through lies. From there, violence takes over, and Taylor's outlook reaches its logical conclusion when he presses the button that destroys the world. He has lived up (or perhaps down) to his own belief, as well as Zaius's, that man is a destructive animal. But it's clear, by *Beneath*'s end, that this destructive quality is not found only in man. It is in whoever trades self-interest for compassion, and faith for curiosity. Thankfully, it is that scientific curiosity that keeps Zira and Cornelius – and the franchise – alive.

There is something gloriously brazen about continuing a franchise after it depicts the destruction of the entire planet. It's particularly brave (or insane) to have apes salvage Taylor's ship and travel back in time, even after establishing that simian society has not even mastered flight. The appearance of Doctor Milo as the scientist behind all of this is a bit of a *deus ex machina* (a rare version that appears at the beginning of a film, not the end), but the major reason audiences believe in this development is that Cornelius and Zira are such rich and positive depictions of scientific inquiry.

Thanks to *Star Trek/Planet of the Apes: The Primate Directive*, a comic book miniseries co-published last year by BOOM! Studios and IDW Publishing, this moment is forever linked to the "slingshot effect" in *Star Trek*. I love this association, because I like to think that the *Trek* and *Apes* franchises inspired generations of young minds to explore science, since both portrayed scientific intelligence as a powerful weapon of its own, a heroic element to which one can aspire. The difference, as portrayed so vividly in *Escape from the Planet of the Apes*, is that in the *Apes* franchise, this weapon is feared.

Escape is widely hailed as the best *Apes* sequel, mainly for the brilliant inversion of the first film's scenario. Instead of talking humans in the world of apes, it features talking apes in the world of humans. The inversion goes deeper. Taylor has a negative outlook but is asked to prove his species' worth. Zira and Cornelius, on the other hand, have a positive outlook – one earned and far from naïve. Compare Taylor's first words to the apes, the immortal "Take your stinking paws off me, you damned dirty apes," to Zira's words to Doctor Lewis Dixon early in the film: "I like you" (Cornelius says he liked Dixon even earlier). The chimps do not find themselves in quite the same situation as Taylor, but they are met with the same mentality: fear and suspicion, mutating into outright hatred. This franchise is usually not subtle about its intentions. When the media asks Doctor Otto Hasslein about what to expect from the Presidential Commission of Inquiry, he replies with only a single word: "fear."

Escape from the Planet of the Apes has ape-o-nauts Cornelius and Zira bring their optimistic viewpoints to a cynical past.

It's interesting to speculate on how Taylor and Hasslein might have interacted on the development of the astronaut's mission. Thank goodness Zira and Cornelius are such major players in this franchise; otherwise, the portrayals of those on the forefront of science would be that of misanthropic men of power. They have accomplished so much, but that has only led them to view their fellow man as inferior. I cannot help but associate these characters, particularly Hasslein, with the fact that these films were created under the administration of President Richard Nixon. The United States was in great turmoil at the time, and the men in charge reacted to it in much the same way that Zauis reacts to Taylor, and that Hasslein reacts to the ape-o-nauts. Nixon's staff took extreme measures to hold onto power, including lying and thievery. While the president in *Escape* seems quite reasonable compared to the paranoiac that was Nixon, Eric Braden's accent and performance for Hasslein certainly remind the audience of Nixon's advisor, Doctor Henry Kissinger.

This gets to what's at the heart of the *Apes* franchise: major events that affect so many lives – perhaps the entire world – often come down to the outlook of those in charge. Do they view the events around them, as well as their innermost selves, with fear-fueled apprehension or with curious yet learned enthusiasm?

Escape leaves viewers with a deeper impression of Zira's and Cornelius's positivity. The film is considered the most light-hearted entry in the franchise, and it is wonderful to see the two apes enjoy "modern" Los Angeles. But revisit those scenes knowing what Cornelius and Zira know: that they are in a doomed society that stands on a doomed planet. They witnessed Earth's destruction, but they do not approach their life on "old" Earth with a sense of melancholy, of which they would be due. Instead, they welcome this world with good humor and warmth. They enjoy this human world, perhaps because they know it cannot last. It starts with their approval of Dixon, and continues with how they win over the press. Cornelius's quip that he talks "only when she [Zira] lets me" should be considered as immortal as "God damn them all to Hell!" That moment, as well as Zira's loving reaction to it, encapsulates what is so wonderful about these two characters, and the fun that these films have to offer. Even the fearful attendees at the hearing cannot help but be charmed.

Escape features Zira's most explicitly feminist moment when she addresses the Bay Area Women's Club, which turns into a look at how both Zira and Cornelius relate to violence. At the club, Zira proudly declares "[Women] have heads as well as hands. I call upon men to let us use them!" This scene then cuts to a boxing match, where Cornelius and Dixon are in an almost cartoonishly masculine environment. Comparing Zira's comment with the footage of two boxers pummeling each other, fans are reminded that it is not just women who are expected to work only with their hands in a stratified society. Boxers often come from disenfranchised communities, and the bloodsport is seen as the only road to success. It's something Dixon may not even realize – it's such an established part of his society that he cheers on the match along with the rest of the fellas. But Cornelius does not hold back in his appraisal, as he finds the tradition "beastly."

The juxtaposition of these two scenes is a reminder of what Zira and Cornelius are always up against. Whether in the world of man or of apes, they find themselves under the rule of those who would use violence – their hands – to impose their will on others. The ape couple always stands against this, not because they consider themselves great rabble-rousers, but because they know, on a deep and personal level, that progress comes from intellect and not from brute force.

This makes the ending of *Escape from Planet of the Apes* all the more tragic. The film's second half becomes so much darker than its first, and it's all due to the bonds of family. Once Zira reveals that she is pregnant, Hasslein enacts his villainous schemes. The ape-o-nauts' "crime" is not one of destruction or even dissent. They simply want to celebrate their love and bring another ape into their world – one that they thought had more time than it actually did. By acting on their passion and romance, they put themselves in the crosshairs.

More than anywhere else in the franchise, the second half of *Escape* is when the forces of intelligence and positivity are savaged by the forces of cynicism and misanthropy. They may be at war in other parts of the movie, but in *Escape*, the forces under which Hasslein operates are fully established in power, and Zira and Cornelius can hardly fight back. A pregnant Zira accepts wine from Hasslein in her hotel room. Here, all the lighthearted "culture shock" moments of the first half culminate in a predator taking advantage of Zira, getting her drunk (and possibly harming her baby) just to get information out of her. But that is just the beginning of Hasslein's cruelty.

It's notable that Hasslein inflicts pain on Zira and Cornelius in a major way, by separating them. He sees their strength is in their bond, their faith in each other. He tries to disrupt that, but cannot. The film then considers a scenario and themes that one would not find in a G-rated sci-fi film these days: Hasslein convinces the government to abort Zira's child against her wishes. The story takes on a feminist bent when Zira fights for her right to choose her own reproductive destiny against the government's edict – though in this case, it is for her right to *keep* her child. Remember, *Escape* was released two years before the U.S. Supreme Court's landmark *Roe v. Wade* abortion decision.

It was while watching the ending of *Escape* that I may have originally deemed this franchise to be the most cynical in the annals of sci-fi history. Zira and Cornelius are trapped by those conspiring against them, and all seemed hopeless. But upon re-watching it, I now notice glimmers of hope. Zira says she was happy to tell the truth about her scientific endeavors with humans. Even with the dastardly way in which the truth is discovered, it lifts the burden of living a compromised life. That idealism in the face of such animosity is extraordinary. Later, the couple asks Dixon for a gun so that they may commit suicide together, if need be. It's a tragic moment, first and foremost, but there is a romance to it, albeit in the *Romeo and Juliet* vein.

This is the most violence that Zira and Cornelius face. It's notable that in these moments, they do not try to continue the cycle of violence. Cornelius accidentally kills a porter, and for the most primal reason known to both man and ape: to protect his mate and their unborn child. Even when asking to be armed, they intend only to turn the gun on themselves, not anyone else. Taylor, on the other hand, is happy to trade gunfire with gorillas, and even to bring about the end of all life on Earth. Later in the franchise, Caesar considers violence a valid option to accomplish revolution. But the final confrontation of *Escape* isn't gun vs. gun, but gun vs. family. Cornelius does shoot Hasslein, but again, it's for the sake of familial bond.

Even the chimps' deaths unfold romantically, with an injured Zira making her way to rest on Cornelius' body as they both die. Perhaps their last thoughts are that despite their murder, their infant son will live on. This dour climax, complete with the death of a regular ape infant, may be the most personal of the franchise's tragic endings. Baby Milo asking for "mama" is both sad and hopeful. Here is a motherless child, but one who may or may not continue the bloodline others tried to destroy. I feel I must be ambiguous, because the life of Caesar née Milo is a fascinating case of nature vs. nurture.

If *Escape* is viewed as the most light-hearted installment in the classic franchise, *Conquest of the Planet of the Apes* may be the darkest (and that is against some stark competition!). I must admit to you, dear reader, that in re-watching the film for this essay, I questioned my entire premise. Maybe this is the dourest sci-fi franchise, and the spark of hope lit by Zira and Cornelius is fully extinguished by Caesar's actions. *Escape* is the least scientifically curious of all entries in the franchise. Earlier, I discussed how violence seems to take over whenever Zira and Cornelius are not around. Here, that phenomenon is writ large. The "future" of 1991 features a human race that brutalizes apes, and thus brutalizes itself by playing the role of cruel taskmaster. In simian society, we see apes' enslavement of humans for scientific discovery (when they're not being used as target practice, granted). In *Conquest*, the enslavement of apes merely leads to them being trained as waiters and barbers. Progress has led to a violent society based on clearly imbalanced transactions of power. Humanity, in *Conquest*, truly lives down to Taylor's idea of it.

The dark turn that humanity takes means Caesar cannot follow his parents' footsteps into the sciences. Rather, Armando, as compassionate as he is, must have Caesar suppress his natural abilities of speech and reason. In comparison to his mother's commitment to the truth, Caesar's fate seems like a cruel joke. But while Caesar may not have known his parents, he has inherited their emotional honesty and this, as it did for them, leads him to challenge society.

There is a moment in *Conquest* that is more emotionally vulnerable than can be found in any other film in the series. When Caesar hears that Armando has died, he cannot react among the humans working for Governor Breck. He walks away, and only when he is alone does he weep for the death of his father-figure. We had never before seen an ape emote like that. As open and warm as Zira and Cornelius were, there is a bit of a "stiff upper lip" quality to them. We never get to see Caesar with his parents, but this scene feels like the link between the generations. Caesar weeps not just for Armando's death, but for the fact that he is truly alone now. It's a testament to McDowall's acting, and to the ingenious idea to have him play both Cornelius and Caesar.

Conquest puts forth the notion that if you add a sensitive soul to a brutal society, the outcome is revolution. Caesar's tactics are completely different than those of his parents. But that is only fitting, since he has been a victim of violence and oppression since (and before) his birth. Hasslein is as much responsible for Caesar as Zira and Cornelius are. Caesar's revolution may not be approved by his birth parents, but that's the whole point. They aren't here, and while the film does not make this explicit, this uprising seems to be a cathartic release for the betrayal and execution of the ape-o-nauts.

Here, I shall put forth my most controversial opinion: I prefer the altered ending of *Conquest* that was shown in theaters, not the original, darker conclusion later restored for Blu-ray release. These films are about hope and misanthropy in battle with each other. While the theatrical ending might be clumsy, it is satisfying to have a film that features a character torn between these two outlooks. By invoking God and destiny, his speech recalls Armando's words in *Escape*, about how he would be happy to live under the fate of ape rule if that rule were under the likes of Zira and Cornelius (it's a testament to the couple's kindness that they don't burst Armando's bubble on that one). This version of the speech sets up Caesar as a conflicted leader, which is made all the more explicit in *Battle for the Planet of the Apes*.

In *Battle*, the passing of generations is felt the most. Caesar doubts himself and wonders if his parents would approve of his ways. He names his son Cornelius, an example of the life-death-rebirth cycle that defines this family (which sadly continues when this Cornelius, too, is murdered by the film's antagonist). *Battle* puts forth one of the most fascinating, if unexplored, concepts of the franchise. The scientist Virgil discusses that there are multiple "lanes" when it comes to time. Could Zira and Cornelius traveling back through time have changed things, so that perhaps the world will no longer be destroyed in their era? After all, in *Escape*, Cornelius talks about Aldo being the ape who changed the course of simian society. Yet in *Battle*, Aldo kills Caesar's son and dies a pariah.

I doubt that Paul Dehn, Arthur P. Jacobs, and everyone else behind the original *Apes* franchise would simply repeat a name for no reason. If ape society is now founded on Caesar's uprising instead of Aldo's, then perhaps peace shall be within grasp, especially since Caesar now has a greater connection to his parents. Indeed, *Battle* is the only film that ends on a hopeful note, with human and ape children living together in peace. The statue of Caesar cries, a powerful but ambiguous image reminiscent of Caesar weeping in *Conquest*. The scene pays tribute to Caesar's past, while preparing the audience for his actions in the future. It's a moment in which his family's bloodline truly resonates.

The original *Planet of the Apes* franchise was viewed as family fare, with all but one film being rated G. That may come as a surprise, since not a lot of G-rated films feature the Earth burning to a cinder. But these are family films, in that they chart the course of a family that changes history. Their challenge lies in being hopeful and wishing for a better world, and the world attacks them for it. For all the losses they suffer, there is a chance that they may have averted the greatest violence of all.

The *Apes* franchise is not to be defined by its cynicism. Rather, it should be praised for exploring what it means to live in a cynical world – and how one can stand against such cynicism, even when all seems lost.

Nothing Ape is Strange to Me: Looking at *Escape* and *Conquest* Through the Eyes of a Zoo Professional

by Corinna Bechko

A Primate Reflected

Apes fascinate us. They are so human... and yet so *not*. Observe an ape closely, especially a chimpanzee or a bonobo, and it can feel like gazing into a clouded mirror. Some people look with love and curiosity, others with disgust and ridicule. As someone who spent five years watching both apes and zoo visitors, I suspect that how people respond has more to do with how they deal with the rest of humanity than what they really think of the chimpanzee or orangutan in front of them.

This ape obsession extends far beyond casual zoo visits, of course. Apes are often used as entertainers, to sell things, and as clownish characters in films, commercials, TV shows, and even street corners in some parts of the world. Most of the time, there's comedy implicit in these displays, as the apes are used as stand-ins for the ridiculous things a human might do if only we were less inhibited. For those of us who have worked with apes in other capacities, there's a great deal of pathos in viewing these performances, too, as we know the price paid by the performer.

To be clear, the apes with whom I worked were in a captive setting, though not one in which any of them were expected to put on a show. In fact, part of what I was studying was how to improve zoo exhibits so that the chimpanzee or orangutan ambassadors living in them could feel more at home. A big part of this was simply space, both vertical and horizontal. Another part was enriching exhibit "furniture," things like puzzle feeders that would engage the user's mind, as well as his or her strength. Even so, many of the behaviors displayed by the apes were interpreted by the public as comical or gross, a result that was quantifiable when we ran a companion study on the manner of reactions that the public had to our chimpanzee troop.

Essay author Corinna Bechko spent time as a behavioral research assistant with chimpanzees at the Los Angeles Zoo – the same zoo featured in *Escape from the Planet of the Apes*.

Some of the things the apes did were born out of boredom, some out of having enough leisure time to figure out innovative techniques to conquer mundane tasks. Still, most of their waking time was spent, as it would have been in the wild, on dealing with other apes. In the zoo, this included humans as well as conspecifics. Not coincidently, this is what most human stories are about, too. We are even more fascinated with ourselves than we are with other species. There's a reason looking at a chimpanzee makes us feel giddy – it's the flash of recognition that often warps into disgust or laughter. That unease is hardly ever handled well in mass entertainment.

Except, of course, on the planet of the apes.

An Insight Flipped, Then Flipped Again

It's no accident that my first real exposure to *Planet of the Apes* in general, and to the third film in the franchise, *Escape from the Planet of the Apes* in particular, came about during my stint as a behavioral research assistant at the Los Angeles Zoo – the same zoo, in fact, that is featured in *Escape*. At the time, I was lead on a study assessing the different ways in which our troop of 13 chimps utilized an old-style "moat" exhibit and a huge, brand-new one signed off on by legendary primatologist Jane Goodall herself. And it's even less of an accident that I first saw the films at a party hosted by a friend and colleague who was then working on her primatology degree. This love for *Planet of the Apes* among keepers and researchers is probably not a surprise. But *why* the people who know apes best love the franchise is a bit more complicated, and worth considering.

Perhaps the most striking thing about the first film is the seriousness with which it treats its subject. There is humor, certainly, but most of it comes out of the banter between Zira and Cornelius, a pair of scientists. The fact that they are chimpanzees is secondary, except for when it slots them into their culture's class system. They are not clowns, never gross or ribald. Instead, they are smart boundary pushers, the most "human" members of the cast.

As science-fiction ideas go, it's pretty simple. "A world where apes evolved from men." That's it. That's the concept. Just flipping our reality that much creates surprisingly rich veins of story to mine. Of course, the chimps, gorillas, and orangutans (bonobos are missing from almost every *Planet of the Apes* iteration, either because they are too poorly known by the general public or because they are too similar-looking to chimps) are played by human actors in realistic costumes and makeup, but the audience accepts them as what they are meant to be. For this to work as a parable and provoke insights into our own humanity, it's important that we laugh *with* the apes, never *at* them.

And that's part of what makes the *Planet of the Apes* franchise so different from almost every other live-action story involving an ape or monkey. Nowhere is this clearer than in the third film of the series, *Escape from the Planet of the Apes,* in some ways the lightest and funniest of the first five movies. By the time we get to this point in the story, we've learned the secret of why humans are no longer in control of the world, learned that ape society has problems of its own, and learned that those problems are nothing compared to the harm that humanity can still inflict on the Earth.

It's rare that a series has to transcend an ending as final as that imposed by *Beneath the Planet of the Apes*, the previous film, in which mutated, bomb-worshiping humans manage, with the help of George Taylor (Charlton Heston), to explode the entire planet. Where do you go with your story when every single character is dead and a prequel is out of the question (since *Planet of the Apes* doesn't work when humans aren't part of the equation)? If you ignore a couple of logical paradoxes, time travel to the past is the inspired answer.

This brings us to the most interesting thing about *Escape*. The human characters start by treating the "ape-o-nauts," Zira, Cornelius, and Milo, as animals. During the course of the film, they come to recognize that the trio are beings with thoughts, feelings, and the ability to reason. And then they begin to fear them, ultimately even to hunt them, leading to one of the most tragic endings in any G-rated film ever. But along the way, we, the audience, are in on the joke. We know that the chimpanzees are intelligent, and are aware of their status as time travelers. We laugh at the humans as they design ridiculous tests for the visitors, and want the chimps to stay one step ahead of any government officials, scientists, or media who get in their way. In short, we identify with the non-humans, and the film never once doubts that this will be the case.

The script has a lot of fun at the expense of humans. Unlike Doctor Zaius's mistrust of Taylor in the original film, these scientists have no context for Zira and Cornelius. And so they continue to underestimate them. A typical piece of dialogue has Doctor Lewis Dixon asking Cornelius if he can read a map. Cornelius's answer? "I'm an archaeologist. I can even draw one!" Stupid human, when will you learn that different doesn't mean inferior?

As the plot progresses, it seems that Zira and Cornelius have little hope of ever fitting into a world ruled by humans. Ironically, the only people who seem to care what happens to them are zookeepers and a circus owner, the very characters who are usually cast as villains in stories centered on animals. But, of course, these are the people who know apes best, and are the least shocked by their displays of intelligence. This is the film's great insight in sending the apes back through time. It is one thing to see a world ruled by apes through human eyes, but quite another to see a world ruled by humans through ape eyes. There is seldom any question of who is the most humane.

Apes Young and Old

From my own experience, I know that most humans consider baby apes to be exceedingly cute. This is part of why it's so common to see infant and juvenile chimps in commercials and films. (Wondering if a young chimp is truly a baby? Look for a white tail tuft. This feature is present at birth, but darkens with age until it disappears entirely in juveniles) Young chimps are very fast learners, picking up cues and behaviors handily. But that isn't the only reason that adults are almost never used as performers. In truth, grown chimpanzees have a mind of their own, and can be quite dangerous. They are stronger, pound for pound, than a human, and they have been known to hold grudges. In the wild, competing troops will even "go to war" with each other on occasion, and sometimes the results can be gruesome. Unlike an angry dog that will bite any leg, hand, or arm that is in its way, chimpanzees can be very focused, aiming for eyes, fingers, and genitals. Such attacks are rare in a zoo setting, where good management practices are the norm, but have been known to occur in situations when the animal was considered a pet and respect wasn't paid to the fact that an adult chimp is an individual being with wants, desires, and needs that extend far beyond food, shelter, and companionship.

That's something that *Escape*, almost alone among films about apes, gets right. When the time travelers first arrive in 1973, they make a pact that they won't allow the humans to discover that they can talk (the fact that their native tongue is English is the subject for another essay). This quickly disintegrates as Zira becomes increasingly annoyed by the way they are being treated, and the assumptions their human captors are making. Why won't she work for bananas? The answer, "Because I *loathe* bananas!", demonstrates that she is an individual, not to mention a woman with very little patience for fools. Even peace-loving Cornelius, when pushed to the limit and needing to protect his family, picks up a gun and is willing to use it. These apes are amusing and smart, but they aren't unreasonable.

In contrast, when it becomes known that Zira is pregnant, and what the future holds for humanity, their fate is sealed despite the fact that no one knows *how* the future will play out. Even as Zira and Cornelius realize what Doctor Otto Hasslein (played by Eric Braeden) has in store for them, Zira is able to take a wider view, reminding her husband that she used to experiment on humans before she learned of their humanity. It can be argued that she is far too generous, since the humans in this instance already know of Zira's humanity, and it makes little difference to them.

Zira, holding a young Caesar, talks with Armando in *Escape*.

The exceptions, of course, are the two zookeepers, as well as circus owner Armando (played by the sublime Ricardo Montalbán). What these three characters know, but the rest of the humans do not, is the full scope of ape behavior. They take it for granted that the chimpanzees will fight for their family members, grieve at the death of loved ones, and do anything at all to keep their children safe. They know that a desperate ape is a dangerous ape, and that compassion shouldn't stop at species boundaries.

As someone who has spent a lot of time watching chimps, I find these impulses deeply satisfying when reflected on the big screen. I have witnessed many of these behaviors myself in real chimpanzees, and it never fails to give me a frisson of recognition.

I vividly recall watching, horrified, as a squirrel once ventured into the large, new chimp exhibit just as I had completed my daily behavioral observation of our troop. The squirrel couldn't find a way out, since the walls, of course, had been designed to repel any thoughts of climbing. The chimpanzees were instantly aware. They are largely vegetarian, but will eat small amounts of meat, especially meat they have hunted, in the wild. In the case of the squirrel, the attack looked incredibly organized, and was over fast. The chimpanzees drew together, locking the squirrel into a tighter and tighter space, until it was lost to view. Then the chimps all sat quietly in a circle, their quarry in the center, until the alpha male raised the now-dead squirrel by the tail. It was then portioned out as each troop member put forward a hand, asking for a taste. Even the infants were given a portion of their mothers' share. (Make no mistake, this is not an activity sanctioned by any zoo, but it was interesting to watch captive apes participate in an activity that is usually only seen in the wild.)

I tell this story, not to vilify chimpanzees in the eyes of squirrel lovers, but rather to contrast it with another instance of group behavior that looked similar, but had a very different purpose. In the second case, the circle was repeated, and the chimps were equally quiet. But this time their postures were hunched, their faces slack. An infant had just died unexpectedly, and the apes appeared to be grieving along with its mother. It's not unheard of for mothers to lose their first baby, even when all concerned are receiving the very best care, so the keepers knew what to do. Instead of hiding the death from the apes or taking away the body too soon, they let the chimps realize that the death has happened. It's obvious that the chimps take some meaning from this, since their demeanor changes drastically. The bonds between chimps can be strong, fortified both in times of bounty and times of sorrow.

In *Escape*, we see this scenario play out twice. Early on, an angry gorilla kills Milo. This scene is one of the film's rare missteps, as gorillas are actually the least likely of the apes to perpetrate this kind of violence. But in the fiction of *Planet of the Apes* it works, since gorillas become militaristic by the time Taylor arrives in the far future. In this case, Zira and Cornelius are horrified, but they don't have much time to grieve.

But it's the end of the film that really captures the way in which apes of all sorts, chimpanzees and humans in particular, relate to death. The family is on the run, beset on all sides, when Cornelius and Zira find themselves at a dead end, trapped on a docked ship. Zira throws her injured and possibly dead baby overboard – an act that seems odd at the time, but makes a terrible kind of sense later. Then she crawls, mortally injured, to join her dead husband. Their lives taken from them, they still manage to find comfort in each other until the very last. It's an effective scene, and one that never fails to make me cry. Most audience members probably think of their own families as they watch, but I can't help but think of the chimpanzees I have known, too. Their grief is no less real than what is portrayed on screen, illustrating our common bond.

Of course, it is fear of what this infant will grow up to be that leads the humans in the story to commit these terrible acts, but it is because Zira and Cornelius are adults that they feel capable of carrying them out. Baby chimps may be adorable, but the general public almost always looks at adults with some degree of apprehension. It's the clouded mirror at work again, as we see ourselves reflected in their actions. Babies can be forgiven their antics, but shouldn't the adults *know better*? After all, they're so like us.

Working at a zoo, you hear some version of this repeated over and over, directed at apes. "Don't put your finger in your nose. You're too old for that!" or "Stop picking on her. You ought to know better!" or even "Ugh, cover that up. That's rude! Don't you know there are ladies present?" These same comments are rarely heard near the giraffes or lions, and almost never near any of the birds. It's as if humans can't comprehend that the mind inside such a similar body might work differently from our own. It's even reflected in the scientific name we have given to the species, *Pan troglodytes.* Pan is the Greek god of the wild, and a troglodyte is a person who lives in a cave — a primitive, basically. Put together, they evoke a mythical wild person, a being who could be civilized, but chooses to be feral, both more and less than human.

Apes on Their Own Terms

It's striking that Armando, the circus owner, tells us that he is a follower of Saint Francis of Assisi, "who loved all animals." Armando is easily the most compassionate character in the story, and the only truly selfless one. When appealed to for help, he doesn't hesitate: "You're asking me to risk imprisonment for the sake of two fugitive apes? The answer is, a thousand times, yes!"

Unlike every other human in the story, Armando never has an agenda for Zira and Cornelius beyond helping them and their new baby to stay alive, healthy, and free. We get the impression that he would do the right thing for them whether they were verbal or not, intelligent or not. His capacity to care about others has nothing to do with their similarity to himself. Instead, he takes each being on its own terms, as an individual with a unique experience of the world. If it wasn't for Armando and the zookeepers, we might despair for humanity after watching *Escape*, but as it is, we are left with some hope.

In the end, even Armando can't keep Zira and Cornelius a secret. The final showdown feels more like noir than children's entertainment, prompting many first-time viewers to exclaim "The baby's dead? No!" But in the coda, we learn that Armando came through after all, placing Zira's baby-toss in a new light. It turns out that another, non-verbal, chimpanzee in Armando's circus had given birth at the same time as Zira, and the infants were switched. Knowing what we do about chimps, verbal or not, this may seem cruel, and out of keeping with Armando's ethos. Surely the other mother grieved for her offspring just as Zira did. But Armando apparently took a wider view, realizing that Cornelius and Zira were something special, and that in the way of time paradoxes, the future might depend upon this intervention. If the world of humans has to end, surely it is better that something else rise up to take its place? If that "other" will be intelligent, sardonic, kind, and thoughtful chimpanzees, so much the better.

I'd go so far as to say that many people who work with animals harbor a secret hope that just such a thing might happen. Being confronted by the non-human brings out the best in some people, allowing them to experience a love and wonder that encompasses not only all of humanity, but the natural world as well. But for others, it brings out the worst. It's seeing what these latter are capable of doing that makes the former despair. Suicide rates among animal care personnel, especially in the rescue community, are alarmingly high. When empathy extends beyond personal friends and family, instances of appalling injustice are suddenly visible. This is true for social workers of all sorts, and becomes harder to deal with the more inclusive the "in-group" becomes.

Harder still is the ridicule that can accompany this inclusivity. Most people who volunteer their time or money have encountered some version of "Why send books overseas when our schools need books, too?" or "Why rescue dogs when there are kids going hungry?" The truth is that suffering manifests in myriad forms, and no one can tackle all of it. Most concentrate on just one or two areas, doing what they can, but almost everyone feels the tug of knowing it's not enough. Here, again, we intersect with Armando's story where it picks up in *Conquest of the Planet of the Apes*, yet another suicide by a good man who wished he could have done more.

Conquest is a fascinating film, and one that, in many ways, does not get the credit it deserves. There are obvious parallels with the Civil Rights Movement of the 1960s, but taken on its own terms (which are admittedly odd – all cats and dogs died, so apes become slaves? I'm guessing there was some heavy genetic manipulation somewhere off screen for that to happen as presented), it makes sense, too. But what's truly moving is the way in which the humans create their own fate, not just by enslaving apes in general, but by their treatment of Armando and Caesar in particular.

Conquest picks up just 18 years after *Escape*, long enough for the world to have changed, but also long enough for Armando to have lovingly raised Caesar as a son. They have lived apart from major metropolitan centers, so they've been spared the full brunt of how terrible life has become for most apes. In truth, Caesar has probably been an adult for years now (chimpanzees grow up a lot faster than humans do), but the story works better if you imagine him to have aged in human terms.

Armando still runs a circus, in which Caesar stars. No one knows he can talk, and that's the danger. If his gifts were to become known, he would meet the same fate as his parents. His foster-father has instilled in him a strong sense of justice, so Caesar cannot sit quietly by when he sees a man abusing a chimp. He is moved to yell an insult, which Armando claims to have uttered himself when they are challenged. He tells Caesar he must straighten everything out with the authorities, and that Caesar must stay quiet and hidden. And so he does, for a time, submitting to humiliating circumstances but keeping his cool even as he outsmarts the humans around him. Meanwhile, Armando learns that the powers that be have never stopped searching for the ape-o-nauts' offspring. He tries to obfuscate, but is cornered by a machine that will force him to tell the truth. Doing so would doom his adopted son, and so he chooses death instead, leaping from a window rather than allowing any harm to come to Caesar.

Armando does his best to hide Caesar's extraordinary gifts in *Conquest of the Planet of the Apes*.

Ironically, it is this act that seals humanity's fate. For Caesar soon learns what has happened, and in an alchemy known to chimps and humans alike, his grief turns to rage. It is because of Armando's treatment, as much as that of the other apes, that Caesar plots a revolt and leads a revolution. Apes rise up against their masters, finally joined together by bonds that cross species lines, and destabilize the governments of the world enough that the future from which Zira and Cornelius sprang becomes reality.

Or does it? In the lore that the ape-o-nauts brought back with them, there was no chimpanzee named Caesar who freed the apes – the simian savior was originally named Aldo. Perhaps the timeline of *Planet of the Apes* is not a closed loop, but rather a helix. What happened once doesn't happen in quite the same way, because a single man was open-minded enough to recognize Zira, Cornelius, and later Caesar as kindred beings deserving of respect and understanding.

Empathy and a Brighter Tomorrow

I don't work in a zoo setting anymore. Since leaving that field, I've moved on to become a full-time writer. Most of my output is comics, including a stint as co-writer on BOOM!'s *Betrayal on the Planet of the Apes*, *Exile on the Planet of the Apes*, and *Planet of the Apes: Cataclysm*.[1] It was while working on those titles that I first turned my attention to the mechanics of the original story, instead of just being enchanted by the premise. I became fascinated by how many different tales could be told using the same basic ideas and themes. At the same time, I was astonished by how easily I could work in the prejudices and bizarre notions about apes that I had witnessed first-hand in my old job. Of course, in our comics it was orangutan, gorilla, and chimpanzee prejudice against humans, but that wasn't a difficult leap to make.

The central concept behind *Planet of the Apes* is so simple that some people do not even consider it science fiction. Could other apes evolve to fill the empty spaces left behind by vanished humans? Is that even remotely possible? The answer, as far as I'm concerned, is "Who cares?" The beauty of the story is in how it allows us the freedom to think about difficult, uncomfortable subjects in a new way, and without the baggage that comes with telling a story in an historical context. The original film meets this challenge head-on, setting out its arguments cleanly and making sure we understand them.

By the time we get to *Escape*, and especially *Conquest*, there is room for more nuance. Both films revisit themes of prejudice and inequality, but now our allegiance is flipped beyond the human. And because we identify with the apes instead of the humans in these movies, the questions they raise about permissible violence, the dangers and rewards of empathy, and calculating when the ends will justify the means resonate long after the closing credits.

---

[1] See the previous volume, *The Sacred Scrolls: Comics on the Planet of the Apes* (Sequart, 2015), for more information about these and other *Apes* comic books.

Was Armando ultimately right? If the world had embraced Zira and Cornelius and had allowed them to raise their baby in peace, would destruction have been averted? Or would that have hastened a future without humans? Doing so wouldn't have been easy. It's hard to look beyond your own reflection to the ape itself. But it can be done. And when it is, it feels like a veil is lifted. The world becomes more interesting, and less deterministic. A world with more Armandos might have less drama and violence, but it would certainly have a brighter future.

The Second American Revolution: Did Another Coup on U.S. Soil Precede the Apes' Own Conquest?

by Jim Johnson

Of the five original *Planet of the Apes* films, *Conquest of the Planet of the Apes* was the chapter that was the most transitionary, bridging mankind's final moments as Earth's dominant species to the genesis of the world's simians taking over that role. As critically maligned as it was at the time, *Conquest* nevertheless largely fulfilled its purpose, revealing the events – or, at least, the most critical ones – that served as the catalyst for this eventual global takeover.

Questions about these exact circumstances had lingered in viewers' minds ever since George Taylor and his crew were first attacked by evolutionarily advanced apes in the very first movie, and *Conquest* was the first of the films to directly answer at least some of them, though Cornelius had provided some degree of verbal explanation to the President's committee in *Escape From the Planet of the Apes*. The first two films – and, to a lesser extent, *Battle for the Planet of the Apes* – established what transpired during the decades, centuries, and millennia after the apes' conquest, but the only indication of what had come before was the modern, everyday world shown as the backdrop of

Escape. However, as the story unfolds in *Conquest*, it becomes very clear that many social standards in the world, or at least in North America, had changed in the nearly two decades since the events of the previous installment.

In *Escape*, the world seemed to be a pretty nice place to live, unless you were a talking chimpanzee and had Doctor Otto Hasslein trying to kill you and your unborn child. Cornelius and Zira had become media darlings, the public seemed to love them, and most everyone treated them with respect, if not outright kindness. In *Conquest*, though, no one really seems to be very nice, except for circus owner and animal lover Armando. North America, the primary locale named in the movie, is a much darker, meaner, and militaristic place come the then-future of 1991. The concrete city seen in the film's opening moments evokes a much colder and more sterile feel, largely free of any greenery – or of any other color, for that matter. The only predominant colors visible, in fact, are on the prison-like jumpsuits worn by dozens of apes, who are being trained and ordered about by baton-wielding handlers, all of whom are adorned as either military police or black-clad overseers.

Cold concrete and prison-esque jumpsuits litter the landscape in *Conquest of the Planet of the Apes*.

As the film proceeds, other elements, like the shrill, ever-present loudspeaker voice of the "watch commander" speaking of unlawful protests and citizen curfews, as well as the sight of law enforcement clad in riot gear, indicate that the land of North America has seemingly become much closer to a fascist police-like state since the end of *Escape*. In the real world, when *Conquest* was released in 1972, the United States and the Soviet Union were in the midst of the longstanding Cold War, and the mindset of the day made the film's setting appear to be one not unlike that of an Eastern-bloc city, or at least Westerners' perception of same. Although nothing is overtly spoken of within the context of the story, it's all too evident that sometime during the years preceding the apes' pending revolution, there was already a transformation of another kind in the United States, be it social, political, or military, that led to the ongoing state of affairs serving as the environment for *Conquest*.

The earlier films were rich with political and social allegories, playing on fears of the consequences of war and nuclear annihilation. While the later ones, including *Conquest*, were more self-referential to the franchise's own continuity, *Conquest* could be interpreted as an allegory to the less catastrophic but very real Cold War, particularly Western fears of it being won by the Eastern bloc, and a possible coup resulting from its aftermath. The film was released right around the time that nuclear détente was being negotiated between the United States and the Soviet Union – negotiations that somewhat calmed society's longstanding fears regarding all-out nuclear destruction, but did little to quell newfound ones of a more covert and subtle Eastern takeover. Just as the ruins of the city below the Forbidden Zone in *Beneath the Planet of the Apes* provided a cautionary extrapolation of the nuclear arms race, the hard-cornered confines of the city in which *Conquest* takes place could easily be the figurative social ruins of an American city that once prospered under democracy but is now crushed under the heels of Eastern domination.

While a full-blown nuclear war seemed less likely by the early 1970s, at least compared to a decade or two earlier, conventional warfare remained a very real concern, as the United States was still embroiled in the final days of the agonizingly lengthy Vietnam War. *Conquest* gives no indication that any kind of nuclear conflict had taken place within the 18 years between its events and those of *Escape*, and the city, as well as the citizens who populate it, all seem blessedly free from any kind of nuclear damage or contamination. But this isn't to say that a conventional war could not have broken out between Western and Eastern armies elsewhere in the world, or even elsewhere within the United States, sometime within that time span, resulting in a loss by Western forces that conceivably could have signaled the end of democracy in America and the installation of a police state.

In the real world, as American forces struggled in Southeast Asia and eventually withdrew, the once-unthinkable notion of the United States losing a war became not only a very real possibility, but a reality. No longer clinging to the false confidence that America's entry into a war ensured an automatic victory, *Conquest* capitalized on that newfound uncertainty, indicating that the near future might not be as devastating as getting nuked, but still reminded viewers that there are other threats outside of America's borders beyond their control, and that if they weren't already concerned about them, then perhaps they should be. The conquest shown in this film could very well have actually been the second revolution on American soil in as many decades.

The vaguely named North American local was, in all likelihood, a deliberate attempt by the filmmakers to convey that the events take place somewhere in the Western hemisphere, and that a specific location bore no relevance to the story itself. But the geographical reference can also be interpreted in another, more nationalism-related context: while "North America" typically refers to the continent, the "North" could be taken as an implication of the United States enduring a postwar split between opposing forces, à la East Germany and West Germany in the aftermath of World War II. Within the context of a possible Eastern takeover prior to the events of the film, the term could be construed as the name given to a portion of the former United States of America, now divided into two (or possibly more) separate and distinct nations.

Conversely, the name could also be taken as that of a newfound nation following an assimilation of Canada and Mexico into the United States, in a manner not unlike the Soviet annexation of the Baltic countries to its west during the Second World War. Either way, when the commonly held continental reference to the name is put aside and instead put within the perspective of international upheaval, the term "North America" can take on a connotation evocative of past Soviet expansionism. The reference made in *Conquest* to Armando's circus travelling primarily through provinces could be an allusion to the Canadian provinces, and an indication that these territories are still part of whatever the new North America constitutes.

While the idea of the United States undergoing a revolution as a result of external intervention is one possibility that can be read into the background of the movie's setting, there are also seemingly unrelated elements in the films that conceivably could be viewed as catalysts for a sociopolitical movement from within the country's own borders. In *Escape*, Cornelius and Zira had become simian celebrities, and the last public perception of them seen in that film was overwhelmingly positive. The findings of the Presidential Commission that deemed Cornelius, Zira, and their then-unborn baby to be potential threats to mankind's future were never shown to be made public. While these findings may have been eventually released to the media, and could have potentially changed or divided public perception at that point, nothing within the scope of *Escape* indicates that the general opinion of the couple had changed before their deaths. It is, therefore, likely that their murders would have generated a great deal of public outrage, naturally directed at their killer, who happened to be a prominent government official.

The seeming assassination of two beloved and unique celebrities by the federal government could have conceivably sparked varying degrees of civil disobedience toward the U.S. government in general, and the President in particular, since Hasslein was a member of his cabinet. An escalation in such acts' severity could, in turn, have triggered a reciprocal escalation of the government's response. A worst-case extrapolation, based on historical evidence of civilian uprisings met with state resistance, would be the government resorting to tactics like restricting protests, enacting curfews, and increasing surveillance – tactics all used by the government of the North American city seen in *Conquest*. Hasslein's extreme actions at the end of *Escape*, and the subsequent fallout from those actions, could have been the seeds of public discontent that gave birth to the more totalitarian atmosphere present in *Conquest*.

Another potential key event capable of initiating national and worldwide upheaval is the relatively sudden and unexpected mass extinction of the world's dog and cat populations.[1] In *Escape*, Cornelius told the Presidential Commission what he knew of the pending extinction, stemming from the spread of a so-called space virus. This story would have been one that was essentially legend from Cornelius's point of view, as this disaster had occurred millennia in his past. His words to the commission, though, turned out to be prophetic from their perspective, as *Conquest* confirmed this disaster early on as having taken place only a decade after Cornelius first spoke of it. The story, legend that it

---

[1] Or near-extinction, given the existence of a dog in the *Planet of the Apes* television series

may have become, nonetheless clearly made it intact through the ages into Cornelius's time; however, there is no indication anywhere within the scope of the films that confirms the plague is a *true* story. The disappearance of mankind's favorite pets is unmistakably and obviously evident, yes, but the reason or the source of it is largely taken on faith.

A destructive element that would cause such selective decimation only to certain species would likely be biological, if other organisms remain untouched by its effects. And it could, indeed, have even been a virus brought down from the skies, as the official and generally acknowledged account goes. But the widely believed story could have also been a cover for a more sinister reality, such as an industrial accident that unintentionally released a weaponized but experimental and unperfected virus, with household pets being the unintended victims. An accident on this scale would undoubtedly create tremendous social turmoil, and if the government were, indeed, responsible for such a disaster, it's not unreasonable to surmise that they might concoct a story to shift blame away from themselves.

The blame could be directed elsewhere, perhaps toward some hapless astronauts who had recently and conveniently returned from a publicly known space mission, rather than on some bungling lab technicians working within what was supposed to be a secret military installation. The slippery slope of broad cover-ups could easily further include stifling the media, squelching outside inquiry, and clamping down on discourse about the disaster – more techniques historically employed by real-life totalitarian regimes very similar to the one that seems to be in place in *Conquest*.

Rather than being brought back by astronauts, a virus from space also could have been a satellite-based attack on the United States by another nation. The catastrophic and unthinkable damage would arguably be construed as a 9/11-level offensive, and recent history shows government tendencies to restrict personal freedoms in the aftermath of such devastating attacks – again, an atmosphere that's discernable within the setting of *Conquest*. Short of anything less lethal than a direct nuclear strike, the United States might not have had a weapon of similar scale with which to respond in kind.

In such a scenario, without a like means of retaliation, a cover story fed to the people, claiming that the virus was not an act of aggression, would serve to calm fears to some degree. This lie would provide the public with the dubious comfort of believing that at least this tragedy was merely an accident and a one-time occurrence, rather than a deliberate attack that could be carried out again, with humans possibly being the intended target the next time. Such a story would also give the populace no direct enemy to rally against, which would thus quell public demand for a military response from the United States that they were unable or unwilling to launch.

The three ape-o-nauts may very well have brought with them the virus that set into motion the death of domestic animals and the enslavement of apes.

Cover stories aside, if the legend of astronauts bringing a spaceborne virus back to Earth is accepted as true, it's interesting to note that those astronauts could conceivably have been Doctors Cornelius, Zira, and Milo themselves. Their arrival in our time could have inadvertently contaminated the planet with this heretofore unknown and slow-acting virus that they somehow picked up during their time in space, resulting in the eventual deaths of all household pets within the span of the next decade. Another possibility is that, rather than *originating* in space, it may instead have simply *traveled* through space, as the virus itself may have actually existed on Earth during Cornelius's and Zira's time two thousand years hence, and their return unwittingly unleashed the plague into the present day.

The virus could very well have been an organism that existed in the Forbidden Zone, where the couple had ventured in the first movie. Cornelius and Zira could have been carriers after being exposed to it during their time in the Zone, and since the virus had no impact on simians, they never would have known that they carried it, nor of its eventual effects on the world's animal population, since they were murdered long before those effects ever became apparent. The virus may even have been mutated by exposure to the same radiation in the Forbidden Zone that mutated the humans who lived there, as seen in *Beneath the Planet of the Apes*, which could have transformed it into an overwhelmingly devastating disease.

Escape showed the present-day world to be one largely similar to our own, and though it offered no perspective on public perception of the government during the course of the movie, it's fair to assume that there was some ongoing state of public distrust, albeit unseen, as there has never been a time in recent U.S. history when public support of the government has been anywhere near unanimous. In the wake of Cornelius's and Zira's deaths at the hands of a Presidential advisor, this distrust and dislike of the government would have only increased, potentially creating an even greater schism between those who distrust the current administration and another demographic unseen in *Escape*: namely, those who might have agreed with Hasslein's views and supported his murderous actions.

Just as the Watergate break-in was the real-life political scandal that polarized the country's population in the years following *Escape*'s time in theaters, the murders of Cornelius and Zira could have subsequently had the same effect on the nation, within the films' continuity. Watergate eventually took down the leader of the free world; the scandal of a Presidential cabinet member going rogue and committing murder would also likely cause some strife in the White House, as well as some potentially severe political and social backlash. This fallout could result in more iron-fisted tactics by the government, leading to the eventual evolution toward a more totalitarian regime as outlined earlier, or it could also result in a more organic evolution of the government, such as ushering in the election of a new President from a different political party, or perhaps even the rise of a new political party altogether.

In *Conquest*, there is mention of Governor Breck's own political party – and while said party is not specifically named, it could indicate the formation of a newer political force within the two decades since *Escape*. When Breck is first introduced in *Conquest*, his predisposed anti-ape sentiment is tangible; he seems to harbor a resentment and even hatred toward the species that is not outwardly explained initially, though Breck himself provides a rather philosophical and idealistic reason at end of the film. Earlier, Breck is mentioned as having political aspirations, and his seeming obsession and disdain toward simians is the trait that's given central focus in the movie. It's possible that an anti-ape doctrine, driven by the Presidential Commission's report 18 years prior, could be a key component of his Machiavellian agenda.

While this is not explored in *Escape*[2], the sudden appearance of talking, intelligent chimpanzees would undoubtedly prove to be a divisive societal issue, especially with the implication that their then-unborn child could prove to be a threat to mankind's future. Overwhelming public support of Cornelius and Zira was the overall sentiment shown in the film, and this demographic is from where any presumed public outrage regarding their murders would commence.

The other, unseen side of the issue, though, would be the reactions of those who did, indeed, feel that the apes were a very real threat, and would, therefore, be much more inclined to support any action that brought about their demise. To this segment of the population, Hasslein would have been seen as a hero, spun as the champion who stood against popular opinion and arguably saved mankind in the process. His own resultant death could have elevated him to the historical status of humanity's hero and savior, and possibly even a martyr. These supporters could very well have been the basis for a political movement, and possibly the birth of Breck's political party, rooted in a kind of human preservationist platform.

When Breck lies defeated and all but deposed at the feet of Caesar, he provides the emperor ape, and viewers, with an explanation of sorts for his beliefs: that apes represent the bestial side of man and thus need to be tamed. Such feelings may indeed be valid, but seem to be a rather vague and shallow reason to use his position as the means to support the subjugation of three entire species, in addition to all of his other presumed leadership duties as governor. A political platform also comes across as a rather extreme means to implement what amounts to an organized and elaborate form of animal cruelty, so there likely exists a more solid and plausible reason for Breck's position that falls more in line with his political career agenda.

---

[2] Though it is an element of the comic book miniseries *Revolution on the Planet of the Apes* (Mr. Comics, 2005-2006), written by Ty Templeton and Joe O'Brien.

As the end credits began to roll in *Escape*, the deaths of the chimpanzee family seemingly close out the perceived threat to mankind's supremacy, but elements from *Conquest* indicate otherwise, Breck's own aforementioned attitude among them. Breck is all too quick to believe that a talking chimp is in his city's midst, after being told of Caesar's accidental verbal outburst in the presence of the police. The police themselves, in fact, all too readily accept the notion that Caesar actually spoke – a notion that should have been immediately dismissed as absurd, especially decades after such an ape had widely believed to have been killed.

This willingness seems to indicate a persistent belief among the population that a talking chimpanzee still exists, which could be fostered by any number of possible factors. Such factors could include a sighting when Caesar was a child, one of Armando's circus hands doing some talking of his own, or conspiracy theorists propagating the idea that baby Caesar was never killed in the first place. All could form the basis for these tenacious rumors, not unlike those of the Bigfoot sighting variety, that would be dismissed by most, yet never quite go away completely. Breck himself, as well as his staff and supporters, could very well be among those believers, which would be consistent with the beliefs of a so-called and ever-strengthening preservationist party.

As Breck and his staff possess a recording of the Presidential Commission's findings from two decades prior, it's evident that this tape has survived intact despite whatever political and government changes had subsequently taken place. This recording could very well serve as a testament of sorts for the foundation of a preservationist-type movement, as the committee chairman not only clearly advises both aborting the fetus and sterilizing Cornelius and Zira, but also warns of the consequences of failing to do so, based on Cornelius's own testimony. As baby Caesar ultimately was *not* killed, and thus no evidence could exist to support this widespread belief, those convinced that mankind was doomed based on the committee's findings would have remained nervously uncertain that their children's generation was ever secure, and only would have felt more threatened when apes became a more prominent part of day-to-day living.

Once the chimpanzee family was slain, thereby eliminating any presumed threat, the testimony provided to the commission by Cornelius could have easily been forgotten. However, a decade later, the global extinction of dogs and cats would have instantly revealed Cornelius's words to be prophetic, and now that testimony would suddenly carry plenty of newfound interest and relevance; whether one believed the baby to be alive or not, there was now undeniable truth that backed up Cornelius's frightening story.

This would undoubtedly have legitimized and galvanized any kind of preservationist agenda that might have existed. If the extinction of two species – a significant part of Cornelius's revelation – had come to pass, then many could just as easily believe the even more frightening aspect about an intelligent ape one day leading a revolution against mankind. This revelation would become all the more believable when combined with the belief, held by many, that such an ape already lived in secret somewhere among them.

The eventual enslavement of apes, also spoken of by Cornelius, seems to play straight into this doomsday prediction, but it presents a curious dichotomy that could be seen as both fulfilling a prophecy and trying to avoid it. Those opposing such enslavement would view it not only as cruel, but also as a move that would set the stage for mankind's downfall. Those in support of it, though, would naturally see it as a means of domesticating and pacifying any potential threat, by taming these wild beasts and presumably neutralizing any collective threat they might ever prove themselves to be.

The domestication of apes could have happened as told by Cornelius, with their being taken in as surrogates to beloved pets lost before this transitioned into a more sinister and sadistic practice. Or, it could have been a practice encouraged by the government, in a deliberate and ironically self-fulfilling response to the threat revealed in Cornelius's statements, to head off any kind of feared revolution by attempting to pacify those responsible for it.

Cornelius's account of the simian uprising to the committee would have come from the historical teachings of the Sacred Scrolls, presumably the only surviving recollection of ancient history known to ape culture within the context of the films. Cornelius spoke of an ape revolt, but less clear is whether the historical writings in the Scrolls spoke of a sole intelligent ape who planned and instigated it. He seems to have no knowledge of any specific timeframe for the uprising, and it's doubtful that the scrolls, created centuries later, could have pinpointed it to a specific year, or even decade. Cornelius and Zira, therefore, would have had no idea that their arrival in 1973 would predate the revolution by less than two decades – or, in fact, that their own unborn child would be responsible for it.

If the Scrolls did mention a specific central revolutionary figure, Cornelius and Zira never showed any indication that they knew that this pivotal figure in their history would have been their own son (despite the Lawgiver having mentioned him by name during his lessons in the bookend scenes of *Battle*). Per their own observations in *Escape*, apes were still primitive in what, for them, were ancient times, so in all likelihood, they presumed that whenever the simian takeover occurred, it was centuries away from the point in time when they arrived, not decades. Cornelius's account of a spaceborne pet plague and man's subsequent enslavement of apes also undoubtedly sounded like a distant concept, not worthy of any kind of serious or immediate concern in 1973.

The Scrolls, or at least Cornelius's recollections of their passages, may have incorrectly recorded one important pivotal moment in ape history, though. According to Cornelius, in his words to the commission in *Escape*, it was an ape named Aldo who first spoke the word "no," when, in fact, *Conquest* showed that Lisa was the first primitive ape capable of this act. The first ape (aside from the ape-o-nauts themselves) chronologically to speak at all was, of course, the time-displaced Caesar, so either this critical turning point was incorrectly captured in the Sacred Scrolls, or Aldo's moment in history was simply not shown in *Conquest*.[3] Those who had paid heed to Cornelius's seeming prophecy about the virus and ape rebellion undoubtedly expected and feared that a talking ape would eventually surface, but none were ever shown to have done so prior to the apes' takeover.

It's entirely possible that, at some point before the uprising, Aldo did in fact first speak, but that this act simply wasn't relevant to the apes' budding coup, and because Caesar himself had taken the lead. While Lisa was the first ape shown to form words, there's no indication whether other apes, unseen in the film, had mustered up that same ability.[4] Aldo may have gotten the credit because, as seen in *Battle*, he had risen to prominence as general of the gorilla army. Whatever legacy he might have left behind, besides that of being the murderer of Caesar's son, could have included a long-held, and possibly self-perpetuated, belief that Aldo was regarded as the first primitive ape to ever

---

[3] *Conquest* would originally have portrayed Aldo's defiance. Near the beginning of the film, Caesar witnesses an ape named Aldo (played by David Chow) being mistreated by his handlers. That Aldo is a chimp, not a gorilla (as Claude Akins' Aldo is in *Battle*), but the movie's script identifies him as a gorilla, indicating that the two Aldos were both intended to be the one mentioned in *Escape*. Why a chimp was used instead, and why he never said "no" in *Conquest*, is unclear.

[4] *Revolution on the Planet of the Apes*, in fact, postulated that Caesar's presence in the past divinely inspired all apes to gain speech capability.

speak, whether or not it was true.[5] Regardless of the truth behind that belief, it's one that nonetheless made it into the annals of ape history.

But because Aldo was *not* acknowledged as the first ape to speak at the time of the revolution in *Conquest*, though, and because there's no public acknowledgment of such an occurrence within the film, Cornelius's account of these events could be interpreted as less than completely factual. This perceived mistake could have provided a false sense of comfort to those who nervously watched the earlier aspects of his recollections unfold; maybe apes had been enslaved, as Cornelius had foretold, but within the scope of *Conquest*, there was no evidence of *any* talking ape that had been publicly observed, short of Caesar himself on the eve of the revolt. Those who had come to believe that ape enslavement would not lead to an ape revolution solely because there had been no evidence of a talking ape would have only discovered that grievous misconception as the revolution was imminent.

The film's linear logic connecting the extinction of dogs and cats to simians being placed in a role of trained servitude (a transition that took less than a decade to transpire) requires some pretty strong suspension of disbelief on the part of viewers. But it's not all that different than accepting the notion that *all* apes could acquire the ability to speak *and* command a pretty good grasp of the English language, as seen in *Battle*, within a comparable length of time. Nothing is said within *Conquest* about other factors beyond a space virus that could have played a role in the ensuing domestication of apes, but that's not to say that such other factors weren't possible.

With the U.S. government, and subsequently the North American government, aware of the commission's troubling findings regarding mankind's potential future, the domestication of apes could conceivably have been a deliberate attempt to stave off a feared simian takeover of the planet, rather than merely the consequences of a massive biological disaster. At the time of the commission's conclusion, though, there was no knowledge that such a virus even existed, let alone that it could kickstart something as preposterous-sounding as a worldwide simian takeover, because apes were still living either in the wild or in zoos at that point. If the U.S. government were so concerned about future simian domination, and were to try to initiate some kind of far-reaching effort to bring apes in from the wild with the sole intent of

---

[5] Malibu Comics featured a cult of gorillas known as Aldonites, who revered him as their savior a century after *Battle*'s events.

domesticating them, the lack of the virus serving as a catalyst would make such a knee-jerk, overly reactive initiative all but implausible.

This type of fearmongering, the kind so prevalent in Breck's attitude and beliefs, becomes a bit more believable if there's a definitive reason for the government to fear an ape takeover, beyond that generated by the words of an intelligent talking ape couple claiming to be from two millennia in the future. If worries about apes taking up arms and fighting at the behest of a leader are so palpable, it may well be because such a fear could be a very real thing if said apes had such training beforehand, perhaps for military or warfare purposes. No such training is mentioned in the films, of course, but it's not unfathomable, given the very existence of Ape Management, to presume that the North American government just might have feared a revolt for reasons beyond apes growing tired of shining shoes or carrying books home from the library.

If the U.S. government had been conducting some kind of covert military program to train apes for a literal kind of gorilla warfare within the timeframe of *Escape*,[6] the arrival of three talking chimps claiming to be from the future would arouse more than just curiosity on the part of government officials. There would likely be some genuine concern, if not outright alarm, over a distant yet not unshakable connection between primitive apes being trained by the government, and three highly intelligent ones washing ashore in one of the same government's very own spacecraft. The subsequent revelation that apes could one day gain the power to take over the planet would be an undeniably disturbing outcome to those in support of a military-backed program to train simians for warfare. To those buying into this doomsday scenario, this revelation could very well be enough to shut down such a program faster than a federal budget deficit ever could.

A surplus of apes forced into an early retirement from the military would be a likely and immediate source of fresh companions for a nation full of grieving pet owners who, following the plague, are looking for pets more personable than lizards or goldfish. Ape Management could conceivably be the likely linchpin between the military and civilian servitude, retraining these apes from warfare to washing clothes, repurposing them as servants rather than soldiers.

---

[6] In fact, *Revolution on the Planet of the Apes* revealed just that, as Area 51 contained a facility in which ape pilots, including Aldo himself, were being trained to fly fighter jets.

Ape Management was most likely borne out of a fear of open revolt, not just of an uprising about shining shoes.

The plague, as tragic as it was, would have played right into the government's hands in this scenario, giving them an excuse and even public support to attempt to retrain these animals, and hopefully forever put to rest the fear of an eventual simian takeover. The North American government would then end up with a country full of apes trained for military action, but now instead serving drinks and lighting cigarillos. A lingering, smoldering fighter or even killer instinct could be readily reignited by Caesar's leadership, meaning that the government would inadvertently have set up the apes' own ability to revolt against them.

Escape and *Conquest* present an interesting question, by asking what a ruling government would or should do if armed with the knowledge and precise circumstances of their eventual downfall. *Conquest* merely shows that ape enslavement has become a reality, but never postulates whether this is due to that knowledge, in spite of it, or simply ignorant of it. Doomsday prophecies are generally scoffed at by many, but one that predicted an extinction-level event a full decade in advance before such a tragedy actually occurs would give even the most ardent skeptics at least momentary pause. Such seemingly ludicrous predictions could easily be forgotten in ten years' time, though, and mankind's subsequent actions could, therefore, unintentionally play straight into it.

If a prophecy like this *is* remembered, its relatively far-flung consequences could easily be a secondary concern next to the more immediate one for a world full of grieving pet lovers looking to fill a sudden void in their lives. Those who place a higher severity on such a prophecy, and support taking a course of action intended to neutralize it, could inadvertently fulfill it instead, while believing that their actions are doing the exact opposite. All of the likely scenarios point to the predictions of mankind's downfall coming true, no matter what is done to prevent them. Perhaps this was another message being delivered by the filmmakers: not only that mankind's actions spell doom for our future, but that we have been preordained to undertake these actions. Beware the beast Man, indeed.

To varying degrees, the original five films provide commentary on the social and political issues of the day, and while *Conquest of the Planet of the Apes* spends most of its time solidifying the movies' collective continuity, there are still implicit references to the state of the era's world affairs. *Conquest*, like the earlier films, plays on the fears of worst-case consequences coming to fruition.

Unlike its predecessors, though, *Conquest* purports the most unsettling extrapolation of all – namely, an extrapolation into a time that its viewers largely would still be around to see. No one had to go to bed at night fearing that an angry, intelligent ape from the future might lead three entire species to depose mankind from the world's throne, but they weren't entirely free of the fear of one day living under some *other* kind of domination, spurred on by the vague but pervasive possibility of change brought on in their lifetimes by a second American revolution.

The Mis-Shape of Things to Come: Paul Dehn's *Planet of the Apes*

by Neil Moxham

Of all the creators of the *Planet of the Apes* mythos, figures like Pierre Boulle, Arthur P. Jacobs, and Rod Serling have received the highest acclaim, as they should. However, as the person responsible for mapping out four of the five original movies, Paul Dehn was also immensely influential. Dehn built upon the iconic legacy of the first *Planet of the Apes* film, but took the sequels in a direction entirely of his own, exploring his thoughts on religion, intolerance, war, nuclear weapons, civil rights, and the politics of protest.

It shouldn't have worked as well as it did. He was middle-aged and quintessentially English, yet was able to consistently connect with a principally young American audience. Dehn was a war veteran who questioned the sanity of those who make war, and he was a writer of the spy genre who had to reinvent himself for science fiction. He was a private man who gave few interviews, adding further to the enigma, but his complex personality can be glimpsed through his poetry, his screenplays, and the memories of a diminishing number of people who knew him personally.

Paul Dehn's remarkable life story sets the context for his writing. He was born in Manchester in 1912 to a family of successful entrepreneurs of German-

Jewish origin. His father aspired to integrate into British society, and so the future screenwriter was enrolled as a boarder at the private Shrewsbury School. Another "Old Salopian" scholar had been Charles Darwin, whose theory of evolution would form such a central part of the *Apes* concept. After Dehn received further education at Oxford, his career was helped along by his godfather, James Agate, another son of the Manchester merchant set who had become a noted drama critic, and he was soon making a living writing film reviews for the London newspapers while stretching his creative muscles writing poetry and song lyrics. This charmed existence was undermined as Europe drifted inexorably toward cataclysm in the 1930s.

The rise of the Nazi ideology of intolerance, and of creating divisions in society, must have been disturbing for a man of Dehn's background, and at the outbreak of World War II he joined the British Army, eventually finding his way into the Special Operations Executive (SOE) – a top-secret spy organization with a training ground at the mysterious Camp X in Canada, and the forerunner of the Special Air Service (SAS). Dehn utilized his writing skills to author a spy handbook covering such topics as parachuting, living inconspicuously behind enemy lines, sabotage, and 21 different methods of silent killing.

To what extent Dehn put these techniques into practice may never be fully known, but he undertook covert operations in Norway and France toward the war's end. In August 1944, Major Dehn and a "boy from Dakota" found themselves in the north-western French town of Saint-Aubin d'Aubigné in advance of the approaching Free French military – "a couple of allies, chance symbol of Freedom new-found," as he remembered in a subsequent poem.[1] Despite this humility, the town later named a square Place Paul Dehn in his honor in 2005.

With the end of the war came an apparent return to civilian life, with Dehn once again working as a high-profile drama critic, but with the added bonus of domestic happiness; in 1944, he had met musician James Bernard, then a member of the Royal Air Force working on decoding the Enigma machine[2], and they began a 30-year relationship, sharing a home together from 1946, albeit surreptitiously. The arts world allowed a little more tolerance toward

---

[1] Dehn, Paul. "St. Aubin d'Aubigné." *The Day's Alarm* (1949). London: Hamish Hamilton.

[2] The 2014 film *The Imitation Game* tells the story of Alan Turing and his attempts to crack the Enigma machine's code.

homosexuals than was typical of mainstream British society at the time, and their discreet and stable living arrangements protected them somewhat from the risk of public scandal. Dehn began to pay more attention to his creative output post-war, writing lyrics, penning radio plays for the BBC, publishing his first book of poetry (dedicated to Bernard) in 1949, and narrating the 1951 short film *Waters of Time*. But his writing would suggest that his faith in mankind's inherent goodness had been fundamentally altered by his wartime experiences and, in particular, by the apocalyptic atom-bombing of Japan.

Dehn and Bernard attempted a collaborative partnership, co-writing a musical and a story that was later developed into the well-received film *Seven Days to Noon*, before opting to focus on their individual talents (Bernard was notable as the composer for numerous "Hammer Horror" films, though he continued to make uncredited contributions to Dehn's writing).[3] In *Seven Days to Noon*, a contemporary government scientist has a crisis of religious conscience and steals a small atomic device, threatening to destroy London unless all such weapons are dismantled. The film introduces some of Dehn's recurring themes, including the moral ambiguity of killing in order to prevent others from being killed and dread of the Cold War arms race. In 1952, just as Dehn and Bernard won a screen-writing Academy Award, the thermonuclear "H-bomb" was developed and tested by the United States, 450 times more powerful than the atomic bomb that had caused so much destruction to Nagasaki, and the fevered competition to create ever-more destructive weapons struck Dehn as utterly insane.

If he was not a card-carrying member of the emerging Campaign for Nuclear Disarmament (CND) or the Committee of 100, he evidently sympathized via some of his parody poems appearing in various publications during the late 1950s (for example, "Lo, it comes, with clouds descending, Pilotlessly dropp'd by plane, And a million lives are ending Underneath the nuclear rain. Alleluja! Now we can have peace again."[4]). He had a particular fondness for twisting the popular and familiar rhymes and songs of British culture into dark and disturbing puns. Many of these verses were collected in

---

[3] Abbott, James. "An Interview with Composer James Bernard." *The Jade Sphinx* blog (2011, recorded in 1996).

[4] Dehn, Paul. "Lo, it comes, with clouds descending." *Quake, Quake, Quake: A Leaden Treasury of English Verse* (1961). London: Hamish Hamilton.

the 1961 book *Quake, Quake, Quake: A Leaden Treasury of English Verse*, accompanied by illustrations of a post-nuclear hell.

Quake, quake, quake
    On thy cold, grey course, O Man,
Eager to do for others
    The service we did Japan.

O hell to the armament race
    For the bomb that is better and bigger!
O hell to the thumb on the switch
    And the finger touching the trigger.

The Christian scientists fire
    Their satellites over the hill;
But O for the touch of a vanish'd Hand
    And the sound of a Voice that is still.

Quake, quake, quake
    On thy cold, grey course, O Man,
Seeking to end the world so soon
    After it just began.

The title poem by Dehn in *Quake, Quake, Quake: A Leaden Treasury of English Verse*, with an illustration by renowned macabre artist Edward Gorey.

By this time, Paul Dehn had also written *Orders to Kill*, in which a World War II agent struggles with his conscience when asked to kill a suspected traitor, for which he won a British Academy of Film and Television Arts (BAFTA) award. Retiring from journalism to focus on screen-writing, Dehn had his breakthrough into the commercial mainstream with his adaptation of Ian Fleming's *Goldfinger* in 1964. Dehn clearly drew on his real-life wartime spy training, adding a new opening scene in which James Bond infiltrates an enemy base, silently killing the sentries. Again, a central pillar of the story is the threat of a nuclear weapon controlled by someone who lacks reason or empathy.

During the next ten years, there followed adaptations of John le Carré's *The Spy Who Came in From the Cold* and *The Deadly Affair*, Hans Hellmut Kirst's *The Night of the Generals*, William Shakespeare's *The Taming of the Shrew*, John Bingham's *Fragment of Fear*, and Agatha Christie's *Murder on the Orient Express*. The common thread running through these adaptations was his injection of intelligent and witty dialogue into each story, linguistic skills honed through his journalistic career. One of Dehn's final projects, before his untimely death from lung cancer in 1976, was writing *The Saboteurs of Telemark*, a 1973 BBC documentary telling the story of an SOE-trained Norwegian resistance unit who sabotaged a plant producing hydrogen-enriched "heavy water" for use in the Nazi atomic weapons program – a plot he most likely had been involved in and was proud of.

All of this, of course, serves as background to the five years Dehn spent expanding the *Planet of the Apes* film into an entire saga.

Dehn had seen and apparently enjoyed the 1968 *Planet of the Apes* film. As an animal lover, he probably approved of the original premise devised by Boulle (another veteran of the anti-Nazi resistance), in which animals have displaced humans at the top of the evolutionary tree. Even more appealing must have been Serling's cinematic twist, implying that this would be Earth's destiny after a nuclear war has ended human civilization.

Dehn's poetry, often covering this latter theme, together with his screen-writing record, prompted co-producer Mort Abrahams to invite him to submit an outline for an *Apes* sequel, and from Dehn's point of view the potential of a big-budget science-fiction screenplay about a post-apocalyptic Earth must have seemed like a logical progression for his writing. "The *Ape* films," he said, "you can take seriously because one can make so many comments about present day life."[5] His first story outline, titled *Planet of the Apes Revisited* (a later version of which would be filmed as *Beneath the Planet of the Apes*), was submitted in September 1968. Abrahams oversaw the script development and supplied some ideas, earning him a co-writer's credit.

Dehn's first innovation was to add a new race of inhabitants to the planet – the mutated, disfigured, unbalanced descendants of the human victims of a nuclear war. Dehn's imprint was all over this new concept, and he set out his sincere belief that "Their evolution, if there should in future be an Atomic

---

[5] Knight, Chris and Nicholson, Peter. "Paul Dehn - Scriptwriter, *Apes* 2, 3 and 4." *Cinefantastique* (1972). Chicago: *Cinefantastique* magazine.

World War, is alas! within the bounds of probability. Their presence in the picture and indeed their location in subterranean New York should be treated as a serious prophetic warning against the Mis-Shape of Thing to Come."[6] He described, in vivid detail, the nightmarish mutation of a people still moulded by a 20th-Century nuclear war millennia after its irradiated dust had settled. Their decline was demonstrated via a sequence of portraits or busts depicting successive generations of the ruling dynasty, from a handsome 20th-Century military leader through stages comparable to the corrupted and homely Hanoverian and Medici royal families,[7] and ultimately to grotesque approximations of humanity reminiscent of the artwork of Henry Moore, Alberto Giacometti, or Elizabeth Frink.[8] Most graphic of all was his description of Mendez, their final ruler:

> a figure who looks like the Grand Inquisitor grotesquely lengthened by a distorting-mirror. The immensely tall, cadaverously lean body is topped by a head discernibly human, though the great aquiline nose suggests an eagle's beak. Even the long fingers are raptorially curved like claws. But the eagle seems blind. Where there should be eyes, there is facial flesh. Then a curious thing happens. Mendez says: "Let me look at you" and turns slowly into profile to reveal that his eyes are at the sides of his face and not in front. He can, like a great bird, look outwards but not forwards.[9]

Others among the community were to have "appallingly mutated" faces; visible veins, arteries, tendons and muscles; sparsely tufted hair; toad eyes; absent noses or chins.[10] And yet, Dehn requested that this catalogue of gruesome deformities should not be sickening enough to repulse the audience, and the final designs for the mutants were much closer to conventional forms; rather, the emphasis was to be on their advanced intelligence and charm. They were to be "as pacifically isolationist as 20th-Century hippies" but, in case any viewers were at risk of sympathizing with this peaceful and charming race of humans, there was a sting in the tail – they were every bit as deluded, irrational, and genocidal as Dehn's contemporary man. Their skewed morality meant that they made a virtue of never fighting, instead compelling others to fight on their behalf, not unlike the great stalemated Cold War powers fighting proxy wars throughout the Third World in Dehn's lifetime.

---

[6] Paul Dehn, *Planet of the Apes Revisited* – Treatment (9-13-1968), p 7.
[7] Paul Dehn, *Planet of the Apes Revisited* – First Draft Screenplay (12-20-1968), p 50.
[8] Dehn, *Planet of the Apes Revisited* – Treatment (9-13-1968), p 24.
[9] *Ibid.*, p 22.
[10] Dehn, *Planet of the Apes Revisited* – First Draft Screenplay (12-20-1968), p 78.

The supreme confidence of the mutant race in their own physical perfection forms part of a wider theme in Dehn's *Apes* scripts – the misuse of religion to justify the most illogical claims and depraved acts. Dehn himself was not particularly religious, yet he acknowledged the function of religion in maintaining a stable society. His scripts are littered with references to religion, drawn particularly from the Church of England faith which, though not his own, was the state church of his country and an important element of his educational experience. The full horror of the mutant society is revealed when Taylor and Brent discover the "degradation of a noble religion,"[11] that noble religion being explicitly Christian in form.

The unmasked mutants partake in a unique religious service in *Beneath the Planet of the Apes*.

In a lengthy sequence, we are shown a mutant congregation at worship in a cathedral. They sing the English hymn "All Things Bright and Beautiful," with the word "Lord" unsubtly replaced by "Bomb" (these verses, in fact, are recycled directly from *Quake, Quake, Quake*). They recite Anglican prayers and passages from the King James Bible, again substituting "Bomb" in place of "Lord," "God," or "Father," and "Holy Fall Out" for "Holy Spirit." The cathedral features the familiar (high alter, sanctuary, prie-dieu, choir stalls, nave, pews and organ loft), but also the sinister – the great cobalt-cased missile forms a huge inverted cross above the altar, and the faithful make a corresponding inverted Sign of the Cross.[12] The Greek letters alpha and omega adorn the fins of the bomb – "the

---

[11] Dehn, *Planet of the Apes Revisited* – Treatment (9-13-1968), p 24.
[12] Dehn, *Planet of the Apes Revisited* – First Draft Screenplay (12-20-1968, revised 2-3-1969), p 48.

beginning and the end," and also a title for Jesus Christ taken from the apocalyptic Book of Revelation. When Brent is asked if he wishes to destroy the mutants' "god," he ruefully comments, "You seem to have destroyed mine," and takes the opportunity to recite another of Dehn's lyrical puns from *Quake, Quake, Quake*: "Onward, Christian soldiers, Each to war resigned, With the Cross of Jesus, Vaguely kept in mind."[13]

The mutants go further in their bastardized Christian worship by associating their physical appearance with divine intervention, perhaps in direct contrast to Biblical passages that condemn as "unclean" anyone who is mutilated, disfigured, injured, or diseased. They are repulsed by our standards of beauty and instead celebrate their scarred faces as evidence of an "inmost truth" imparted by the Spirit of the Holy Fall Out, to be revealed only to the Bomb itself, their Creator, during sacred worship.

The "First Year of the Bomb" is considered the starting point of their culture, replacing the birth of Christ.[14] Dehn strengthens his point by comparing the mutants' religion with that of the apes. They are mirror images of each other in many respects; each society is utterly convinced that they have been created in the image of their god, and that their god will guide them to final victory. Using language similar to Mendez (who is addressed as "Holiness"), an ape minister reminds his flock that apes are God's Chosen, destined to be Masters of the Earth and blessed with a "bodily beauty" lacking in their enemies,[15] and it is this unshakeable faith that gives Zaius – a genuine believer – the courage to challenge the mutants' sacrilegious illusions.

The same minister invokes his god's blessing on the ape army's Holy War, while a mutant illusion of a human army clad in gleaming armor with gorillas crucified on the sacred inverted cross adds to an evocation of the Crusades.[16] Zaius is particularly incensed to find busts of human faces, deeming them "obscene" to his faith. The finer details of the mutants' and apes' theology

---

[13] Dehn, *Planet of the Apes Revisited* – First Draft Screenplay (12-20-1968), pp 65-66.

[14] Dehn, *Planet of the Apes Revisited* – First Draft Screenplay (12-20-1968, revised 2-3-1969), p 64.

[15] Dehn, *Planet of the Apes Revisited* – First Draft Screenplay (12-20-1968), pp 32-33.

[16] Dehn, *Planet of the Apes Revisited* – Treatment (9-13-1968), p 29; Paul Dehn & Mort Abrahams, *Beneath the Planet of the Apes* – Final Shooting Script (4-10-1969, revised 5-28-1969), p 91.

aren't spelled out, but again they mirror each other intentionally. To one, the Divine Bomb is a "Holy Weapon of Peace," yet merely the instrument of their god rather than a god itself, whereas to the other, the Lawgiver is a prophet of their god, fulfilling a similar symbolic role. Taking his cue from the overtly biblical Sacred Scrolls mentioned in the first film, Dehn recognized the sinister potential of depicting a form of worship only slightly removed from that familiar to the mainstream audience.

In later films, Dehn alluded further to the origins of these respective faiths. In *Escape from the Planet of the Apes*, for example, Cornelius repeats that his contemporary gorillas and orangutans believed that their god created apes in his own image – much to the consternation of a 1970s Christian Cardinal[17] – though he implies that chimpanzees were less devout, and later comments that the destruction of the Earth had been caused by "God... if there *is* a God."[18] At the height of his rebellion, Caesar promises that apes shall found their own religion,[19] a faith born of political pragmatism rather than any type of sincere conviction, and we subsequently get an introduction to this new dogma in *Battle for the Planet of the Apes*, with the Lawgiver's monologue describing man's betrayal both of the apes and of their common god, and the prophesied coming of their saviour, once again invoking biblical language and imagery.[20]

However, in Dehn's original outline for that film, we see an orangutan leader (Zeno, intended as the future Lawgiver) affirming that god created apes in his image, while in contrast a chimp leader (Pan) echoes Cornelius: "If I knew there were a God, I would pray to Him."[21] The same outline includes an elderly woman secretly teaching a group of human children the symbols and prayers of Christian worship, a practice outlawed under Caesar's new regime, with an implication that this will shape the faith of their mutant descendants.[22] In the final script, even the most loyal humans of Ape City are reluctant to fully give up

---

[17] Paul Dehn, *Escape from the Planet of the Apes* – First Draft Screenplay (revised 10-22-1970), p 22.

[18] Dehn, *Escape from the Planet of the Apes* – First Draft Screenplay (revised 10-26-1970), p 45.

[19] Paul Dehn, *Conquest of the Planet of the Apes* – Final Shooting Script (1-18-1972, revised 1-27-1972), p 86.

[20] Paul Dehn, John William Corrington & Joyce Hooper Corrington, *Battle for the Planet of the Apes* – Revised Screenplay (12-20-1972, revised 1-5-1973), pp 1-2.

[21] Paul Dehn, *The Battle for the Planet of the Apes* – First Draft Story Outline (7-5-1972), pp 61-64.

[22] *Ibid.*, p 27.

their old customs, as shown when MacDonald and friends continue to eat meat covertly,[23] and the wise orangutan Virgil pointedly, almost accusingly, asks MacDonald how a benevolent god could "allow the branch of one of His own trees to crack and cripple an innocent child?"[24] Mandemus, for his part, displays an attitude at odds with both Christianity *and* Caesar's new religion: "If we knew for a fact that there was an after-life and that the after-life was Bliss Eternal, we'd all commit suicide in order to be able to enjoy it."[25]

Simultaneously, the first Mendez of the mutant dynasty chooses to launch an enduring philosophy rather than launch their ultimate weapon: "This bloody chain-reaction has got to stop... before anyone knows where they are there'll be nobody left to know anything... anywhere. Only nuclear dust, falling through space like dead stars."[26] He vows: "It must never be exploded. It must be respected – even venerated. For one of its ancestors made us what we are... And what we are, shall, from this day forward, be called beautiful."[27]

Within context, each of these new religions is formed for rational and practical reasons, yet we, the audience, already know the punchline – that they will ultimately set Earth's surviving races on a path to mutual annihilation. It is a bitter commentary on the destructive potential of creed, and yet Dehn was not entirely negative on the subject, as shown by Armando's taking inspiration from the animal-loving St. Francis of Assisi.[28]

Overall, Judeo-Christian references are to be found throughout Dehn's scripts, particularly in regard to the story of Caesar: the saviour of an enslaved people who is prophesied even before his birth, the rulers of the land ordering his death, only for his mother to place him in the care of an adoptive parent, after which he instinctively defends his oppressed brethren, enters the inner circle of the oppressors, and finally leads the slaves to freedom. The template is drawn substantially from the story of Moses (known as the "Lawgiver of Israel") and also from that of Jesus – as the U.S. President points out in an argument

---

[23] Dehn, Corrington & Corrington, *Battle for the Planet of the Apes* – Revised Screenplay (12-20-1972), pp 23-24.

[24] *Ibid.*, p 77.

[25] *Ibid.*, p 28.

[26] Dehn, Corrington & Corrington, *Battle for the Planet of the Apes* – Revised Screenplay (12-20-1972, revised 12-27-1972), p 59.

[27] Dehn, Corrington & Corrington, *Battle for the Planet of the Apes* – Revised Screenplay (12-20-1972), p 100.

[28] Dehn, *Escape from the Planet of the Apes* – First Draft Screenplay (revised 10-2-1970), p 84.

against the apes' summary execution, "Herod tried that, and Christ survived."[29] Later, Caesar reveals that "Armando once told me the story of Judas,"[30] Lisa sits over her dead son Cornelius like Mary over Jesus in the Pieta,[31] and some apes are "awed, almost religiously so, by the realization that Aldo has become the Cain of Apes."[32]

Perhaps inevitably, given Dehn's direct experiences, the brutal depths of human intolerance seen during the mid-20th Century feature prominently in his scripts. Both apes and humans are, at various times, measured against Nazi standards. General Ursus is described as "yelling like Hitler in the Sportspalast on the eve of the Second World War" and, like Hitler, his reason for launching a war of conquest is to create "living-space" for his loyal followers. They, in turn, beat their chests in an "equivalent to the Nazi *'Sieg hiel!'*", while the ape intellectuals have to be prodded into conformity by police enforcers.[33] Ursus refers to humans as infections, parasites and pollution,[34] and to the purity of ape civilization being overwhelmed and degenerated by "weak and hairless" humans breeding in great numbers.[35]

Meanwhile, Zaius herds humans into camps for experimentation: "The Concentration Camp parallel," Dehn emphasises, "should be discernible."[36] Nazi symbolism is even more evident in Dehn's *Conquest of the Planet of the Apes*, in the young and charismatic but utterly ruthless Breck, in the sleek and functional architecture of his so-called Modern City, in his black-uniformed militaristic security police, in the austere, color-coded clothing of the human and ape castes, in the apes being transported in cramped and dangerous cages toward

---

[29] Dehn, *Escape from the Planet of the Apes* – First Draft Screenplay (revised 10-23-1970), p 37.

[30] Dehn, *The Battle for the Planet of the Apes* – First Draft Story Outline (7-5-1972), p 55.

[31] Dehn, Corrington & Corrington, *Battle for the Planet of the Apes* – Revised Screenplay (12-20-1972, revised 1-2-1973), p 71.

[32] Dehn, Corrington & Corrington, *Battle for the Planet of the Apes* – Revised Screenplay (12-20-1972), p 103.

[33] Dehn, *Planet of the Apes Revisited* – Treatment (9-13-1968), pp 11-13.

[34] Dehn, *Planet of the Apes Revisited* – First Draft Screenplay (12-20-1968, revised 2-3-1969), p 11.

[35] Dehn & Abrahams, *Beneath the Planet of the Apes* – Final Shooting Script (4-10-1969, revised 4-18-1969), pp 18-18A.

[36] Dehn, *Planet of the Apes Revisited* – Treatment (9-13-1968), p 13.

imprisonment and torture,[37] and in the emphasis on rigid government control – both of the apes through Ape Management and of poorer humans through the restriction of working hours and of labor rights.[38] Respected books – the Bible, as well as the works of William Shakespeare, Charles Darwin, John Milton, Theodore Dreiser, John James Audubon, Oswald Spengler, and Margaret Mitchell – burn during the ape uprising: "As once in the book-bonfires of pre-war Nazi Germany, an entire cultural heritage is going up in crackling flames."[39]

Caesar himself, in Dehn's unused *Battle* outline, becomes paranoid through a combination of absolute power and personal tragedy, and begins "yelling like Hitler" about conspiracies against him.[40] Ultimately, it is Aldo who echoes the Nazis on screen, drilling his gorillas until they "resemble a line of German soldiers in their exact symmetry,"[41] and later ordering the human minority to be locked up in the horse corral, which "should, in some vague way, make one think of a concentration camp... elite troops standing guard, automatic weapons cradled in their arms, black uniforms and boots, legs spread wide. Behind them, we see humans standing against the wire, looking out hopelessly."[42]

Dehn saw the moral ambiguities of war, and of combating violence with violence, whether through killing in order to save lives or through maintaining the balance of peace by building nuclear weapons. In his first *Apes* story, the screenwriter had Taylor agreeing to spy on behalf of the mutants, in the grudging belief that only with their victory could a swift and permanent peace be brought about.[43] Later, Dehn created a multi-layered persona for Doctor Hasslein that goes beyond that of a one-dimensional villain. Instead, we understand why Hasslein does what he does, and can almost sympathize with

---

[37] Dehn, *Conquest of the Planet of the Apes* – Final Shooting Script (1-18-1972), p 6, pp 26-28.

[38] Dehn, *Conquest of the Planet of the Apes* – Final Shooting Script (1-18-1972, revised 1-24-1972), pp 14-15, 38.

[39] Dehn, *Conquest of the Planet of the Apes* – Final Shooting Script (1-18-1972), p 76.

[40] Dehn, *The Battle for the Planet of the Apes* – First Draft Story Outline (7-5-1972), p 50.

[41] Dehn, Corrington & Corrington, *Battle for the Planet of the Apes* – Revised Screenplay (12-20-1972), p 64.

[42] *Ibid.*, p 84.

[43] Dehn, *Planet of the Apes Revisited* – Treatment (9-13-1968), pp 13-14.

his logic when he concludes that the descendants of the space-apes will enslave our own descendants:

> Who cares whether, long, long after we're dead, a Man who might have been another Shakespeare, another Buddha, even another Christ will be crawling the face of this earth on all fours like a dumb brute unable to do more than grunt or slobber. ... Scientists are entitled to consciences. And my conscience bleeds when I confront these Apes and deduce the future of Mankind – however distant. If it's fanatical to feel pity for the unborn, then I'm a fanatic. Somebody has got to begin to care.[44]

Hasslein pleads his case with apparent conflicted feelings: "I've wrestled with this, and I don't know... If I urge the destruction of these Apes, am I defying God's will or obeying it? Am I God's enemy or His instrument? ... We condoned the attempted assassination of Hitler because he was evil." To which the President counters: "But would we have approved of killing him in babyhood when he was still innocent? Or killing his mother when she was still in her womb? Or slaughtering his remote ancestors?"[45] Hasslein is a man willing to commit unspeakable acts for what he believes is the greater good, contrasting directly with the religious Armando, to whom a clear conscience is all that matters: "I hate those who try to alter Destiny, which is the unalterable will of God. If it is Man's destiny to one day be dominated, then please God let him be dominated by such as you."[46]

Ultimately, both the President and the Presidential Commission tend, however reluctantly, toward Hasslein rather than Armando, perhaps reflecting the compromised ethics of western society.[47] The decision to sterilize the apes and kill their child (closely mirroring the plot of the original *Planet of the Apes* novel) seems obscene to the cinema audience, yet it is not unlike the cold pragmatism of their own governments during times of crisis.

In *Escape*, Dehn portrays Cornelius as a touchstone of moral empathy, lacking the scientific detachment of Zira and finding a human boxing match "beastly," but he is pushed into an ethical quandary when he accidentally kills his human guard. Cornelius is racked with guilt over having taken a life,

---

[44] Dehn, *Escape from the Planet of the Apes* – First Draft Screenplay (revised 9-29-1970), pp 71-71A.

[45] Dehn, *Escape from the Planet of the Apes* – First Draft Screenplay (revised 10-6-1970), p 40.

[46] Dehn, *Escape from the Planet of the Apes* – First Draft Screenplay (revised 10-2-1970), p 84.

[47] Paul Dehn, *Escape from the Planet of the Apes* – Final Screenplay (10-28-1970, revised 11-27-1970), pp 77-77A.

especially that of a generally kind man, but soon afterwards, he kills again while protecting his family from Hasslein. There may be a point beyond which even the most conscientious become driven more by necessity than by principle.

Caesar later reaches that same point, though without displaying the same angst as Cornelius. Poisoned by rage over the torture administered to both himself and Armando, Caesar coldly and needlessly murders his unconscious guard and escapes.

MacDonald is virtually alone in consistently displaying empathy for the suffering of any creature, ape or human. Having already saved Caesar's life, MacDonald finds himself trying to save Breck's as well. The violence meted out by the revolting apes against Breck's regime is "demented" and "manic" but, by the standards of Caesar's increasingly human logic, entirely justified. As originally scripted, Caesar oversees Breck's brutal murder without mercy. Begged to show humanity, Caesar points out that he "was not born human" – which is literally true, yet Caesar *was* born with the intelligence and the capacity for vengeance that are all too human.[48]

Long after the heightened emotions of the ape revolution, Caesar continues along this path, declaring that with humans brought under ape control, "The world can now breathe again. It cannot now be destroyed by those who walk upon it. ... we stand upon the brink of an Era of Peace."[49] But he disregards his oath to avoid war after he first encounters the mutated humans,[50] and he breaks his own fundamental code of honour – "Ape shall not kill ape" – when he is provoked by Aldo's murder of his son (much as Cornelius had been provoked to kill). After all of this, Caesar then overrules Mandemus in deciding that the ape community still needs to keep their weapons arsenal, even though they believe their enemies to have been defeated – a reversal of his decision, in the theatrical release of *Conquest*, to have his followers lay down their arms after storming Ape Management, despite the continued danger of human retaliation. Though wise, Caesar has become as unprincipled as any human leader before him; with intelligence comes compromised ethics.

---

[48] Dehn, *Conquest of the Planet of the Apes* – Final Shooting Script (1-18-1972, revised 1-27-1972), pp 84-86.

[49] Dehn, *The Battle for the Planet of the Apes* – First Draft Story Outline (7-5-1972), pp 4-5.

[50] Dehn, Corrington & Corrington, *Battle for the Planet of the Apes* – Revised Screenplay (12-20-1972), p 65.

Dehn had an appreciation for the simple instincts of animals, free from the complications of human interaction. He refers to the mutants as having re-achieved the telepathic abilities that were lost when humans ceased to be animals,[51] and Caesar finds that the apes of Breck's city are already communicating their defiance through speechless "grunting sessions" led by the surly Aldo who, in turn, instinctively recognizes Caesar as a natural leader and one who can coordinate the apes' resistance simply by "willing" their actions.[52] Caesar explains this remarkable talent to MacDonald by comparison with the Emperor moth – a small, mindless insect that can apparently communicate with another moth over a distance of 80 miles.[53] The increasing ability of the other apes to speak and reason, however, correlates with their ability to question and challenge Caesar's natural leadership. Cornelius had claimed that "one reason for Man's original downfall was your peculiar habit of murdering one another. Man destroys Man. Apes do not destroy Apes."[54]

Likewise, Caesar comments that "the human way is violence and death," but MacDonald perceptively notes that with Aldo's killing of Caesar's son, the apes have "just joined the human race."[55] In an early version of *Beneath*'s script, this dynamic is spelled out in reverse when Brent questions Taylor's plans to teach the mute human tribes to speak:

> And learn to differ? And learn to quarrel? And learn to hate? And learn to kill? As it was in the beginning? World without end? We'd be starting all over again. ... [Animals kill], but singly. Not collectively. One cat hates one dog. But who in hell ever heard of an army of cats declaring war on an army of dogs? Collective hatred is for those who talk. Be merciful, and keep these ones dumb. Leave them in ignorance.[56]

---

[51] Dehn, *Planet of the Apes Revisited* – Treatment (9-13-1968), pp 7-10.

[52] Dehn, *Conquest of the Planet of the Apes* – Final Shooting Script (1-18-1972, revised 1-24-1972), p 53 (although Aldo appears in this screenplay as a gorilla, the ape called by that name on-screen is a chimpanzee, establishing that the Aldos in *Conquest* and *Battle* are separate apes).

[53] Dehn, *Conquest of the Planet of the Apes* – Final Shooting Script (1-18-1972), p 85.

[54] Dehn, *Escape from the Planet of the Apes* – First Draft Screenplay (revised 10-26-1970), p 45.

[55] Dehn, Corrington & Corrington, *Battle for the Planet of the Apes* – Revised Screenplay (12-20-1972), pp 103-111.

[56] Dehn, *Planet of the Apes Revisited* – First Draft Screenplay (12-20-1968, revised 1-7-1969), pp 105-106.

In the final scene of that film, Dehn's over-riding anxiety of nuclear Armageddon is at its most vivid. The Doomsday Bomb scorches the entire planet into a cinder: "Earth's rim whitens to incandescence and a soundless explosion sends a column of fire and cloud mushrooming up ... the bright, white light of Earth's final holocaust."[57] He notes, "There are no End Titles. There is nothing more. The film, itself destroyed by the atomic catastrophe, is over."[58] The screen becomes a white silence (just as *Conquest* later ends with black silence). It's the bleakest possible outcome, and one Dehn feared was all too plausible in the Cold War era, even anticipating it occurring just 20 years into his own future; in *Beneath*, he predicts that an atom bomb would consume New York circa 1995[59] (later revised to 1990[60]), while in *Battle* he describes a worldwide nuclear catastrophe in the aftermath of the 1991 ape rebellion.[61]

Doctor Otto Hasslein often voiced what could have been Paul Dehn's own opinions in *Escape from the Planet of the Apes*.

---

[57] Dehn, *Escape from the Planet of the Apes* – First Draft Screenplay (revised 10-21-1970), pp 1-2.
[58] Dehn & Abrahams, *Beneath the Planet of the Apes* – Final Shooting Script (4-10-1969, revised 4-18-1969), p 109.
[59] Dehn, *Planet of the Apes Revisited* – Treatment (9-13-1968), pp 7-9.
[60] Dehn, *Planet of the Apes Revisited* – First Draft Screenplay (12-20-1968), p 41.
[61] Dehn, Corrington & Corrington, *Battle for the Planet of the Apes* – Revised Screenplay (12-20-1972, revised 1-5-1973), pp 1-2.

Dehn felt that most people regarded nuclear annihilation as some far-off abstract fantasy "at the back of everybody's mind. One doesn't want dire threats, one wants to see what could happen after an atomic war a hundred years hence."[62] Hasslein could have been voicing Dehn's opinions directly when saying, "That's what I'm afraid of. Later. *Later* we'll do something about pollution. *Later* we'll do something about the population explosion. *Later* we'll do something about nuclear war. We think we've got all the time in the world – but how much time has the world got? And how can we give it more? ... Somebody has to begin to care."[63]

Dehn feared that not enough people *would* care, and so Caesar, like Hasslein before him, could foresee "the inevitable day of Man's downfall: the day when you will finally and self-destructively turn your weapons against your own kind. The day of the writing in the sky, when your cities lie buried under radioactive rubble, and the sea has become a Dead Sea, and the Land a wasteland."[64] In spite of all these warnings, man might continue along the path to nuclear oblivion, toward the full horrors that haunted Dehn:

> The surface of the world was ravaged by the vilest war in human history. The great cities of the world split asunder and were flattened.
>
> London, Rome, Athens, Rio, Moscow, Tokyo, Peking.[65]
>
> We catch the classic Hiroshima glimpse of a stray human backed against a stone wall. Then his body vanishes and only his silhouette remains burnt into the wall ... which splits. The screen bleaches to a white, blinding incandescence; and the thunder of crashing masonry deafens us, as the now invisible city founders.[66]
>
> It is the total desolation of one of man's great cities. It is massive, silent, utterly dead. A monument to all twisted and contradictory ideas and passions that drove mankind to suicide.
>
> The City did not simply blow apart, it melted. Glass, masonry, steel, all were dissolved by the enormous temperature at the center of the H-bomb... Buildings have crumpled and flowed into one another so that, in

[62] Knight & Nicholson, 'Paul Dehn - Scriptwriter, *Apes* 2, 3 and 4' in *Cinefantastique* (1972).

[63] Dehn, *Escape from the Planet of the Apes* – Final Screenplay (10-28-1970, revised 11-5-1970), p 93.

[64] Dehn, *Conquest of the Planet of the Apes* – Final Shooting Script (1-18-1972, revised 1-27-1972), pp 85-86.

[65] Dehn, Corrington & Corrington, *Battle for the Planet of the Apes* – Revised Screenplay (12-20-1972, revised 1-5-1973), pp 1-2, p 30.

[66] Dehn, *The Battle for the Planet of the Apes* – First Draft Story Outline (7-5-1972), p 28.

large measure, the City is a single piece of an undifferentiated slag. Portions of this mountain of glass look rather like a glacier, with cars, trolleys, etc., melted and stuck to it.[67]

Perhaps the most frightening aspect of Dehn's post-apocalyptic vision is the tension of a 2,000-year wait for the final act. The world is held in limbo for centuries with the clock frozen just before midnight, and countless generations are condemned to live in this twilight; Brent encounters mutant children singing a macabre death-rhyme (again borrowed from *Quake, Quake, Quake*): "Ring-a-ring o'neutrons, A pocketful of positrons, A fission! A fission! We all fall down."[68] These doomed children are still as aware of their precarious existence as the founders of their community were two millennia earlier.

One point Dehn was very definite about was that in any future human society, no matter how unsavory, race would become an irrelevance. He had noticed that in the original film, only a single human character – the astronaut Dodge – was non-white, and he retrospectively suggested that Dodge's body had been put on display in a museum because he had black skin unique to that era's humans. In contrast, the mutant community created by Dehn is ethnically diverse, with "skins dappled in various racial combinations; black-and-white, brown-and-yellow, black-and-brown, white-and-yellow. The same permutations can be seen in their hair: blonde negroes, red-haired Pakistanis."[69] The mutant children are "of many races, all beautiful," and Brent's and Taylor's mutant inquisitor, Ongaro, is described as a "magnificent negro."[70]

Dehn also hoped that the 1973 society encountered by Zira and Cornelius would include a number of successful black VIPs and lawyers,[71] that Breck's 1991 city would be inhabited by "Anglos, Blacks, Orientals," including black

---

[67] Dehn, Corrington & Corrington, *Battle for the Planet of the Apes* – Revised Screenplay (12-20-1972), p 30-31.

[68] Dehn, *Planet of the Apes Revisited* – First Draft Screenplay (12-20-1968), p 50.

[69] Dehn, *Planet of the Apes Revisited* – Treatment (9-13-1968), pp 7-9.

[70] Dehn, *Planet of the Apes Revisited* – First Draft Screenplay (12-20-1968), pp 50-52.

[71] Dehn, *Escape from the Planet of the Apes* – First Draft Screenplay (revised 10-22-1970), pp 19-21.

business tycoons,[72] and that the 2670 community descended from that established by Caesar would include black children.[73]

All of these casting decisions were specified by Dehn in his scripts, conscious that any allegory about racial intolerance would be undermined by a lack of diversity on-screen. Indeed, a crucial element of *Conquest* requires Caesar to have a human ally, someone prominent enough in Breck's regime to be able to save his life, yet with an instinctive sympathy for Caesar's plight. Thus, MacDonald is an African-American in an officially egalitarian society, but below the surface old prejudices remain, as two policemen make insinuations about why he seems lenient toward ape slaves. Breck respects MacDonald as an administrator, but leaves him out of the loop on morally questionable security matters like the Achilles List of troublesome apes, probably because Breck is aware of his qualms. "Stop being so touchy," the governor berates him. "We've all been slaves at one time or another. I can trace my family back to Breckland in Suffolk, England. We were slaves, then. To the goddam French..."[74]

It is, indeed, the bitter legacy of slavery that troubles MacDonald; the images of an intelligent being like Caesar being auctioned like a racehorse, of brutal conditioning to serve the needs of the master, of the selective breeding of docile apes, and of living beings quantified in monetary terms are particularly pointed. MacDonald, as a "descendant of slaves and savages,"[75] empathizes with Caesar, while his brother's house in *Battle* contains "a yellowing photo of Martin Luther King in a corroded frame. Above the mantel, an educational diploma from a Negro University."[76]

Dehn was well aware that his films were tapping into an undercurrent of the Civil Rights Movement. "It's a very curious thing," he commented frankly, "that the *Apes* series has always been tremendously popular with Negroes who

---

[72] Dehn, *Conquest of the Planet of the Apes* – Final Shooting Script (1-18-1972, revised 1-24-1972), p 6, p 14.

[73] Dehn, Corrington & Corrington, *Battle for the Planet of the Apes* – Revised Screenplay (12-20-1972), p 114.

[74] Dehn, *Conquest of the Planet of the Apes* – Final Shooting Script (1-18-1972, revised 1-24-1972), p 15A, pp 52-52A, p 44.

[75] Dehn, *Conquest of the Planet of the Apes* – Final Shooting Script (1-18-1972, revised 1-31-1972), p 39, pp 29-31, pp 36-37, pp 69-70, p 84.

[76] Dehn, Corrington & Corrington, *Battle for the Planet of the Apes* – Revised Screenplay (12-20-1972), p 23.

identify themselves with the apes. They are Black Power just as the apes are Ape Power and they enjoy it greatly."[77]

Cornelius stated that his ancestors "became alert to the concept of slavery and (as their numbers grew) to slavery's antidote, which is unity. They began to assemble in small bands. They learned the art of corporate and militant action. They learned to refuse."[78] Breck, in due course, identifies a "rising tide of disobedience – of downright defiance – among the servant apes," leading to the rebellion that Caesar considers "the only means left to us."[79]

In Dehn's original concept for *Battle*, the pitfalls of intellect are again shown as Caesar continues a form of segregation and authoritarian rule in the conquered city; the human and ape species are segregated by dress, just as they had been under Breck, and Caesar has become "Emperor-King of the Apes," immortalized in statue and coinage. His court officials must give him "that slight inclination of the head which serves for a royal bow in England," signifying a very rigid hierarchy. The public restrooms are now segregated according to "Ladies," "Gentlemen," and "Humans," just as under Breck they had been "Men," "Women," and "Apes," and as bombs begin to fall on the city, only those humans of practical use to the apes are considered worth saving.[80]

Further contemporary references found their way into Dehn's scripts: chimpanzee students are seen staging a "pathetic" peaceful protest against General Ursus' war;[81] Zira and Cornelius arrive in 1973 just as (human) students are rioting at Berkeley University;[82] Zira speaks in support of women's liberation;[83] the impact of the space-apes' arrival is compared to the Bay of Pigs

---

[77] Knight & Nicholson, 'Paul Dehn - Scriptwriter, *Apes* 2, 3 and 4' in *Cinefantastique* (1972).

[78] Dehn, *Escape from the Planet of the Apes* – First Draft Screenplay (revised 10-21-1970, revised 10-26-1970), p 47-48.

[79] Dehn, *Conquest of the Planet of the Apes* – Final Shooting Script (1-18-1972, revised 1-24-1972), p 24, p 61.

[80] Dehn, *The Battle for the Planet of the Apes* – First Draft Story Outline (7-5-1972), p 1-8, p 12, p 10, pp 17-18; Dehn, *Conquest of the Planet of the Apes* – Final Shooting Script (1-18-1972, revised 1-26-1972), p 12.

[81] Dehn, *Planet of the Apes Revisited* – First Draft Screenplay (12-20-1968, revised 2-3-1969), pp 73-74.

[82] Dehn, *Escape from the Planet of the Apes* – First Draft Screenplay (revised 10-20-1970), p 2.

[83] Dehn, *Escape from the Planet of the Apes* – Final Screenplay (10-28-1970, revised 11-27-1970), p 40A.

invasion;[84] the ape revolution is likened to the Attica Prison riots;[85] and Aldo's horseback gorillas are called "Ape City's Hell's Angels."[86]

Given his residence in Britain, beyond the immediate prism of U.S. culture and politics, the global upheavals of the time are also likely to have influenced Dehn's writing. He incorporated an international dimension in the contrasting television news coverage of the space-apes' arrival, ranging from the very restrained British ITN *News at Ten*, through gradually less restrained German, French, and Japanese reports, to the sensational American news. Dehn's *Apes* scripts were written during an era that covered Enoch Powell's inflammatory anti-immigration rhetoric, the rise of the British National Front, the eruption of sectarian violence in Northern Ireland, the 1968 student riots across western Europe, and the crushing of the reformist government of Czechoslovakia by the Soviet army, and echoes of each can be discerned in his stories.

Notably, the original ending of *Beneath* saw the "left-wing intellectual" chimpanzees take over Ape City from the "'right-wing" orangutans and militaristic gorillas[87] and, in scenes often echoed in recent history, use pickaxes to destroy a statue of Ursus dominating the main square.[88] Similarly, Aldo leads what equates to a typically human military coup against Caesar. Dehn alluded to his own contribution to contemporary culture when he described Caesar's escape from certain death on the torture table as "an exit that Bond might have been proud of."[89]

Indeed, Caesar, like Brent and Taylor, conceals himself among his primitive brethren with all the operational skill of James Bond – or perhaps even of the wartime Paul Dehn himself. Inevitably, Dehn's personal interests must also have bled into his fiction, and there are some tantalizing hints embedded: an author named Minnie Sokolsky[90] (the Sokolsky Opening is a chess move also known to aficionados as the Orangutan Opening); background characters with the

---

[84] Dehn, *Escape from the Planet of the Apes* – First Draft Screenplay (revised 10-23-1970), p 38.

[85] Dehn, *Conquest of the Planet of the Apes* – Final Shooting Script (1-18-1972), p 70.

[86] Dehn, Corrington & Corrington, *Battle for the Planet of the Apes* – Revised Screenplay (12-20-1972), p 15.

[87] Dehn, *Planet of the Apes Revisited* – First Draft Screenplay (12-20-1968), p 71.

[88] Dehn, *Planet of the Apes Revisited* – Treatment (9-13-1968), p 41.

[89] Dehn, *Conquest of the Planet of the Apes* – Final Shooting Script (1-18-1972), p 68.

[90] *Ibid.*, p 11.

unusual names Mr. and Mrs. van Thal[91] (Herbert van Thal was James Agate's publisher, and someone Dehn would likely have known); and General Mendez of the U.S. Army, originally conceived of as the founder of the mutant society[92] (Colonel Louis G. Mendez was one of the leaders of the U.S. invasion of Normandy in 1944 and, like Dehn, has had a French town square named in his honor). It seems likely that there are a lot of subtle references and tributes threaded throughout Dehn's original scripts, the significance of many now forgotten since the deaths of Dehn and his circle of friends.

One of those who knew Paul Dehn best was his niece, the poet and dramatist Jehane Markham, who, in e-mail correspondence with this author, said that she remembers him as "incredibly kind and generous both with his money and his advice and support of my work, when I was beginning to write professionally."[93] Markham added that he had a "penetrating understanding of human frailty,"[94] something that has hopefully been shown in this examination of his enormous contribution to the remarkably enduring *Apes* franchise. That understanding of human frailty is at its most insightful in an early version of *Beneath the Planet of the Apes*, during which Brent frequently seems to voice the opinions of the screenwriter, but it is ultimately Taylor, in a climactic and impassioned final speech, whose mask slips to reveal Paul Dehn's inmost self:

> Listen. The whole stinking, rotten history of this stinking, rotten planet is the history of leaders keeping their people in ignorance. Ignorance that the earth moved around the sun. Ignorance that men were descended from monkeys. Ignorance about the mass-murder of Jews in gas-chambers. Ignorance of what the Bomb would do, when we dropped it on Hiroshima. Zaius kept the Apes in ignorance – and they died for a false God who taught them they were the Master Race. Mendez kept the Mutants in ignorance – and the poor bastards were burnt alive by a monstrosity they'd been falsely told was their own Creator. Two thousand years ago, you and I were kept in ignorance about germ-warfare and nerve-gas and all the other cancerous and obscene secrets that governments used to sweep under their ceremonial red-carpets, while the bloody bugles blew a lie: that it was sweet and proper to slaughter our fellow-men. If we're told

---

[91] *Ibid.*, p 39.
[92] Dehn, *Planet of the Apes Revisited* – Treatment (9-13-1968), pp 24-25; Dehn, *The Battle for the Planet of the Apes* – First Draft Story Outline (7-5-1972), p 14.
[93] Markham, Jehane. Email conversation (27 May 2015).
[94] Markham, Jehane. Email conversation (13 May 2015).

the whole truth, we can at least protest. We can at least rebel. But if we're *not* told … one madman can kill millions.[95]

With sincere gratitude to Jehane Markham for her assistance, and to Hunter Goatley and the contributors to his Planet of the Apes *Archive website (pota.goatley.com/scripts.html).*

---

[95] Paul Dehn, *Planet of the Apes Revisited* – First Draft Screenplay (12-20-1968, revised 2-3-1969), pp 106-106A.

Time and the Planet of the Apes

by Joe Dilworth

Time has played an important role in the *Planet of the Apes* film franchise, whether involving characters moving backward and forward through it, or just the story advancing years beyond the timeframe in which they were made. The end result is that the five original films do not necessarily follow a linear pattern from one to the other. Indeed, they actually seem to form a contained loop.

However, there are arguments to be made that time and events are altered by certain actions in the movies – or, at the very least, that a paradox is created or even an alternate universe. A lot of this ambiguity derives from an individual's ideas and perceptions of the fictional conceit of time travel, as well as interpretations of key scenes depicted on screen and referred to as happening off screen. Examining the facts as presented does very little to clear anything up – in fact, it only seems to muddy things further.

"I leave the 20th Century with no regrets..."

It all started with a man smoking on a spaceship. To be fair, the story of *Planet of the Apes* began with Pierre Boulle's novel *La planète des singes*, but as far as movie-goers were concerned, it really began in 1968 with Charlton Heston puffing a cigarillo on a then-futuristic spaceship bound for the stars.

Very few details are given as to exactly what sort of mission Heston's George Taylor and his slumbering fellow astronauts are on, but the crucial information concerning the tale to come are provided in those opening moments. The audience is told that the unnamed ship is travelling rapidly away from the planet Earth, and that while six months have barely passed for the crew, their home planet (due to the effects of time dilation) has aged some seven centuries. And Taylor is so cool and collected about all of it, even if he does wax poetic about life, the universe, and everything.

This opening prologue provides some concrete numbers as far as dates and the future, though subsequent information already starts the confusion train. Taylor says that his crew – Dodge, Landon, and Stewart – are an hour away from being six months into their journey, with the onboard calendar showing July 14, 1972, thus marking 14 January 1972 as the departure date. Taylor also makes mention of Doctor Hasslein's theory of time, stating that, as the ship is travelling near the speed of light, more than seven hundred years have passed on Earth. Indeed, a second display shows the Earth date to be March of 2673. The loneliest man in the universe then joins his crew in the long winter's nap of suspended animation for the remainder of the journey to wherever it is they are headed.

Taylor's ship calendar marks time, both actual and dilated, in accordance with Doctor Hasslein's theory of time.

Twelve months later (mere seconds of screen time), the ship crashes on an unknown planet and all but one of the crew, Stewart, the lone Eve amongst the three Adams, escape. As Taylor abandons the literally sinking ship, he sees the Earth-relative date on the chronometer. It is right around Thanksgiving in the year 3978. Once the three survivors successfully escape their ship, they begin to get their bearings and speculate on where they might be. Here is where things get a little odd.

The surviving crew acknowledge that they have been travelling for eighteen months at nearly the speed of light. Basic science tells us that a light-year is the distance light can travel within a year. A generous estimation would thus be that the crashed ship has travelled nearly one and a half light-years. However, the three astronauts speculate that they have travelled around three hundred and twenty light-years to the Bellatrix system. The math doesn't add up.

Still, science fiction has always enjoyed a rather special relationship with real-world math and science. Most sci-fi films deal with ideas that can only really be speculated about anyway. There are no time machines or spaceships that can warp through space at speeds equivalent to or faster than the speed of light. The effects on people and the environment around them can only be guessed at or theorized anyway, so the second part of the name "science fiction" should lend itself to the story-bending science to fit the narrative. *Star Trek* is famed for its "technobabble," which allows for plausible, yet nonsensical starship jargon to be used in a convincing way. If every other franchise can fib its way through unproven science, then surely *Planet of the Apes* can as well.

At any rate, the end of the film reveals that Taylor isn't trapped in a madhouse however many light-years from home, but is actually on Earth of the far distant future. The ship he was on travelled for eighteen months, presumably nine months away from Earth and nine months back. During those eighteen months, more than two thousand years transpired on Earth and, in that time, humans became mute, feral, and reduced in population, while apes learned how to speak and emerged as the planet's dominant species.

Also of significance is the chimp Cornelius reciting the words of the Lawgiver from the Sacred Scrolls, specifically "Beware the beast Man, for he is the Devil's pawn. Alone among God's primates, he kills for sport or lust or greed. Yea, he will murder his brother to possess his brother's land. Let him not breed in great numbers, for he will make a desert of his home and yours. Shun him; drive him back into his jungle lair, for he is the harbinger of death." These stark words would be repeated throughout the next two films, and the Lawgiver himself would make an appearance in the fifth movie, though not necessarily beating the same drum, as it were.

All of the preceding raised many questions that went unanswered in the original film, but that was not the point of it. It was about race relations and how we treat one another. However, a sequel was on the way, so perhaps we would learn about how a ship was able to travel in a loop back to Earth to a future that saw a radically different population.

"As suggested, I took an Earth-Time reading just before re-entry..."

Beneath the Planet of the Apes begins with a concise summary of the first film, focusing mainly on the revelation of the mysterious planet being future Earth. Soon after that, we are introduced to two more astronauts who have crash-landed. The commander, known only as Skipper (a military term for a vessel's captain), dies shortly after the unceremonious landing, leaving his crewmate, Brent, as the lone survivor. The short scene between the two astronauts reveals a few oddities that are difficult to reconcile with what we know from the first film.

The most striking revelation is Brent declaring the year to be 3955. He says he took an Earth-Time reading before they crashed and noted the year – but this is a full twenty-three years before Taylor's arrival. Even though it is established that Brent and Skipper departed after Taylor and company, travelling through time doesn't necessarily mean that they have to arrive in the order in which they left. Brent certainly could have crashed a couple of decades prior to the earlier ship. The problem with this is that when he encounters Cornelius and Zira in Ape City, they have already experienced the events of *Planet of the Apes*. It seems highly unlikely that Brent wandered around for more than twenty-years before encountering any apes, nor does he visibly age.

Adding to the confusion, the shooting script for the first film gives the date as 3975 when Taylor looks at the Earth-Time display. Why three years were added when the film was made is anyone's guess. The year 3975 is also used in the first script for *Beneath the Planet of the Apes* by new screenwriter Paul Dehn, who would conceive the stories for the subsequent sequels as well. 3955 is eventually used in this film and for the rest of the series (sort of – more on that point soon), but 3978 is generally considered by fans and scholars of the *Apes* series as the year in which Taylor fell from the sky.

The most likely possibility, other than the obvious scripting gaffe, is that Brent's instrumentation malfunctioned at some point before the ship reached the end of its journey through time. It's even possible that the clock on the first vessel malfunctioned at some point as well, and that both crews ended up even farther into the future than the late 40th Century. As with any continuity glitches in any franchise, it is up to the individual to reconcile this dating issue as they see fit. Or to ignore it.

Worth noting is that Doctor Hasslein's theory of time has now become a "Hasslein Curve," something that Brent states he and the Skipper passed through. Strangely, while Taylor and his crew were well aware that more than a century had passed on Earth for every month they spent in space, Skipper and Brent both seem astonished at being more than two millennia in the future. Skipper laments that his family is long dead. As the two astronauts were supposedly on a rescue mission to find Taylor's crew, it seems odd that they would not at least have been warned about possible time-dilation effects. Alternatively, if they were not travelling at the same near-light-speed velocity as the first ship, how were they expected to find them? Again, this can probably be attributed to the aforementioned "special relationship" between films and actual science and, more prominently, to the narrative needs of the script.

Beneath ends far more bleakly and finitely than its predecessor, and would seem to make this film series a duology. The Earth, all the characters and, indeed, all life are obliterated at the end, after all, which should have truncated the possibility of any further sequels. However, this is science fiction and the biggest time-travelling twist was yet to come.

"We have returned to Earth nearly 2,000 years before its destruction..."

Escape from the Planet of the Apes turned the whole franchise on its ear. With no more future left to tell, the producers decided to take the series back in time, but still in the future. The 1971 film contains a news broadcast that quite plainly states it is two years after the two spacecraft from the previous two films were lost. As they were both launched in 1972, the setting of *Escape* is thus 1974. The film begins with the ship that ferried Taylor and his crew to the stars returning home with some very different occupants.

That same news broadcast also states that both ships were seemingly lost upon entering orbit. This actually explains why Brent and Skipper were surprised about the passing of several centuries on Earth while they were on what they thought was a rescue mission. If Earth lost communication with Taylor's ship right after takeoff, it would be reasonable for ANSA[1] to send a rescue ship as soon as possible. This would also explain the two-man crew of

---

[1] The films' fictional counterpart to the real-world National Aeronautics and Space Administration (NASA)

the second vessel – there would be no need to explain relativistic time travel to them, as they were only supposed to search for the first ship.

At some point after it crashed, Taylor's ship was recovered from its watery resting spot by the chimp Doctor Milo. Between that point and the Earth's destruction, Milo was able to repair the ship, make it space-worthy, and figure out a way to launch it into Earth orbit. This seems pretty incredible, but it should be noted that he would have had a second ship, the one carrying Brent and Skipper, to scavenge for parts. It is also easy to assume that he had access to the Forbidden Zone, which possibly contained a treasure trove of information and materials that Milo could have used. Taylor's ship appeared to be completely intact, aside from the blown hatch; it merely sank into a lake. Drying it out and replacing any damaged systems with those from Brent's craft doesn't seem too farfetched. Repairing the ship would only be marginally improbable, but not impossible.

Getting it into space, on the other hand, would seem unachievable given the level of technology that ape society exhibited. Again, we aren't given a lot of information on Doctor Milo, so we have no idea what his areas of expertise are or what resources and information he had at his disposal. For all we know, he may have been keenly up to date on past, advanced human technology and had found and learned to use all sorts of tools. The whys and wherefores of it all are ultimately unimportant, as all that really matters is that Milo, Cornelius, and Zira were about to escape the planet before it was torn asunder.

Zira refers to the year from which the apes come as "3950-something." She specifically recalls seeing this date onboard the spaceship in which they traveled back in time. As this is Taylor's ship, though, the date she saw on the instrumentation should have been 3978, as that was clearly displayed on screen in the first film. It seems Dehn, being the scriptwriter for the previous film and this one, decided to stick to the incongruous date he set in *Beneath*. It is unknown what his thinking was in regard to changing the date from 3978 to 3955, but as a simple explanation could be used in the previous film, a similar one could be applied here. If we assume that the reading on Brent's ship is due to an instrument malfunction, it could also be assumed that maybe Milo needed to replace the readout display in Taylor's ship with the one from Brent's. Who knows why this would be necessary (water damage, perhaps), but it provides a quick and easy solution to the continued continuity mix-up.

It would seem that the Hasslein Curve works in two directions. Either it is a two-way road, like some sort of temporal wormhole, or the Earth's destruction caused it to reverse itself. Either way, the chimpanzees were flung backward in time, almost to the point from which the original time travelers originated. Highly coincidental, to be sure, but, again, we are dealing with a hypothetical concept, so the only rules that apply are what we have been shown thus far. Milo and his compatriots left the future an indeterminate amount of time after men from the past arrived, themselves arriving at a somewhat determinable time after the humans left. That makes for a confusing sentence, but doesn't go against time travel as established in the prior films.

Consideration should be given to the possibility that the very event of Earth's destruction caused the time anomaly to begin with. It would stand to reason that such a catastrophic cosmic event would play havoc with the laws of physics. It isn't unreasonable to postulate that it could tear a whole in the fabric of space-time and propel a ship back in time, starting the whole cycle. If this seems like far-fetched science-fiction claptrap, that is what we are dealing with, after all. No other explanation is given for the time-travelling shenanigans, and this one doesn't go against anything already established.

Similarly, there is no explanation on "present-day" Earth regarding how the United States has technology capable of propelling ships in interstellar travel. There are no signs of other advanced technology, or of society being further advanced than in the real world, so this goes unexplained. This is yet another situation in which the needs of the story demand that Earth have sufficient technological research to make this type of space travel possible, and is ultimately unimportant in the overall scheme of things. It's still fun to speculate that maybe ANSA received better financing and was more rapid in its advancement and successes than the real world's NASA. It's still a little difficult to explain why space technology advancement hasn't trickled down to other forms of technology as it usually would, but, again, that's an unimportant detail.

We finally get to meet Doctor Otto Hasslein, the supposed originator of the Hasslein theory of time and the Hasslein Curve. The scientist has another theory, one postulated in the real world, that gives the first hint that our travelers from the future might be making changes by their mere presence. The Many-Worlds Theory is an idea of quantum mechanics which essentially theorizes that every decision we make creates a parallel world to account for every outcome. It's a little more complicated than that, but that is the basic principle. It's why we had a goateed Spock in the classic *Star Trek* episode "Mirror, Mirror," and also accounts for the infinite Earths that are occasionally put into crisis in the pages of DC Comics' many comic books. All of this makes Hasslein's ensuing actions a little strange.

Hasslein is the President's senior scientific advisor and has enough of an analytical mind to come up with theories on time travel and infinite parallel universes. Yet when he is entering the committee that will be questioning Cornelius and Zira, he states that he expects fear to be the outcome. Indeed, his subsequent behavior becomes increasingly fearful and somewhat erratic as the chimps reveal future history. He argues more and more forcefully for action to be taken against the two apes, especially when it is revealed that Zira is close to giving birth. Ultimately, the scientist himself fatally shoots Zira and what he thinks is her infant son, and most likely would have done the same to Cornelius if the ape hadn't killed him first. Not very fitting behavior for a man dedicated to the sciences and exploration.

Much is revealed about the future of Earth, at least in broad strokes. In the near future, dogs and cats died out from disease and man took apes as pets. In just under two centuries, the new pets learned to do things like cook and clean and shop. After three more centuries, they began to recognize their servitude for what it had become – forced slavery. Cornelius tells of the day that a singular ape, Aldo, finally stood up and spoke the word "no" to his oppressors, and thus began the ape rebellion. Over time, apes became the dominant, intelligent species, while humans became mute and dumb.

Hasslein becomes convinced that Cornelius's and Zira's soon-to-be-born son will lead the future revolution, and that they must be killed to change the future. Again, it seems strange that a scientist would leap to euthanization in such a short span of time instead of exploring any other means of altering the situation, especially events that are many decades into the future. Even the soldiers and politicians around him, who are much more inclined toward quick, dispassionate action, are interested in finding a more peaceful solution.

While it does appear that the newborn ape was killed, the coda of the film shows us that he was instead switched out for a regular circus ape baby and already has the ability to speak. As the baby, once grown, will learn of his parentage in subsequent sequels, and discover what was done to them, it is quite possible that Doctor Hasslein's rash actions may have brought about the very devastation he irrationally tried to prevent.

"We shall found our own armies, our own religion, our own dynasty – and that day is upon you... now!"

If *Escape from the Planet of the Apes* was about prophecies and foreshadowing events to come, *Conquest of the Planet of the Apes* was where some of them paid off and it took a giant leap toward completing the loop back to the first movie. We once again move into the future, nearly two decades, to the year 1991. As foretold, a plague has wiped out all cats and dogs, and man has taken apes as pets. (One has to wonder why on Earth mankind would still do this, given their advance knowledge of where this would likely lead.) Slave labor seems to be fully in effect, as apes perform all sorts of menial and dangerous tasks for their human masters. The planet, or at least the United States, appears to exist in some sort of police state, possibly as a result of whatever event caused the elimination of canines and felines.

Lisa, the first ape to say "no," as seen in *Conquest of the Planet of the Apes.*

However, instead of the five centuries relayed in the previous movie, the apes breaking free of their human masters happens much, much sooner. It is not an ape named Aldo who incites his brethren to rise up, but instead it is

Caesar who ignites the flames of freedom — which starts, interestingly enough, after he witnesses a chimp named Aldo being abused by human handlers. And contrary to the history related by Cornelius, it is Lisa, not Aldo, who is the first to utter the word "no." She does so to prevent her fellow apes from killing Governor Breck, and this has the effect of causing Caesar to back down from a call to slaughter the humans (in the theatrical version, at least), and instead decide to lead and dominate them with compassion, in the hope that one day, both species could walk upon the Earth in unity.

Interestingly, the original ending for this film did have Caesar calling for full-on rebellion and the deaths of all the humans, but the final ending was added after test audiences found the original far too dark. The end result is that we have the rise of the apes happening much sooner than it originally did, and the possibility that a world solely dominated by apes may not come to pass. This is pretty compelling evidence that by travelling to the past, Cornelius and Zira have altered the destiny of their society and have perhaps created a very different Earth of the 40th Century that might be more welcoming to time-lost human astronauts. Fortunately, we would have one more chance to see if things continued to play out along this altered path.

"But as I look at apes and humans living in friendship, in harmony, and at peace, now some 600 years after Caesar's death, at least we wait with hope for the future."

Battle for the Planet of the Apes not only ends the original film series, but gives us the final compelling evidence that Cornelius, Zira, Caesar, and Milo have changed the future of Earth and altered their own past. However, there is a hotly debated coda that can be interpreted in two conflicting ways, either proving or disproving that the first two films will still culminate in the planet's destruction. While this may be the least well-received of the original five films, it has perhaps sparked the most arguments and debates among Apes fans since it first screened in 1973.

The main action in the film takes place an unspecified number of years after the previous movie, and is bookended by a scene set in 2670, featuring the mythic Lawgiver. Before we delve into the rather significant sequence in the 27th Century, the other timeframe has some very relevant bits to explore. The Earth has been ravaged by nuclear war, presumably initiated by the humans in response to the worldwide ape uprising. Caesar has founded the first Ape City, where he is maintaining a tenuous peace between humans and apes, though the simians are clearly in charge. The military is led by an ape named Aldo – this one a gorilla. While not enough time has passed for him to be *the* Aldo who originally caused the ape revolt, his actions indicate he certainly could be an ancestor. (Of course, the same could be said of his chimp namesake from *Conquest*, since Cornelius never specifies Aldo's species in *Escape*.)

While no date is given for the "present-day" parts of the film, there are some lines of dialogue that offer significant clues. MacDonald states that there have been twelve years of peace, so we know that more than a decade has passed since the rebellion in 1991. Mandemus, meanwhile, claims to have guarded the ape armory for Caesar for 27 years. Assuming he has been there since just after the rebellion, this would put the year at 2018. As the actor playing Caesar, Roddy McDowall, was 45 years old at the time, the year 2018 would just about correspond with Caesar being that age. Rich Handley hedged bets slightly by assigning a date of 2020 in his comprehensive book *Timeline of the Planet of the Apes*.[2] The framing sequence is shown by on-screen titles to be in the year 2670, which the Lawgiver says is around 600 years after Caesar's death, so given that Caesar most likely lived well past the titular battle, the year 2020 fits rather nicely.

As an aside, there is a sequence cut from the film that would have shown the beginnings of the mutant cult who worshipped the Alpha-Omega Bomb that Taylor detonated to destroy the Earth in *Beneath the Planet of the Apes*. It is unknown why this was removed from the film's initial release, as it would have provided a richer subtext to the film and additional ambiguity as to whether or not Caesar's actions would ultimately prevent Earth's fiery fate in 3978. Thankfully, the lost scenes were restored for the movie's Blu-ray release.

In uncovering a murderous plot by the treacherous Aldo, Caesar realizes that apes are no better than humans, and that "Ape shall never kill ape" should extend to include their former masters (humans are, after all, apes). This golden rule of the apes previously seemed to have been attributed to the Lawgiver, so it is significant that Caesar is the one to originate it. Also, the first two films showed plenty of statues of the Lawgiver within Ape City, but in this film we see a statue of Caesar in 2670. It would seem that Caesar has replaced the Lawgiver as the most significant individual in ape society.

---

[2] Handley chose 2020 to accommodate the events of Marvel Comics' "Quest for the Planet of the Apes" storyline, which set Mandemus's assignment to the armory two years after the events of *Conquest*.

In contrast to the Lawgiver's words being discussed in the first two films, in 2670 we see the orangutan relating lessons learned from the actions of Caesar, and it is general knowledge that he was the child of two apes from the future. This is yet another indicator that times have changed. Most significantly, the Lawgiver is teaching a group of ape *and* human children together, and they appear to be social equals. Not only that, but humans can still apparently speak. The words of the Lawgiver are very different than his words quoted in the first movie about the beast Man, the Devil's pawn. He speaks of unity between the species, and of peace and friendship.

Finally, we close on the statue of Caesar, which sheds a single tear. This is the shot mentioned above that has been debated, sometimes heatedly, among fans for the past 40 years and counting. Some say it symbolizes Caesar's hope for a peaceful future between man and ape being realized. The other side of the argument is that the tear symbolizes despair that the peace between the species is ultimately doomed to fail because we will loop around to the events of the first two films unaltered.

Much may have changed in the timeline, as evidenced by the Lawgiver teaching lessons to ape and human children, in 2670, in *Battle for the Planet of the Apes*.

Both sides have equal merit, and it is a tribute to the filmmakers that these films are as scrutinized, debated, and theorized about as they are decades after they were made. Scriptwriter Paul Dehn stated, in a subsequent interview, that he intended the tear to signify that the hope for peace was ultimately doomed to failure, as the events of 3978/3955 would still occur as shown.[3]

[3] Russo, Joe; Landsman, Larry; and Gross, Edward. *Planet of the Apes Revisited* (St. Martin's Griffin, August 2001).

In the original film, Zaius claims ape society began only 1,200 years prior, per the Sacred Scrolls, but that would be a century after the setting of *Battle*'s bookend scenes. The eight centuries following Caesar's rebellion are thus unaccounted for in the Scrolls. This could explain the inconsistencies, with the events of the past being wiped away by the authors of a religious text a few generations after the Lawgiver's lifetime. The Sacred Scrolls' writers may have chosen, for the good of apekind, to eliminate all mention of Caesar and his parents, to rewrite history so that Aldo (one of the film Aldos, or maybe a descendant) was revered as a savior, to bury the knowledge of humanity's true nature by establishing the Forbidden Zone, and to change the Lawgiver's teachings to match their anti-man sentiments. Dehn's statement would seem to support this closed-loop line of thinking.

The scriptwriter would seem to have the final word on the matter, so perhaps we should accept that the whole timeline of the *Planet of the Apes* is one fatalistic loop and that fate, however dire, is unalterable. As there were never any additional films to fill in the gap between *Battle* and *Planet*, it is left up to the audience to decide whether it all turned out OK or went to hell. At its best, science fiction should make a person question and ponder and wonder what happens next.

Given that scale, *Planet of the Apes* and its four sequels provide some of the best science fiction and the most intriguing storytelling. With the original series of films, as well as with the current reboot series, we can once again wonder what happens next.

It's a Madhouse Every Week! Television Journeys to the Planet of the Apes

by Dayton Ward

After five feature films, one might have argued, in the early 1970s, that the *Planet of the Apes* franchise was approaching its nadir. However, plans to extend the successful series to television had been brewing even before the last of the movies went into production. Arthur P. Jacobs, the man originally responsible for bringing his adaptation of Pierre Boulle's *La Planète des Singes* (*Monkey Planet*) to 20th Century Fox, had considered a TV series while the fourth movie, *Conquest of the Planet of the Apes*, was still being filmed. When that movie proved a box office success and the studio expressed a desire for yet another sequel, plans for a TV incarnation were put on hold.

Following Jacobs' death in the summer of 1973 and shortly after the release of *Battle for the Planet of the Apes*, Fox acquired from his production company the rights to the films, and to create new material based on the property. CBS then purchased the broadcast rights for the first three movies. Following their rating successes, the network began working with the studio to develop a new television series.

FRIDAY

Planet of the Apes

"All humans look alike, you know that." . . . "Bad enough having humans in the house . . . but wash first. There's a smell about you." . . . "These humans are dangerous! They think they are as good as we are. They stir up trouble." The speakers are gorillas. The time is 2000 years from now, and apes rule the earth, while human beings are considered "a lower species." Into this upside-down world come a pair of 20th-century astronauts, who are stranded there after passing through a time warp. The anthropoid leaders (Booth Colman and Mark Lenard) are determined to hunt down these two alien troublemakers, and the astronauts are just as determined to keep themselves from being enslaved or killed. They are befriended by a chimp (Roddy McDowall) who is very broad-minded about being seen in the company of his zoological inferiors. All of this outlandish monkey business is, of course, based on the "Planet of the Apes" movies. The films were immensely popular in their TV showings, and now CBS yearns to ape their ratings every Friday. Debut: CBS, Sept. 13. *Pictured (l.-r.) James Naughton, Roddy McDowall, Ron Harper.*

58   TV GUIDE SEPTEMBER 7, 1974

This advertisement, from the 7 September 1974 issue of *TV Guide*, heralds the coming of Peter Burke and Alan Virdon to the planet of the apes.

Genesis

For the most part, the five *Planet of the Apes* films had worked together to tell a self-contained – if not always internally consistent – circular story. While developing concepts for the television series, much thought was given to where to place it within the "future history" established by the movies. There was even consideration of creating overt links to the events of the first film. Rod Serling, creator of *The Twilight Zone* and *Night Gallery* – who, with Michael Wilson, had penned the screenplay for the original movie – was tapped to create a series writer's guide, as well as develop scripts for the show's first two episodes.

Serling's draft for the pilot episode features astronauts Alan Virdon and Stanley Kovak crash-landing on a future Earth while searching for another spacecraft that has gone missing, commanded by an astronaut named Taylor. Despite the obvious connection to Charlton Heston's character George Taylor from the first two films, the names of the other astronauts from the lost ship (Thomas, LaFever, and Bengsten) differ from those of their movie counterparts (Dodge, Landon, and Stewart).

Upon their arrival, Virdon and Kovak are befriended by a benevolent chimpanzee, Galen, and end up being pursued by Doctor Zaius, a senior member of the ape "High Council," as well as General Ursus, who commands the ape police garrison. Serling's script also refers to the deaths of Taylor and a chimpanzee called Zira, indicating that while the series may have wanted to tie to the films' events, it was intended as more of an adaptation than any direct continuation.

As the series began to take shape, mentions of Taylor and Zira were removed from the concept, along with other obvious ties to the movies. Stanley Kovak became Peter Burke, and Ursus evolved into another gorilla, Security Chief Urko[1]. The characters of Virdon and Galen survived largely unchanged, whereas Zaius was somewhat tempered in comparison to his silver-screen incarnation. Here, he serves to rein in Urko, who is very much in the mold of General Ursus from *Beneath the Planet of the Apes*, with no regard for humans in general and the renegade astronauts in particular. Urko is convinced that Virdon and Burke, given sufficient time, might incite the local humans to rise up against their simian masters.

The Doctor Zaius of the films was of similar mind and so, too, is his television counterpart, Councilor Zaius. Still, while he wants the astronauts captured or killed, he understands they possess knowledge that has otherwise been lost to time. Though he believes that gaining insight into the technological achievements of past eras might serve to advance ape society, this Zaius is also

---

[1] Who would himself evolve into a similar character, General Urko, on the animated series *Return to the Planet of the Apes*

worried about avoiding the mistakes that so plagued humanity before its eventual downfall.

Prior to his casting as Alan Virdon, actor Ron Harper was known to American television audiences for his portrayal of Lieutenant Craig Garrison in 1968's *Garrison's Gorillas*, an ABC series set during World War II and inspired by the popularity of the Lee Marvin film *The Dirty Dozen* from the previous year. James Naughton was already an accomplished stage actor before landing the role of Peter Burke, and had ended a turn on the short-lived television series *Faraday & Company*, one of four shows in rotation as part of the *NBC Mystery Movie* series. Portraying the fugitive astronauts was each actor's first time working with a science-fiction film or TV series.

On the other hand, Roddy McDowall was something of an old hand, having appeared on such series as *The Twilight Zone*, *The Invaders*, and *Batman* throughout the 1960s as part of a career spanning more than 30 years. After portraying Cornelius in the original *Planet of the Apes* film and *Escape from the Planet of the Apes*, as well as that character's son, Caesar, in the fourth and fifth movies, McDowall had already cemented his place as the figurative – if not literal – face of the entire franchise. For the new television series, he would play Galen, another compassionate chimpanzee who becomes Virdon's and Burke's traveling companion and fellow renegade.

Likewise, Mark Lenard was familiar to genre audiences, having provided two different yet equally memorable guest performances on the original *Star Trek* series. In the first-season episode "Balance of Terror," he portrayed a Romulan commander who engages in a lethal game of cat and mouse with Captain James T. Kirk and the U.S.S. *Enterprise*. However, it was his later portrayal of Sarek, father of Mr. Spock, in the episode "Journey to Babel"[2], that would endear him to fans for all time. Lenard's commanding presence and distinctive voice were instrumental to realizing the character of Urko, the militant gorilla obsessed with finding and executing the fugitive astronauts.

Rounding out the main cast, Booth Colman brought with him an extensive stage, film, and television career that featured numerous portrayals of authority figures, which served him well in the role of Councilor Zaius. In an odd bit of

---

[2] The first of multiple appearances by Lenard as Sarek, which would also span an episode of *Star Trek: The Animated Series*, three *Star Trek* films, and two episodes of *Star Trek: The Next Generation*.

trivia, Colman studied as a young actor under Maurice Evans – who, of course, portrayed his protégé's film counterpart in the first two *Apes* films.[3]

Arrival

Premiering on the evening of Friday, 13 September 1974, the first episode of the *Planet of the Apes* television series, "Escape from Tomorrow," wastes no time introducing us to astronauts Virdon and Burke and thrusting them into their tumultuous new situation. Similar to what happened to Colonel Taylor and his crew in the original film, our two new heroes are part of an interstellar exploration mission, traveling this time from Earth to Alpha Centauri. Their spacecraft encounters difficulties and crashes on what they at first believe to be an alien planet. As happened with Taylor's shipmate Stewart, Virdon and Burke lose a fellow astronaut, Jones, who is killed in the crash.

Astronauts Jones, Virdon, and Burke crash in the TV series' premiere episode, "Escape from Tomorrow."

---

[3] "Actor Booth Colman Dies at 91." *Variety* (21 December, 2014): variety.com/2014/film/people-news/actor-booth-colman-dies-at-91-1201384795/.

After being found by a local human, Farrow, who pulls them from their wrecked ship and takes them to a subterranean chamber that serves as his home, Virdon and Burke soon learn that they've traveled forward in time from the year 1980 and returned to an Earth of the distant future[4], where humankind has fallen from its place atop the evolutionary pyramid and is now ruled by intelligent simians. Unlike the first two films, humans in this time period still possess the ability to reason and talk, though they are subservient and most work to serve ape interests.

What is carried over from the movies, however, is the rampant paranoia the astronauts' presence evokes in Zaius, who is alarmed upon learning of the crashed spacecraft and immediately issues orders for Virdon and Burke to be apprehended. They cannot be allowed to remain at large, spreading their knowledge of past human civilization. To this end, Urko is more than happy to see them killed at any cost, but Zaius is adamant that they be taken alive. Upon their capture, the astronauts are brought before Zaius and a council of apes, where they are condemned for the actions of humans from centuries past. Urko is convinced that they possess the intelligence and ability to spur rebellion among the human populace, and therefore must be put to death. Virdon and Burke are jailed to await their fate.

As Taylor was befriended and rescued by the compassionate chimpanzees Cornelius and Zira, Virdon and Burke avoid murder when young Galen sees them about to be shot by one of Urko's soldiers. Galen, an assistant to Zaius for all of a few hours, is branded a traitor and thrown in jail to await execution for treason, prompting the astronauts to break him out before they all make their escape. Now on the run with Urko and his soldiers in pursuit, the fugitives and Galen make one stop: the crashed spacecraft. Virdon is determined not to leave the ship's flight data – recorded on a magnetic disc – for the apes to find and possibly destroy. His hope is that somewhere, some pocket of civilization might possess technology capable of reading the disc's stored data, allowing him and Burke to recreate or reverse the events that hurled them through time. The central goal for the series is now set, with Virdon, Burke, and Galen trying to stay one step ahead of Zaius and Urko while searching for a way home.

---

[4] Possibly to 3085, though that date is open to debate since that may simply be when the chronometer on the astronauts' craft (called *Probe One* in production materials) ceased to function.

What Kind of a Planet of Apes *Is* This?

Though much more restrained in approach than the five feature films, the *Planet of the Apes* TV series still found ways to touch on themes put forth in its cinematic predecessors. The lessons aren't quite so heavy-handed, perhaps as a result of studio or network concerns, but the show's writers still found ways to work in a message here and there. Racism is a common element, of course, as personified in the casual treatment of humans by apes as lower-level beings.

Indeed, in this case one could argue that the allegory is even more accurate, given that humans in the series retain a reasonable portion of their intellect, as well as the power of speech. They're not so easy to dismiss as the primitive, even savage "animals" seen in the first two movies. Because of this, the issues that receive greater attention – albeit on oblique terms – revolve around social inequality and injustice. As the series progresses, first Galen and then a growing list of apes come to understand the truth of humanity's downfall and realize that apes and humans might one day be able to live and work together, provided they can find common ground. More than one episode ends on a hopeful note to that effect, which is almost cruel when considering whether the television series fits into the film continuity and, if so, what most of us know will happen about 900 years later. (Hint: "Boom.")

Starting with the first episode, the series dangles a few tantalizing plot nuggets that do more to evoke questions rather than supply answers so far as its placement within the larger *Planet of the Apes* framework. This hasn't stopped devoted fans from making uncounted attempts to integrate the series' characters and events into the "future history chronology."[5]

There are references to "another ship" and other astronauts who apparently landed 10 years prior to the arrival of Burke and Virdon, and Zaius says that Urko killed at least one of these "renegade humans." The dialogue is sufficiently vague that it invites the possibility of another astronaut who might still be alive, but it's a plot point that is never revisited after this first episode. Despite this being something of a holdover from Rod Serling's original concept and script, Virdon and Burke display no knowledge of another expedition or missing spaceship in the finished episode.

---

[5] See the timeline by yours truly published in Paul A. Woods' *The Planet of the Apes Chronicles* (Plexus Books, August 2001), as well as Rich Handley's *Timeline of the Planet of the Apes: The Definitive Chronology* (Hasslein Books, November 2008).

There is no mention of characters or events from any of the films, despite the astronauts having departed Earth almost a decade after the time of Taylor's flight. Likewise, the duo exhibit no knowledge regarding the arrival of Cornelius and Zira on 1973 Earth, as depicted in *Escape from the Planet of the Apes*, and have never heard of talking apes. They are stunned to discover that they have crashed on an Earth of the distant future, long after human civilization's collapse and the rise of the apekind. Zaius, despite his name being carried over from the films, is quite obviously not meant to be the same character, even though he occupies the same basic role as a "defender of the faith."

This is most evident in "Escape from Tomorrow," when the orangutan scolds Galen on matters of heresy and the dangers of pursuing forbidden knowledge. Later, when Zaius tells Virdon and Burke about humanity's demise, it echoes the conversations between his film counterpart and Taylor in the original *Planet of the Apes*. Likewise, the notion of preventing the astronauts from using their advanced intellect to perhaps undermine ape society and inspire the humans to revolt against their masters will be mentioned several times throughout the course of the series.

Even the circumstances surrounding the major linchpin in the *Planet of the Apes* mythology – humanity's demise and the rise of the apes – is subject to revision, in the form of the "ancient" history book Farrow shows Virdon and Burke. The book contains a photograph of the New York cityscape from the year 2503, centuries after the astronauts' departure from Earth, and long after the time of Caesar's ape uprising, along with the subsequent nuclear war that devastated the planet.[6] The simian rebellion's genesis is chronicled in *Conquest of the Planet of the Apes*, whereas *Battle for the Planet of the Apes* begins several years after the nuclear conflict that leaves much of human civilization in ruins, but well before the date of the supposed photograph in Farrow's book.

In fact, "Escape from Tomorrow" introduces a seeming continuity problem in its opening moments, when we see a young chimpanzee child playing with a dog. According to *Conquest*, all dogs and cats died or had to be killed as a consequence of a plague brought back from yet another space mission. However, it's entirely possible that a sufficient number of our canine and feline

---

[6] In reality, the "photograph" is an illustration, but Virdon says, "This picture was taken 500 years after we left." The shot of the supposed "picture" was likely inserted during post-production, as doesn't appear to match the page in the book Virdon is studying.

friends survived the disease, particularly in the wild, and that the population was restored, at least in part, during the course of the intervening centuries. Still, it's suggestive of an alternate take on the basic *Planet of the Apes* premise for purposes of television (or "alternate timeline" for the geeks among you... and, really, if you're reading this book, that's you, too).

Further, there are other apparent inconsistencies with respect to the level of technological advancement Virdon and Burke left behind in the 20th Century, or even what may have been achieved following their departure. In "The Trap," Burke is buried with Urko during an earthquake, falling into the ruins of a subway station beneath the streets of San Francisco. There, he shows the gorilla examples of lost human achievements. Everything from atomic-powered subway cars to pills that substitute for entire meals to disposable clothing – it all seems out of place with the Earth depicted in the third and fourth films.

On the Run

In a manner similar to how another CBS series, *M*A*S*H*, used as inspiration Robert Altman's 1970 film along with the novel on which that movie was based, the *Planet of the Apes* TV series ultimately wasn't developed as a strict continuation of the storyline put forth in the five theatrical films. Instead, it adapted and reinterpreted the basic premise to a weekly television format. Much of what appears in Rod Serling's writer's bible and his early drafts of the first episode's script was changed by the time the series went into actual production, though many of the ideas he put forth still served to define the show's basic concept and recurring plot points.

Alan Virdon and Peter Burke each possess individual traits previously exhibited by astronaut George Taylor in the original *Planet of the Apes* film. Virdon, the commander of his crew's ill-fated mission, is separated by more than a thousand years from the wife and son he left behind. On the one hand, he does share Taylor's need to know what brought about the collapse of human civilization in the first place. This sentiment echoes Taylor's questions at the end of the original film, when he tells Zaius that he needs to understand how he came to be on a "planet where apes evolved from men." Of course, Taylor doesn't yet know the truth at that point, and once he finds it there's some suggestion that he might continue to search for more answers, even if he's resigned to his own fate. Virdon is similarly driven to learn what happened in the centuries since he left Earth, though he has no intention of accepting his situation while there remains even the slightest hope of returning home.

Meanwhile, Burke exhibits more of Taylor's temperament. He's definitely a realist, if not an outright fatalist. In the first few episodes, in particular, Burke often expresses a resignation to their situation, viewing with unrestrained skepticism Virdon's belief that there might still exist some remnant of an advanced civilization, somewhere on the planet. Despite his doubts, Burke still supports Virdon's quest and the hope that fuels it, compelled by loyalty to the other man who is both his friend and the group's undisputed leader. In "The Legacy," he even tells Galen, "When you joined this outfit, you got stuck obeying orders from the commanding officer, Colonel Alan Virdon." Beyond that, Burke's certainly not interested in living on any terms the apes might provide. His main concern is keeping himself and his friends alive, and to find some safe haven where they might live free of ape pursuit.

Adopting the formula which had served *The Fugitive* so well throughout the life of that series[7], each new episode of *Planet of the Apes* sees Virdon, Burke, and Galen venturing to some new village or region, with Urko and his gorillas never too far behind. They typically encounter a group of humans or – on rarer occasions – apes in need of assistance. On several of these occasions, the astronauts' advanced scientific and engineering knowledge plays a key role in the story, allowing them to construct or otherwise devise a solution to the problem of the week. In a few of these cases, the fugitives even manage to leave things a bit better than they found them.

In "The Good Seeds," Virdon brings his childhood upbringing on a family farm to bear in several instances, when he's able to show an ape family several tried and true agricultural techniques and other, smarter ways to carry out work on their farm. The lessons Virdon imparts meet much resistance, as the apes tend to be set in their ways and fearful of change. Like so much other knowledge from human civilization, even these simple methods have been lost throughout the centuries, replaced by superstition and uncertainty in the face of the unknown. Virdon and Burke must battle generations of ingrained tradition over everything from how to water crops to moving hay to building a fence. The ape family's patriarch, Polar, and particularly his son, Anto, resent having their beliefs challenged, even when the astronauts demonstrate easy techniques for improving their crop yields and their general quality of life.

---

[7] And would later inform *The Incredible Hulk*, *The A-Team*, *Starman*, *Kung Fu*, *The Invaders*, *Blake's 7*, and other shows

On the other hand, such societal fallacies come in handy once in a while. Earlier in the same episode, the fugitives are traveling during a cloudy evening, using a compass Virdon has crafted to keep them moving in a set direction. We learn that either apes have not learned how to create such devices, or else it's yet another piece of long-lost knowledge; either way, it is considered taboo to travel at night if the stars are not visible. It is this cultural restriction, as well as the fear attached to it, that hampers the efforts of Urko's soldiers to maintain their pursuit.

Combating a variety of erroneous beliefs is a recurring problem as the fugitives move from one place to the next. When they happen across a seaside fishing labor camp in "Tomorrow's Tide," they discover that the human workers and their ape masters worship the sharks that lurk in the nearby ocean. Humans who are too old or otherwise unable to work spearing fish in order to meet the village's demanding quotas are tied to wooden rafts and sacrificed to the sharks. Unaware of these cultural practices, Virdon and Burke rescue an older man, Gahto, who's been condemned to the "gods of the sea." This causes some initial uproar until the astronauts concoct a scheme to show both ape and human villagers how to catch even more fish. They teach Gahto how to build a net, then demonstrate how it can snare many more fish than simple spears, thereby pleasing the gods without the need to sacrifice workers who are too old or injured to work.

Baseless fears even extend to medicine. After Virdon is shot by a gorilla patrol in "The Surgeon," he requires an emergency operation to save his life. Galen and Burke get him to an ape hospital, where Galen convinces a doctor and former flame, Kira, to operate. When Burke suggests a transfusion to combat the blood loss Virdon will suffer during the surgery, Kira replies that an earlier attempt to transfer blood between two humans resulted in the recipient's death. The conclusion was that such transfusions were "against the laws of nature," and the donor, the daughter of one of the hospital's human servants, is ostracized because of the belief that her blood is "evil." Burke quickly realizes that the girl was a mismatched donor, and conducts tests to determine each servant's blood type. The girl's type is compatible with Virdon's, the operation is a success, and the ape doctors learn that many more lives can be saved thanks to proper blood transfusion during surgery.

Then there are those who use superstition and ritual to control others. In "The Liberator," a human named Brun, the self-proclaimed "master" of a mining labor camp, uses the fear of godly punishment to keep slaves in line while working in the mines. As part of his rules and laws, he routinely "sacrifices" transgressors and others to gods that supposedly live in a temple and possess the power to kill unseen. Burke and Virdon soon discover that Brun is using ancient military gas canisters to poison the sacrificial victims, and is wearing a gas mask beneath his ornate ceremonial face mask. Brun's larger plan is to use the gas against the apes, but when Galen accidentally starts a fire in the temple, the gas supply is destroyed and Brun dies. It's one of the rare times during the series when present-day humans or apes are threatened by something from humanity's past.

In Search of Emerald City

Virdon and Burke finding such links to the world they left behind is a notion visited only on rare occasions throughout the series. That they would do this as part of a larger quest to find some remnants of advanced human civilization is a premise first put forth in Rod Serling's original series concept pitch. Serling's initial story notes also included the idea of the astronauts retrieving the magnetic flight recorder disc from their crashed spaceship, in the hopes that the data encoded on it might provide a means of returning home. Of course, this requires technology capable of interpreting that information, which Virdon is driven to find. From Serling's original concept document[8]:

> Rumors of an advanced pocket of civilization give Virdon the hope that he might find a group with the scientific capability of building a space ship and by feeding the disk into a computer, find the means of returning them to their own time period.
>
> It is this hope that causes Virdon to cling desperately to the magnetic disk and continue his journey from one place to another on the PLANET OF THE APES.

As we know, the magnetic disc concept survived and plays a major role in "Escape from Tomorrow" as well as in the series' second episode, "The Gladiators," in which Virdon loses the disc and the astronauts spend the rest of the story attempting to get it back. Unfortunately, the disc is never mentioned again. Likewise, the idea of the fugitives finding some representation of past human civilization largely falls by the wayside as the series progresses, with two notable exceptions. First is "The Trap," in which they find the ruins of San Francisco, but their efforts to find any clues as to a possible outpost of advanced humans are sidetracked by an earthquake that traps Burke

---

[8] Serling, Rod. *Planet of the Apes – Concept."* Date unknown.

underground with Urko. They never get to explore the city before being forced to flee in order to avoid capture and execution at the hands of Urko's soldiers.

The series' one major attempt to follow this plot element is "The Legacy," in which the astronauts and Galen learn that they are near the ruins of another immense city. Upon their arrival, they realize they have found what remains of Oakland, California, and stumble into the former headquarters of what had been a government think tank in their era. Hidden in the bowels of the building is a machine representing a technology more advanced than anything with which the astronauts are familiar. It's a holographic projector that, once activated, plays a recorded message alerting any viewers that scientists, in anticipation of the coming "holocaust," have taken steps to preserve the vast wealth of human scientific knowledge. This information has been placed in caches hidden in cities around the world, including one location in Oakland.

Virdon is certain this is the first substantial clue they've been looking for, and might well hold the answers to getting them back home. When the projector's power supply gives out, he and Burke devise a plan to rig up a battery using available materials in order to reactivate the machine and learn the location of the hidden information.

Even Burke, ever the realist and skeptic, is motivated to restore the projector and find the cache. Following the usual sorts of circumstances that routinely plague the fugitives – including Virdon being taken prisoner for a time by Zaius and Urko – they find the hidden storehouse but are forced to abandon it to the apes in order to avoid capture. It is a bitter carrot dangled before our heroes only to be snatched away, and such a prize never again presents itself throughout the remainder of the series. One has to wonder how long it would've taken the writers to revisit the premise had the show not been cancelled, or even survived to complete its first season.

Fates Untold... Sort Of

Unfortunately, it didn't take long for *Planet of the Apes* to fall into a pattern of repetition on "*The Fugitive* formula" that drove most episodes, from which there seemed very little variation and no chance of escape. The basic template called for the astronauts and Galen to encounter some group of humans or apes in sore need of a bit of knowledge which might make their lives better, or perhaps they just required a swift kick in the pants for one reason or another. Many of these setups also called for one of the fugitives to be captured, if not by Urko (and occasionally Zaius), then by the particular episode's guest ape or human, necessitating a rescue by the remaining two companions. If someone wasn't taken prisoner, then they were injured in some manner. Occasional variations allowed for the prisoner *du jour* to be captured *and* injured.

The repetitive nature of the show's plots, along with somewhat lackluster production values and a large per-episode budget – a significant portion of which was devoted to ape makeup – and low ratings stemming from a Friday-evening timeslot that pitted it against the top-rated sitcom duo of *Sanford and Son* and *Chico and the Man*, all served to undermine the series. *Planet of the Apes* was cancelled without fanfare following its 14th episode, "Up Above the World So High."

Galen, Zaius, and Urko hold a tense-looking conversation in the woefully short-lived television series.

Depending on which source you consult, this episode aired either on 6 December or 20 December 1974. To this day, there remains debate regarding whether the show's penultimate episode, "The Liberator," actually was aired as scheduled on 6 December, and consensus throughout the years seems to have concluded that it aired in some markets while being preempted in others. Regardless, there was no actual series finale. "Up Above the World So High" ended in much the same fashion as the rest of the episodes, with the fugitives having escaped capture – or worse – and heading off toward whatever unknown fate might await them.

As with the rest of the *Planet of the Apes* franchise, the television series generated a modest array of merchandising, including a quartet of episode novelizations written by noted science-fiction author George Alec Effinger, as well as action figures and playsets, bubble-gum cards, and assorted other items. The adventures of Virdon, Burke, and Galen weren't completely over, either, thanks to a Power Records album release featuring four original audio stories based on the television series.[9] The characters also appeared in comics and short fiction stories created for a trio of hardcover "annuals" produced between 1975 and 1977 by British publisher Brown Watson. During this same period, a Spanish-language publisher, Editorial Mo.Pa.Sa., released *El Planeta de Los Simios*, a comic book based on the series and sold only in Argentina. The title only ran for seven issues. [10] Good luck finding them.

In 1980, 20th Century Fox repurposed selected episodes of the television series as a package of five TV movies to air in syndication. These telefilms were titled *Back to the Planet of the Apes*; *The Forgotten City of the Planet of the Apes*; *Treachery and Greed on the Planet of the Apes*; *Life, Liberty and Pursuit on the Planet of the Apes*; and *Farewell to the Planet of the Apes*. The five theatrical motion pictures had already been sold to various markets for airing as part of a block of *"Planet of the Apes* Week" programming, and these new telefilms offered local stations the chance to "Go Ape" for just a little while longer.[11]

It was because of this decision that the fates of Virdon and Burke ultimately received something resembling resolution. Viewers watching the new package on ABC-owned stations got a special treat in the form of Roddy McDowall reprising his role of Galen in ten short segments that book-ended the telefilms. Depicted as being many years older, Galen introduces each movie and offers a hint about his adventures with Burke and Virdon. At the conclusion of the final

---

[9] "Battle of Two Worlds," "Dawn of the Tree People," "Mountain of the Delphi," and "Volcano"

[10] Both the annuals and the Argentine comics were discussed at length in this anthology's companion volume, *The Sacred Scrolls: Comics on the Planet of the Apes*, and can be found online at http://potatv.kassidyrae.com.

[11] Houston, David. "Packaging Apes for TV Profit." *Starlog* #45 (April 1981).

TV movie, *Farewell to the Planet of the Apes*, the aged chimpanzee provides this simple yet cryptic declaration as to what finally happened to the astronauts:

> Virdon and Burke? They found their computer in another city, and disappeared into space as suddenly as they arrived. What about me? I certainly could have gone with them, back to your time; your world, where apes are kept in zoos. Tell me, now: would you have come to my world willingly? You will... eventually, of course.

These opening and closing segments only aired on the ABC stations, and only during the telefilms' initial broadcast. They weren't included on the 2001 "Complete TV Series" DVD set, though low-quality versions of the videos can be found on sites like YouTube and Vimeo.

Ultimately, the *Planet of the Apes* television series was a case of striking after the iron had cooled. In the wake of five motion pictures throughout the course of six years and all the associated merchandising, fans and studio executives at 20th Century Fox were likely suffering from "franchise fatigue," even if that term was decades away from being coined. By late 1974 and with the show's cancellation[12], a reasonable person might conclude that the reign of the apes was finished.

And that person would have been wrong.

---

[12] On television, at least. In 2017, Titan Books published *Planet of the Apes: Tales from the Forbidden Zone*, a licensed short-fiction anthology edited by Rich Handley and Jim Beard, featuring four original tales picking up where the TV series left off, written by Robert Greenberger, Will Murray, Andrew Gaska, and yours truly.

Escaping to Tomorrow: The TV Series Novelizations

by John Roche

The first episode of the *Planet of the Apes* television series to be aired in those hallowed, halcyon closing months of 1974 was titled "Escape *from* Tomorrow." While that may have adequately summed up the aspirations of our astronaut heroes, the title of the second TV series novelization has always been closer to the mark: *Escape **to** Tomorrow* neatly encapsulates what the *Apes* TV show was all about – leaving behind the real world of today and escaping into a future of high excitement, gripping action, and no small amount of humor.

The sad, premature demise of the TV series after only 14 episodes left a void that could have been unbridgeable had it not been for the special little legacy bestowed upon an unworthy humanity in the shape of the four novelizations written by George Alec Effinger, containing adaptations of eight episodes (more than half the number aired). While Mego figures for the TV series would arrive (misspelled "Verdon" figure included!) and Topps' glorious set of 66 trading cards had a mini narrative tale printed on the backs, in the absence of the actual TV episodes, the adaptations were the only way in pre-VCR days to re-live the actual stories. Reading and re-reading the novelizations was formative for my young mind – Alan Virdon, Peter Burke, and Galen were role models and friends who have never left me and walk with me still.

George Alec Effinger, a native of Ohio, was a worthy member of the quite breath-taking group of authors selected by Award Books to pen their *Apes* line. Luminaries such as Jerry Pournelle, John Jakes, and David Gerrold delivered wonderful novelizations of the three movies adapted by Award[1], while Effinger was a Hugo and Nebula Award science-fiction author, whose 1972 novel *What Entropy Means to Me* is well regarded to this day.

Effinger wrote briefly for Marvel Comics in the early 1970s, and went on to write his Marîd Audran trilogy of novels in the following decade. Indeed, Effinger even came back to the concept of two astronauts lost in time and space with his short-lived comic, *Neil and Buzz in Space and Time*[2]. For his *Apes* work, the author was, naturally, working from scripts penned by others and, indeed, he subsequently expressed surprise at just how little assistance he was given in getting access to the scripts to actually adapt them. Be that as it may, Effinger clearly received at least eight of the scripts, though the selection, in itself, raises a number of questions.

Award Books was an imprint in the 1970s that served up such wonders as adaptations of the films *Enter the Dragon* and *The Return of Sabata*, science-fiction anthologies like Hans Steffan Santesson's *Gods for Tomorrow*, and an invitation to probe the unknown with Eric Norman's *The Abominable Snowmen* and Brinsley Le Poer Trench's *The Sky People*. The *Apes* novelizations were part of the glorious era of cheap cash-in merchandising that the '70s seemed to do so well. Indeed, the *Apes* movie and TV series novels really had no business being as good as they are. It is to the eternal credit of the authors that *Apes* was privileged to have writers capable of elevating themselves above the pulp merchandising premise and deliver, instead, some enchanting books.

The TV series adaptations are contained in four books, at two episodes per volume. The running order bears little relationship to that of the broadcast series, or even the production order. For example, the first story adapted, "The Cure," was the 12th episode broadcast, whereas the final story novelized, "The Gladiators," was actually the second broadcast. We never get to see how our astronauts arrived on the planet of the apes, since the opening episode, "Escape from Tomorrow," is not among the adapted stories. Indeed, this glaring

---

[1] *Escape from the Planet of the Apes*, *Conquest of the Planet of the Apes*, and *Battle for the Planet of the Apes*, respectively. Michael Avallone had previously adapted *Beneath the Planet of the Apes*, but for Bantam Books.

[2] Fantagraphics Books, April 1989, illustrated by Bill Spicer and Henry Mayo

omission is so surprising that the suspicion arises that the pilot's origin story must surely have been considered for adaptation. Barbara Hamblin, Effinger's widow, kindly agreed to look through his papers for me to find out if there was any hint of other adaptations. Sadly, her search proved fruitless.

The basic structure of the TV series sees two American astronauts, Virdon (played by Ron Harper) and Burke (James Naughton)[3], travel forward in time to the year 3085 (although it may be later!), where they encounter a sympathetic chimpanzee named Galen (portrayed by the wonderful Roddy McDowall). The trio become fugitives from an ape authority led by Councillor Zaius (Booth Colman), an orangutan leader of the government, and Security Chief Urko (Mark Lenard), a gorilla leading the armed military police.

The series was beautifully shot and superbly scored, with striking credits and excellent performances from the leads. Sadly, however, the cost of making the show, combined with poor scheduling resulting in modest viewing figures, as well as unsympathetic executive "suits" making decisions in the background, led to the very premature cancellation of the series. Any retrospective criticisms of repetitive plots and scripts misses the simple fact that *Planet of the Apes* was the greatest TV series ever made.

For this young fan, the disappearance of my favorite-ever TV show was a shock. In the United Kingdom, we adored our *Apes*. Viewing figures of 12 million during the battleground Sunday-night primetime slot were indicative of how well received the franchise was in Britain, where Marvel's *Planet of the Apes Weekly* comic was a top seller. The Topps trading cards were traded and fought over on school grounds, and a plethora of masks, Mego figures, and hardback annuals helped the *Apes* phenomenon to carry on for some years – indeed, in the U.K., the final *Apes* annual appeared in the summer of 1977, three years after the show itself had departed the airwaves.

While the British annuals contain a simian treasure trove of TV series-based tales, in the form of comic strips and text stories, the lack of the live-action series on our screens was a desperate loss. Staggering blindly across a Forbidden Zone of cultural desolation, where the beast, Man, had seen fit to destroy my precious *Apes* TV show, I was in utter despair until one day, shimmering like a mirage in the distance, a flash of blue caught my eye as I was out foraging for emotional sustenance. Given renewed hope, I stumbled forward into the arms of my saviour, George Alec Effinger, scribe of the

---

[3] A third crewmember, simply called "Jonesy," dies in transit.

Lawgiver and imparter of the Holy Word. In the midst of my agony and trauma, I had discovered his TV series novelizations.

Or, to be more precise, I'd found the second novel, *Escape to Tomorrow*, among a stack of books at my local general store. The TV series novels were designed in an eye-catching manner, with primary colors surrounding an image from the show. *Man the Fugitive* (red and yellow) was the first volume, adapting the episodes "The Cure" and "The Good Seeds." Next up was my epiphany tome, *Escape to Tomorrow* (blue and white), adapting "The Surgeon" and "The Deception," followed by the yellow and green *Journey into Terror*, containing "The Legacy" and "The Horse Race" (sporting, oddly enough, a cover picture of Zon from "The Deception," adapted in the previous book). Finally, belatedly and, to this writer, mind-blowingly only discovered in the internet age, there was the hard-to-find fourth volume, *Lord of the Apes*, slightly different in design, sporting a yellow cover, and containing "The Tyrant" and "The Horse Race." Four Gospels – sorry, novels – eight episodes, and a lifetime of wondrous escapism and joy.

Our first novelization encounter with our heroes, therefore, opens with "The Cure," based upon the teleplay by Edward J. Lakso, a tale about a malaria outbreak in a human village which the fugitives assist in curing. The choice to lead with this episode could partially be explained by a curious quirk of the entire TV series, whereby one of the most recognizable and famous characters, Zaius, the orangutan President of the Supreme Council, only ever appeared in six out of the 14 episodes. In the media and marketing – Topps cards, posters, etc. – Zaius is a very visible figure. Therefore, from an editorial point of view, if the intent in the opening tale was to introduce the main cast, the choice of episodes was very restricted. In fact, Zaius only appears in three of the eight adaptations. As "The Cure" is one of the orangutan's most prominent appearances in the series, this may account for why it was first up in the novelizations. Likewise, for the next two volumes, the first story in each features a major appearance by Zaius. By the fourth novelization, however, the councillor is entirely absent.

The adaptation of "The Cure," in the first book, *Man the Fugitive*, sets a tone for the written series that is neatly captured by John Warner in his review of the book in issue #7 of Marvel's *Planet of the Apes* magazine of the time: "[...]when you are introduced to the two astronauts, you are immediately sympathetic, empathizing with what they are going through – hunted fugitives, running with no place to run, hoping when there is no hope."[4] In other words, Effinger makes our heroes *real*. He gets inside the heads of our protagonists, human and ape alike, and lets us see the planet of the apes through their eyes.

For example, in "The Cure," we are told that Virdon has a daughter back home (who is never mentioned in the live show, which establishes only a son) and this adds depth to his close friendship with Amy. "Virdon touched the girl's hair. It was exactly the same color... he forced the thought from his mind." There is a sexual guilt-trip tension that underlies Effinger's treatment of the relationship that is ignored in the TV episode. These adaptations are no mere dumbed-down cash-in fodder – they have bite.

The second adaptation, "The Good Seeds," based on Robert W. Lenski's teleplay, contains more internal trips down memory lane for Virdon and Burke and is also a supreme example of Effinger's skill at breathing life into every character. The five members of the Polar family are all fleshed out, with each chimp given time to explore his or her hopes, regrets, fears, and joys, and each being truly memorable, not just background noise for our heroes. Polar, the beleaguered rough farmer patriarch, shares a scene with his wife, the city-girl Zantes, in which he gripes about the fancy city life she has missed since marrying him (and without reducing them to *Green Acres* stereotypes in the process). Zantes soothes Polar, saying, "I knew then, and I've never regretted it for an instant." It's a small moment, but it's an example of how deftly Effinger elevates his characters.

Effinger was able to take us inside the heads of not only apes and humans, but animals. The opening scene of "The Deception," in *Escape from Tomorrow*, is given to us through the eyes of a squirrel, who observes our heroes' arrival. Later, Effinger describes the bored familiarity a horse displays when not reacting to a violent fight between Virdon and his gorilla owner, Krono.

"The Deception," from the much amended teleplay by Anthony Lawrence, Joe Ruby, and Ken Spears, allows Effinger to explore a tender, if doomed, love shown by the blind chimpanzee Fauna for Burke, whom she believes to be a fellow chimp. The author handles this with a lightness of touch and a sensitivity that makes the ultimate reveal of the truth all the more sad: "Slowly his hand moved closer to hers. Burke's face was shiny with perspiration. He only had to

---

[4] Warner, John. "Man the Fugitive." *Planet of the Apes* #7 (Marvel Comics, April 1975).

move his hand a few inches, but in his heart, it felt as though he were trying to move a mountain."

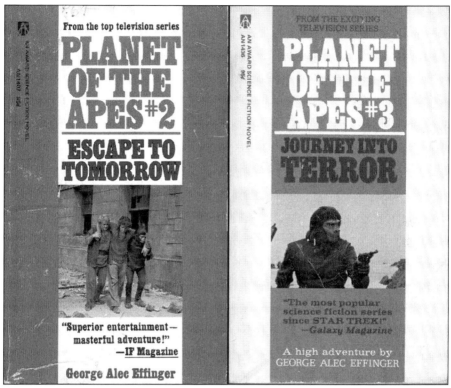

Books two and three of the *Planet of the Apes* television series novelizations by George Alec Effinger

This deftness with romance is also reflected in the first story in book #2, "The Surgeon," in which Galen encounters a past love, Kira, and must work through her revulsion at his fondness for humans to secure medical treatment for the wounded Virdon. Based on Barry Oringer's teleplay, Effinger's adaptation contains some wonderful scenes that exist only in his words – including an opening walk and talk along a dried river bed, a lovely scene in which Galen prepares "chamomile for a bullet wound," a thrilling race through Central City on a medical cart, and a charming closing scene on a mountain path in which another quirk of the script adaptations arises. The final script for "The Surgeon" has a young lady, who gives her blood to save Virdon, reveal her name to be Arna. However, an earlier draft of the script uses the more memorable Prunella Alexandrina, which she says is "an ordinary name around here," much to the amusement of the astronauts. Interestingly, it is the earlier

Prunella version that Effinger uses, which gives credence to his comments that getting scripts from the studio wasn't easy.

Effinger fills in the gaps for our heroes' life stories. "The Deception" contains a scene in which the astronauts realize they are at Hanson Point, where Burke once carved his initials with a redhead, Jan Adams, 2,000 years earlier. As Burke traces those letters with his hand, Effinger notes, "There were other initials carved there, too, most of which hadn't been there before; he wondered whether human or ape hands had made them." Effinger had a way of melding emotions in these books so that it didn't matter whether it was an ape or human involved – both were real and powerful. (Incidentally, Jan Adams reappeared decades later in Andrew Gaska's novel *Conspiracy of the Planet of the Apes.*) This "familiar location" idea recurs in book #4, *Lord of the Apes*, when Burke and Virdon recognize a hill as one they once called Jenning's Nose, while storing re-liberated grain in "The Tyrant" (teleplay by Walter Black).

Journey into Terror, the third volume, opens with "The Legacy," from a teleplay by Robert Hamner. As well as maintaining the policy of opening with a Zaius story, the adaptation offers subtle hints at how three guys can, occasionally, annoy one another. Galen, after viewing a projector message from the past, expounds about the futility of making images bigger and says that it is very simple to make images smaller: "You just walk away." In response, Burke quietly mutters, "That's a thought," but is glad Galen doesn't hear him. This tetchiness is also alluded to in "The Gladiators," adapted in book #4, when Virdon is exasperated at Burke's rash intervention into the fight between Dalton and Tolar, necessitating Virdon's help. Virdon, Effinger writes, "was of half a mind to let the impetuous astronaut take a bit of a beating first."

Such insights and internal monologues abound in the four books, taking us to memories and places the live series never could. The entirely rounded and vibrant world created by Effinger gives rise to a curious phenomenon. While, for example, I read and re-read Alan Dean Foster's *Star Wars* novelization to shreds, and only saw the movie once, it has always been the movie images that are burned into my mind. With the *Apes* TV series, however, if an episode was adapted by Effinger, the image I have in my mind's eye is the book, not the televised episode. Therefore, although the broadcast episode of "The Deception" has our heroes fishing off a bridge just before the human Jasko is murdered by Dragoons, *my* version is Effinger's far more engaging swim in a lake, with an amusing tale of Zaius and Jasko talking over their back fence. The

Effinger adaptations really are that effective that they can overwrite the actual episodes, and that is a tribute to just how alive he makes these characters.

The second episode adapted in *Journey into Terror* is "The Horse Race" (teleplay by David P. Lewis and Booker Bradshaw), in which Effinger gives us a deliciously devious and nasty Urko, toying with the human blacksmith Martin over the fate of his captive son, Greger.[5] The episode also introduces one of the series' few recurring characters, Prefect Barlow, a chimp who, in his own way, is as devious as Urko (though arguably kinder). However, Barlow's appearance in the third volume causes a major issue for book #4, when he "reappears" in an episode that has already happened prior to "The Horse Race" – namely, "The Gladiators," the second episode broadcast (teleplay by Art Wallace).

Unfortunately, internal story points dictate that Barlow in "The Gladiators" *must* have already met out heroes in "The Horse Race," though that simply can't work in the context of the novels. And so, in Effinger's adaptation, there has to be some re-jigging and Barlow is re-named Irnar (possibly a pun on the word "earner," for reasons discussed below). *Lord of the Apes* is an anomaly; whereas the first three books came out in rapid succession in late 1974 and early 1975, the fourth edition appeared in 1976 (nearly two years after the show was cancelled!), sporting an all-yellow cover with a different design.

Why this should have been so is unclear; the three novels based on the animated *Return to the Planet of the Apes* came out in 1976, and Award may simply have decided to cash in (hence, Irnar/earner) on the free publicity. However, the print run seems to have been very low and the volume is extremely rare today. That this final book contains no Zaius tales suggests it was a holdover, as the first three all featured Zaius in the lead story. Indeed, it is arguably the least engaging book of the four, possibly because Effinger had not had full opportunity to polish the draft – his adaptation of Walter Black's "The Tyrant" is very disjointed and episodic, hinting at attempts to deal with script amendments. Interestingly, while the gorilla bad guy, Aboro, is an intelligent villain in the televised episode, with a dimwitted aide named Daku, the scripts started with an intelligent Daku and a dim Aboro – and Effinger's adaptation falls somewhere in between, as if the scripts had not yet been solidified when the scribe was working on the adaptation.

---

[5] This spelling appeared in both the novel and the script, so I choose to adhere to that instead of the version in the episode's credits, Gregor.

A German edition of *Man the Fugitive* (translated as *Hunt on the Planet of the Apes*) seems to be based on the likeness of Claude Akins' General Aldo, from *Battle for the Planet of the Apes*.

Still, regardless of the reasons, *Lord of the Apes* is a wonderful bonus[6], and it seems doubtful that it was distributed in any numbers overseas. The very existence of *Lord of the Apes* does raise an interesting question, though: were there any *other* scripts adapted by Effinger waiting to be published? The lack of the pilot episode has already been discussed, and in "The Horse Race," Virdon asks whether Venta is "a special production area," and whether they will "need special identification" to go there. The question of such areas and identification only arises in the sixth episode, "Tomorrow's Tide," which possibly hints that Effinger may have seen or even begun to adapt that episode as well. Sadly, we may never know.

If you've never read these novelizations, hunt them down. Four books, eight wonderful adaptations. The first three can still be readily found cheaply online, and the fourth pops up occasionally, but usually at a higher price.[7] It is a fond dream of mine that somewhere in the United States, collecting dust in a filing cabinet or a locked desk, rests George Alec Effinger's adaptation of the TV series pilot, "Escape from Tomorrow," with "Tomorrows's Tide" as the follow-up for a fifth volume in the series. Because dreaming is what Effinger has always helped me to enjoy, allowing me to ecape to tomorrow and the planet of the apes. And for that, I shall always be in his debt.

---

[6] I only discovered it in the 1990s, in fact, thanks to the dawn of the internet.
[7] If you can't find the original novelizations, you're in luck – Titan Books plans to repackage them later this year in a single edition, *Planet of the Apes Omnibus, Volume 3.*

Saturday-Morning Simians: Animating the Planet of the Apes

by Zaki Hasan

It was September 1987 when what would turn out to be a nearly three-decades (and counting) love affair with *Planet of the Apes* began most unexpectedly for me. I was seven years old and living overseas when Saudi Arabia's Channel 2 aired the entirety of the animated *Return to the Planet of the Apes*. From the very first shot of the intro, the series both scared the crap out of me and had me utterly transfixed. Although I'd never seen it, I was somewhat familiar with the franchise's barebones concept, but it was this cartoon that was the entrée to an entire lifetime of immersion in Ape-dom.[1]

It was only several years later, after I'd tracked down a copy of the original 1968 *Planet of the Apes* on grainy, fourth-generation VHS (and then followed the breadcrumb trail to its coterie of sequels), that I came to understand just how different this version was from the live-action entries that had preceded it. Yes, it was plagued by a low budget, but it also benefitted from terrific designs and direction by *Jonny Quest* creator Doug Wildey, and a fairly mature storyline (considering the audience and the era).

---

[1] I can draw a straight line from that first viewing to the garage-full of *Planet of the Apes* merchandise that has long since forced me to park my car on the street.

Also, unlike the other TV series, *Return to the Planet of the Apes* took chances with its status quo, something that was very much in the vein of the films, but practically unheard of for kidvid... which may also explain why it didn't last very long. While it was gone after a brief 13 episodes (one less than the previous, live-action TV series that had aired the previous season), the animated *Apes* is nonetheless an important part of the voluminous *Planet of the Apes* catalog, and one that's worthy of further examination.

Before we discuss the show itself, let's take a look at the lay of the land for the *Apes* brand leading up to its premiere. In fall of 1974, following months of hype and riding the coattails of what was at that time a franchise whose success was virtually without precedent, the *Planet of the Apes* live-action TV series made its much-anticipated debut on CBS... and promptly fizzled in the ratings. In hindsight, knowing how it was greeted with viewer apathy and boxed in by high budgets, it's no great shock that the weekly *Apes* was dead-and-gone inside of a mere 14 episodes.

But what *is* somewhat of a shock is that even *that* wouldn't prove to be the end of *Planet of the Apes* on the small screen (then again, this is the same franchise that found its way to three more sequels after literally destroying the Earth, so maybe it's not that shocking after all). Sure, the other TV show hadn't done that well, but the franchise was still a proven commodity, and 20th Century Fox was making a mint on the *Apes* merchandise that was lining toy aisles. As such, it's understandable that they weren't quite ready to throw in the towel on their golden monkey just yet.

Of course, given that tune-in for the live-action skein was highest among the pre-teen set, it also makes a certain amount of sense that Fox next set their sights on Saturday morning for what would turn out to be the *Apes* franchise's final curtain call (at least for a little while). When you think about it, this was actually a pretty brilliant maneuver — albeit in concept more than execution. After all, every successive entry following the first one was faced with pulling off a comparable amount of chills and spills while faced with a comparably reduced budget (by the fifth installment, 1973's *Battle for the Planet of the Apes*, it looks like they had about $1.50 to put the thing together).

In fact, while the live-action TV show was fairly expensive for its time, it still looked pretty chintzy given all that it tried (and failed) to pull off. The lead characters basically spent the entirety of the series running from one end of the Fox lot to another, then back again. The beauty of turning it into a cartoon was that whatever flights of fancy the folks behind the scenes could think of was only a brushstroke away. When NBC's *Return to the Planet of the Apes* premiered on 6 September 1975, it definitely stood out from a Saturday-morning pack that included *Speed Buggy* and *Hong Kong Phooey* on ABC, and *Shazam!* and *Scooby-Doo* on CBS.

Taking a cue from its forebears, *Return* dove headfirst into some remarkably dark terrain that harkened back to the first two features, but it would have no easier a go of it than the previous show. Before we get to the end, though, let's go back to before the beginning. There's a fairly prestigious lineage behind *Return to the Planet of the Apes*. In addition to 20th Century Fox, the series was co-produced by DePatie/Freleng Enterprises, itself headed up by founders David H. DePatie and Isadore "Friz" Freleng, who'd previously found success with United Artists' *Pink Panther*.

But while Depatie/Freleng (DFE) certainly had credibility in the industry, they were still a fairly unorthodox choice to handle the honors on the animated *Apes*, especially given their focus on humor and lack of expertise in producing adventure cartoons. That's where a key participant enters our narrative: Doug Wildey. Given that he'd created what is pretty much the definitive action-adventure cartoon of the 1960s in Hanna-Barbara's *Jonny Quest*, it's entirely understandable that DFE turned to Wildey to produce and direct *Return to the Planet of the Apes*. While DePatie and Freleng are credited with developing *Return*, much of its creative identity sprang from Wildey.

Putting to use his many years of experience drawing comic strips, Wildey tried like heck to push against the boundaries of the *very* limited animation that the miniscule budget forced him to use (so much for anything he could imagine being only a brushstroke away). Of course, the biggest limitation Wildey faced, right off the top, wasn't so much a budgetary one but a *thematic* one. As was evident to anyone who'd bothered to watch the movies beforehand, *Planet of the Apes* is practically built on tackling mature, often unsettling subject matter.

The first film has one character lobotomized and another stuffed and mounted. The second features mutated zealots worshipping an atomic bomb. The third and fourth put us on the side of an ape revolution that displaces human beings from their place at the top of the pecking order. And the fifth sees a child murdered. This wasn't exactly feel-good stuff, and I highly doubt NBC executives were thinking about that when they added it to their weekend lineup, nestled comfortably between *Run, Joe, Run* and *Westwind*. In fact, Wildey found himself bedeviled almost immediately by the so-called "Emulative Clause" the network had in place governing children's programming.

In essence, the rule was centered on the notion that if any action or violence in the program might conceivably be copied by a six-year-old, it had to be removed. This basically ruled out gorilla soldiers being armed with the rifles and clubs that were part and parcel of the whole "apes hunting humans" thing (which is itself kind of the foundation on which the entire *Planet of the Apes* enterprise is built). A workaround Wildey found was to have his apes armed with old-timey tanks and Howitzers, because it seemed unlikely a six-year-old would have one of those lying around.

(It's also worth mentioning here that the animal-like humans are referred to as "humanoids" throughout the run, most likely to differentiate them from us, lest the kids watching it accidentally begin to ponder the broader implications of losing their perch atop the animal kingdom.)

Nonetheless, even if Wildey may have felt a tiny bit constrained by some of the (admittedly draconian) content restrictions that were placed on him, he still found plenty of ways to skirt their edges and make *Return to the Planet of the Apes* exactly as engrossing and unsettling to its target demographic as the movies were for theirs. In fact, the opening title sequence manages to set the tone for us right off the bat. First, we hear the unsettling chords of Dean Elliott's theme music, then we see the barren desert landscape, punctuated by several ape-constructed scarecrows.

As the camera continues to pan, it comes to rest on an array of gathered apes just as the music hits a nightmarish crescendo. From there, we cut to a rapid-fire montage of various hand-drawn images from the movies filling the screen. And then, finally, we hear announcer Ted Knight (he of *Mary Tyler Moore* and *Too Close for Comfort* fame) shout the title of the program that we're watching. Seriously, it's no exaggeration to say that this was nightmare-inducing stuff for me even as a seven-year-old. I have very distinct memories of lying awake at night, terrified to move, supremely confident that there were gorillas hiding in my closet.

And that was all thanks to this show. I was afraid of it – but I didn't hate it. I *loved* it. And honestly, it's really odd that I did. The animation, which leaned heavily on Wildey's *Jonny Quest* style for the character designs, was often pedestrian by even the standards of the mid-1970s era that birthed it (much less the late '80s era, during which I finally watched it). But somehow that animation, detailed and yet paradoxically discursive as well, wasn't so much a bug as it was a feature, one that drove home the essential surreality of the situation as our heroes attempted to escape the dystopian nightmare in which they were trapped.

While we're on that subject, let's talk about the characters and the setting. Clearly casting as wide a net as possible, *Return to the Planet of the Apes* liberally pulled from all previous iterations of the franchise, ending up as sort of a samplers' platter for *Apes* aficionados. Movie stalwarts Cornelius and Zira (Edwin Mills and Philippa Harris) – last seen riddled with bullets in *Escape From the Planet of the Apes* – can be seen occupying the same frame as the TV show's Urko (Henry Corden, a.k.a. Fred Flinstone), while ever-dependable Doctor Zaius gets his third onscreen incarnation here, this time voiced by Richard Blackburn (who also provided Bill's voice for about half of the run).

Return to the Planet of the Apes utilized the same lost-astronaut trope as the films, but was the first incarnation to feature a major African-American character.

As far as the human leads, the cartoon utilized the same "astronauts lost in time" premise that had proven effective in the first two movies, as well as the previous TV series (and the Pierre Boulle novel, naturally). Our heroes are Bill Hudson, Jeff Allen, and Judy Franklin (though only Hudson's full name is ever uttered onscreen). Their spacecraft, the *Venturer*, launched in 1976, is propelled into the 3970s milieu of the first film.[2] This, in turn, ends up proving out the "Time Thrust" theory proffered by one Doctor Stanton, who one can only presume was a drinking buddy of the movies' Doctor Hasslein.

It's worth mentioning here that Jeff, an African-American, is the first black character in the franchise to make more than one appearance. (It's also worth

---

[2] The fact that the first film gives the date as 3978 while the subsequent sequels peg it as 3955 remains one of the most baffling continuity errors in the *Apes* canon – and there are a few!

noting that he's voiced by actor Austin Stoker, who portrayed Caesar's first assistant MacDonald in *Battle for the Planet of the Apes*.) As for Judy (Claudette Nevins), she's the first female astronaut to make multiple appearances in any *Apes*. And while her early disappearance in the first episode may be a bit jarring, Judy gets plenty more to do as things progress (and one assumes her original function on the space voyage had a little more heft to it than merely serving as the crew's "new Eve," à la Lieutenant Stewart).

Regardless, after the crew's ship (a space capsule in the *Mercury* mold) crashes in the water (and following a brief aside as we join the in-session ape council as they debate how to handle the "humanoid" threat), the three astronauts begin their long journey through the vast wasteland which longtime fans have come to know as the Forbidden Zone. What's interesting here is how closely the early beats of the cartoon echo those of the original film – albeit without the same sense of the unknown hanging in the air. Those of us in the audience are several steps ahead of the characters already, as far as where and when they are, so it's really just a waiting game until they catch up to us.

That said, you really do have to give it up to Wildey for pushing against the prevailing norms of TV animation at the time, and for being willing to give over several valuable minutes of screentime to an extended sequence with our heroes traipsing across the desert – no dialogue, only visuals telling the tale. This evinces a remarkable trust in the audience (children, mind you) to keep up on their own. The Forbidden Zone trek serves not only as a terrific showcase for Elliott's haunting music, a combination of the atonal styles that feature composers Jerry Goldsmith and Leonard Rosenman pioneered, but also for how they strove to turn the (at times too apparent) animation limitations into less of a disadvantage.

Driving home the desolation and hopelessness of the astronauts' situation, in the same way director Franklin Schaffner did in the film's early goings, were long shots of the landscape. These were detailed paintings, often still images with no animation, with only stylized outlines of our characters working their way through the desert to their predestined ape encounter. As it turns out, the makers of the cartoon had learned a lesson that even the folks behind 2001's abortive *Planet of the Apes* remake didn't: it's not about how quickly you get to the apes, but how you set up the stakes for the human characters.

In *Return to the Planet of the Apes*, it's only at the very end of the premiere episode ("Flames of Doom," penned by animation veteran Larry Spiegel) that our heroes are finally caught up in the apes' hunt (of course, the need to simplify the animation results in the apes being utterly oblivious to the super-intelligent humans in their midst wearing space-age NASA clothes). This, in turn, leads into something even more unexpected for Saturday morning: a cliffhanger. Just about every episode teed you up for the next with some dangling plot threads, which virtually demanded the loyalty of anyone who was watching, lest they be utterly perplexed by the intervening plot developments of any episodes they may have missed.

While *Return* was bedeviled by the limitations of its budget at every turn, one area in which budget didn't have any impact was in the depiction of the ape society. For the films, production designer William Creber was tasked with taking the highly advanced simian society that Boulle depicted in his original novel and finding a way to make it play on the screen, leading to the troglodytic Ape City that's become at least as iconic as the ape makeups designed by John Chambers. But in *Return*, Wildey finally gave Boulle his due.

The Ape City in *Return to the Planet of the Apes* actually resembled a city, like in novelist Boulle's original vision, complete with Parisian influences and all the conveniences of 1970s living.

This was an Ape City that truly deserved the second half of its moniker, looking like it was inspired by the same Parisian environs that may well have been Boulle's backdrop as he penned his momentous tome. Although horses and wagons had previously been the primary means of conveyance (with the eerie sight of gorillas on horseback in movie one losing none of its ability to unnerve even this many decades later), these apes were gifted with all manner of motorized vehicles, not to mention television, radio, and all the other comforts of mid-1970s living.

Mind you, this doesn't come off as silly as one might think. An ape society that's more closely a simulacrum of our own only drives home the essential unease underlying the entire premise. Also upping the heebie-jeebie factor was the inclusion of the mutants from *Beneath the Planet of the Apes*, albeit in an altered, "sanitized for TV" form. Led by the mysterious Krador, these mutants – called "Underdwellers" here – don't worship an ancient atomic bomb (so no unmasking reveal, à la *Beneath*), but they view Judy as prophesied savior returning to aid them, due to a statue of her bearing the inscription "USA," which is why they call her "Usa" (pronounced "oo-sah").

By the time the Underdwellers are introduced in episode three, "The Unearthly Prophecy," it's clear that the producers aren't so much beholden to the extant *Apes* mythology as they are using it as a jump-off point for whatever gonzo stories they felt like telling. Again, what's so notable in the early episodes is how much effort is put into arc-building and serialization, something almost never seen in kidvid before stuff like *Avatar: The Last Airbender* came along.

Heck, the very first episode drops a hint about the presence of another astronaut from a previous expedition, one Ronald Brent, and has the confidence to not even follow up on that lone breadcrumb until eight episodes later – an eternity in TV time! (The Brent we finally meet in episode nine, "Trail to the Unknown," has the surname of James Franciscus' character John Brent in *Beneath*, but the appearance and personality – minus the misanthropic cynicism – of Charlton Heston's George Taylor.)

Given the heavy serialization early on, it's perhaps understandable that producers chose (or, perhaps more likely, were mandated) to ease off a bit and tell some solo stories with a clear beginning, middle, and end. This (plus NBC airing the episodes willy-nilly out of the intended sequence) can help account for such sudden detours as Bruce Shelly's "Terror on Ice Mountain," which has Bill and Cornelius building a hot air balloon so that they can hide a valuable ancient book high atop a mountain (running across a giant Kong-esque ape called Kygor in the process).

The following episode, "River of Flames" (written by Jack Kaplan and John Barrett), is also a one-off, involving Bill and Jeff rescuing the Underdwellers from an impending lava flow, but it is notable for adding Judy back into the rotation as a regular. From episode eight onward, the final six episodes are once again heavily serialized, depicting the gorilla army's efforts to acquire ancient airplane technology, as well as our heroes' efforts to move the vulnerable tribe of humanoids to a place of safety.

By the time the first season wrapped, there was a certain measure of closure, sure, but there was also clearly more story yet to tell. In fact, Wildey (who passed away in 1994) said as much in later interviews, discussing extensive plans to bring the conflict between apes and humans to a head and bring things to a very definite conclusion.[3] It might have been interesting, and NBC purportedly mulled a short order of three more episodes to wind things up, but the ratings simply weren't there to justify NBC taking a chance on another batch of episodes.

And so, our *Return to the Planet of the Apes* was only a brief sojourn rather than an extended stay. And unlike TV's Virdon and Burke before them, we never did get any finality for Bill, Jeff, Judy, *et al.*, despite the publication the following year of three novels by authors William Rotsler and Donald J. Pfeil (both writing pseudonymously as William Arrow) that adapted and expanded on the teleplays for nine of the thirteen episodes (and placed them in the intended order, which heightens the serialized nature of the story).

The muted finale of *Return to the Planet of the Apes* aired on 29 November 1975, marking the end of the franchise's extraordinary run since 1968. Dean Elliott's library music would later be heard in DFE's *Fantastic Four* in the late 1970s, as well as Ruby-Spears' *Thundarr the Barbarian* in the early '80s. Ruby-Spears also pitched a new animated *Planet of Apes* at the same time, this one based on the live-action series (for which Joe Ruby and Ken Spears had written). This proposal had concept art by none other than comic book legend Jack Kirby.

That show didn't go anywhere, but whispers of a new *Apes* cartoon series began once again in the mid-'90s for the Fox Kids network, just as the studio was actively mulling plans to revive the movies. This, too, didn't go anywhere (most likely because it took so long to get the remake off the ground), leaving *Return to the Planet of the Apes* as the one and only time the hoary brand hit animation. And with the benefit of hindsight, I suppose it's not that difficult to see why *Return* failed to find its footing.

---

[3] Russo, Joe; Landsman, Larry; and Gross, Edward. *Planet of the Apes Revisited* (St. Martin's Griffin, August 2001).

Even now, the show occupies a kind of strange middle ground: too kiddie for adult audiences, but too mature for young audiences. With long stretches of dialogue centering on military overreach and societal ills juxtaposed with sea monsters, flying dragons, and giant ice apes, it did stake out a unique place in *Apes* lore all to itself – and actually still does. In the decades since *Return to the Planet of the Apes* put the pin on the franchise's classic era, the *Apes* brand has soldiered on. It has been restarted, re-imagined, and rebooted, but never re-animated.[4]

---

[4] Yet.

All the World's a Stage:
The *Planet of the Apes* Live Shows

by Dave Ballard

"See the Apes Live!" the ad promised, "At These Rodeos Now Touring the Country."[1]

I frowned, turned to my father, and asked… "Dad, what's a 'roedeeoh'?"

He pulled his attention away from the newspaper he had been reading, thought for a moment, and replied, "It's like a circus for Americans… where cowboys show off."

As definitions go, maybe that wasn't the greatest, but back then it was pretty much all I had to go on.

It was 1975. Back in its homeland of the United States, the *Planet of the Apes* television show had already been canceled, but thanks to repeated showings, Britain was still firmly in the vice-like, hairy grip of apemania. I was 14 years old and probably just a little older, a smidgen wiser, a dash more discerning, and a few pounds heavier than your average *Apes* fan. Somehow, I'd managed to see four of the five movies at the cinema (and I count seeing astronaut Brent being shot in the head as the moment when my childhood abruptly ended), so by the time the TV show came along, I was already an

---

[1] From an advertisement published in *Planet of the Apes Weekly* #40 (Marvel UK, July 1975).

established fan. I had been collecting the Marvel UK reprinted comics, and that was where I'd seen the advertisement that prompted my question to my father.

"Roedeeoh."

It was a strange word, not even British, which was why no one in my family had even noticed I was pronouncing it all wrong. It had come along during a time of change in the air. Something wasn't right with my beloved apes, you see. The first two movies had clearly been meant for an adult audience. The TV show was at least partly intended for an adult audience. And Doug Moench's opening phases of the "Terror on the Planet of the Apes" and "Future History Chronicles" comic strips were also clearly aimed at adults.

But things... they were a-changing.

Herb Hirschman, the television show's executive producer, had expressed frustration that the series had failed to attract the right audience. Speaking about the show, Hirschman told the authors of *Planet of the Apes Revisited*, "My interest was making the show for adults and hopefully the kids would enjoy it too. But the focus changed."[2]

And boy, was he was right. On British TV, the series, originally screened at 7:20 pm, was now being repeated on Saturday mornings at around 10 am – a primetime children's programming slot. There was even a cartoon series on its way, for Christ's sake!

Suddenly, *Planet of the Apes* was just for kids!

I wasn't sure when it had happened, but happened it had. Many years later, movie director J. Lee Thompson said of *Battle for the Planet of the Apes*: "Right from the start, Arthur [P. Jacobs, the film series' producer] said 'We're going to make a kid picture and something that will appeal to families.' It had no real political implications; it was simply a kids' science-fiction film."[3] Did the decline begin right there?

So these roedeeohs left me wary and unconvinced. When the reports started coming in, via the *POTA* Fan Club newsletters and the letters column of the weekly comic, it was clear, even to a 14-year-old, that this wasn't *Planet of the Apes* as I knew it – and certainly not as I wanted it to be.

---

[2] Russo, Joe; Landsman, Larry; and Gross, Edward. *Planet of the Apes Revisited* (St. Martin's Griffin, August 2001).
[3] *Behind the Planet of the Apes*, dir: David Comtois and Kevin Burns. Image Entertainment, 1998.

So I was aware of these live appearances, but, coming from a low-income, car-less family, anything that wasn't a short bus ride away may as well have been on the surface of the Moon. In the following weeks, I read eyewitness accounts, and eventually I saw photos.

The acronym "WTF!" wouldn't become popular until around 40 years later, but it might just have been invented right there and then. No way was that Galen! Just where did Urko find those trousers? And what kind of rifle was *that*?

So, due to the lack of adult material being offered, my interest in *Planet of the Apes* had begun to wane. My Fan Club membership lapsed, and my subscription to the comic was canceled. (They had started re-printing reprints anyway.) The TV show had disappeared from the airwaves and into memory, and I discovered Clint Eastwood, Spaghetti Westerns, and Hammer movies instead. (Girls were still a few years away.) I never forgot *Planet of the Apes*; I just put it aside for many years – but those rodeos? They were always going to remain a mystery to me...

Or so I thought.

Cue strings being plucked on a harp and pages flying off the calendar as we enter a Hasslein curve and find ourselves in the mid to late 1990s.

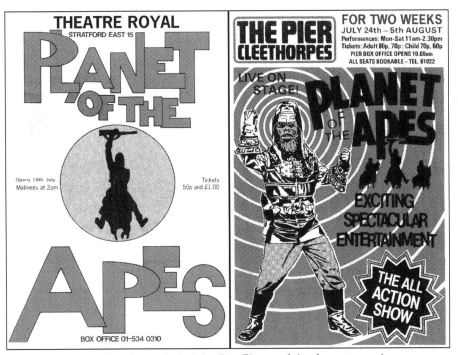

Two posters heralding the arrival of the live *Planet of the Apes* stage show

With the advent of the internet, fans of a feather flocked together and fragments of information regarding the live *Apes* appearances slowly began to assemble themselves into a clear account. Years later, a breakthrough came and a group of fans managed to contact some key personnel behind these shows. What follows, then, is the story behind one of the mythology's more peculiar offshoots: the story behind *Planet of the Apes'* live appearances in the United Kingdom.

A Vehicle for Stunts

In October 1974, the *Apes* live-action TV show began to air in the United Kingdom. It was a ratings smash and proved far more popular with British audiences than with those back in its native country. In the United States, your average *Apes* fan would probably have already seen one or more of the movies on TV before the series – but in Britain, the opposite was generally true. I clearly remember many of my schoolmates not being aware that *Apes* movies even existed! So here in the U.K., the TV show was, for many, our first exposure to the mythos. No doubt, this was a contributing factor to its increased popularity on this side of the pond – familiarity had yet to breed contempt.

Britain just couldn't get enough. Only after the show proved to be a hit did the movies begin to be screened on British television. They also returned to the big screen, often in double bills or marathons (giving me the opportunity to finally catch up with *Conquest of the Planet of the Apes*, the one I had somehow managed to miss the first time around). Marvel Comics had their U.K. weekly reprints selling by the lorry-load. Posters, toys, model kits, and every other kind of *Apes* merchandise you could possibly imagine was to be found on shelves everywhere, from the big department stores to the humble corner-of-the-street news agents.

Later, in 1975, the *Planet of the Apes* TV series was enjoying repeated airings that struggled to cope with demand. There were, after all, only so many times you could repeat a mere 14 episodes. There was an obvious demand for something new...

Enter Television Character Promotions (TCP).

TCP was a small public-relations firm that shrewdly secured the rights from 20th Century Fox to use characters from the TV show for a series of promotional appearances across the length and breadth of the United Kingdom. They were a small family concern, headed by husband and wife team Mike and June Caulfield. Along with arranging the live appearances, Mike and June, in association with brother Pete Caulfield, secretary Sally Skinner, and Marvel Comics, also found the time to run the official *Planet of the Apes* Fan Club.

If Herb Hirschman and the production team behind the *Apes* TV series were concerned with the notion that the television show was attracting the wrong kind of audience (i.e. kids), TCP was positively embracing it, and the company used the Fan Club, via its newsletters, to promote an ever-expanding number of live appearances.

The first of these took the form of meet-and-greets, with fully costumed characters from TV (never the movies – still an unknown to most U.K. children) showing up at store openings, supermarket promotions, and the like. These modest beginnings grew into what TCP called "rodeos": stunt-filled arena "re-enactments" featuring fights, chases, captures, thrilling escapes, and explosions (or cowboys showing off!). These re-enactments were invariably a support act for a much larger event.

Mike McCarthy, the source for most of what we know about these shows, was about to prove himself to be a major factor in the continuing development of these live events. He had moved to London in 1971 to train as an actor and, upon leaving drama school, went to work with renowned theatre director Joan Littlewood at her theatre in Stratford, East London. It was while working on a project there that he first met Mike Caulfield.

McCarthy told *Simian Scrolls* magazine:[4]

> He was performing there as one of the attractions, regularly turning up on a white horse while dressed as Urko. When Mike realized I had theatre skills, he recruited me to help improve the staging of the arena show. The arena shows were just a very basic action sequence that involved the astronauts being captured by Urko and his cohorts, and Galen somehow rescuing them. It involved a lot of chasing on horseback (trying to catch the escaped astronauts in a net). Lots of audience interaction and involvement. There was also a voiceover and music soundtrack to enhance and explain the action. The arena show was definitely a vehicle for stunts and had a very thin storyline.

The shows ran for a duration of around 30 minutes. Costumes were something of a mixed bag, being approximations of what the characters wore on TV, cobbled together from various sources (Army fatigues, modified boots, Lee Enfield rifles, etc.). A discerning 14-year-old may have balked at these

---

[4] *Simian Scrolls* issue #18. Summer 2015: http://pota.goatley.com/scrolls/simianscrolls_18.pdf. All McCarthy quotes are taken from this interview.

inaccuracies, but no one else seemed to mind. The complex Hollywood prosthetics were replaced with pullover ape masks – probably sourced from Don Post Studios.

"They were pullover masks, but very tight-fitting," McCarthy said. "We used to apply black and red stage make-up under the eyes to blend the flesh with the mask and give the eyes a bloodshot look"

Thanks to my connections made through the *Simian Scrolls* fanzine, I had the opportunity to correspond with another cast member, the delightful Rory Lister. Rory was able to confirm many of McCarthy's recollections, as well as fill in some gaps in our collective knowledge.

Lister became involved with the show at the end of 1975. A friend of his had been offered the role of an astronaut for one of the rodeos, but was unable to take the part due to other commitments, and had suggested Rory as a replacement. Rory recalled:[5]

> We were to be part of the Circus Hoffmann Christmas show at Newcastle's City Hall, and began to rehearse... above a pub in Hammersmith late November that year. We drove to Newcastle to begin the shows and were billeted in caravans next-door to the venue. To say that conditions were grim would be an understatement – it was freezing cold and the only place to have a decent wash was in the public bath house.

Grim conditions were also recalled by Pete Caulfield, who, for one performance on 7 June 1977, stood in for one of the astronauts. As Caulfield told the *Planet of the Apes* Fan Club at the time:[6]

> The day started off nice enough but as the crowds gathered around the arena, the sky darkened. As the soundtrack began so did the first spots of rain. As the apes entered the arena on horseback, the storm began with vengeance. It was all very well for those hairy great gorillas, all clad in their leather tunics etc., but poor old Astros, we only had thin jump suits on. As soon as we stepped into the downpour, we were soaked to the skin.

Ahh, the great British summer!

---

[5] *Simian Scrolls* issue #17. Summer 2012:
http://pota.goatley.com/scrolls/simianscrolls_17.pdf. All Lister quotes are taken from this interview.
[6] In the July/August 1977 Fan Club newsletter:
http://pota.goatley.com/uk_newsletters/uk_fc_7707.pdf

WARRIOR GORILLA

© 1974 Twentieth Century Fox Film Corp.

Stage show writer Mike McCarthy poses as a "Warrior Gorilla" for this promotional photo given out at the arena show.

Perhaps the best way to envisage one of these shows is through the eyes of an audience member. Andrew Shakespeare, a member of the *Apes* Fan Club, was there and left us this account of a Hoffman Circus appearance:[7]

> Inside the tent there was a *Planet of the Apes* stall where I bought a colour picture of Dr. Zaius and one of Urko, a black and white one of Galen and a Dr. Zaius badge.
>
> There was an interval during the performance and in it one could have their photograph taken with Galen.
>
> After the interval the Apes came into the ring, then the Astronauts and Dr. Zaius and Urko. When the audience saw the Gorillas and their leader they started booing, then gave a cheer as the renegade ape, Galen, hopped into the ring. The gorillas caught the astronauts and put them in a cage then started chasing Galen, firing their guns at him. Galen climbed on one of the poles and then, when he came down again, was chased through the audience. A gorilla rushed up to where I was sitting and fired his rifle. It gave out a terrific BANG! Galen escaped the gorillas and jumped back into the ring, where he knocked down Dr. Zaius.
>
> Quickly he released the astronauts as Urko rode up. An astronaut pulled him off his horse and they started fighting. Soon Urko was lying flat on the ground and Galen rode off with the astronauts leaving Dr. Zaius, Urko and the gorillas either tired (tied?) or knocked out. At the end of the performance the Apes gave their autographs. I have got Galen's five times, Urko's four times, Zaius' once and another gorilla's (Virgil) three times.
>
> I had a lovely time and it was very enjoyable.

Unpredictable weather aside, McCarthy recalled, these re-enactments proved incredibly popular and regularly attracted crowds numbering in the thousands. "When we were performing the outdoor arena shows, the arrival on site of the *Planet of the Apes*-branded caravan would be greeted with crowds. When I was in costume as a warrior ape, I would spend hours after the show signing autographs. Out of costume, I would be ignored. Strange, that. So, yes, it was obvious to us that this was *big*."

So big, in fact, that plans were soon put in motion to bring *Planet of the Apes* to the London stage.

He's Behind You!

Caulfield quickly saw the potential of taking the personal-appearance productions a step further. McCarthy, who also had the contacts at the theatre

---

[7] In the May 1976 Fan Club newsletter:
http://pota.goatley.com/uk_newsletters/uk_fc_7605.pdf

to get things staged, was intrigued by his ideas and offered to write a script for a stage show. As McCarthy recalled:

> This was written as a family adventure show. I remember writing the stage play with the Pierre Boulle novel at my side, so I guess I tried to base much of the story on that. I no doubt enhanced the story to make it appropriate for the stage. I was also quite political at the time, so there was an anti-fascist undercurrent to the story.
>
> The script was definitely an amalgam of the novel, TV and film, so in that sense, it was a conscious effort to mix and match. The other factor I had to consider was that I was writing primarily for a family audience, and that may have affected what I chose to include and exclude.

It was proving much easier for TCP to secure vacant afternoon matinee slots in theaters, a time generally aimed at family audiences, so the show became deliberately targeted toward children. Ape voices and dramatic music were all pre-recorded at a London sound studio. (Producer Mike Caulfield provided the Urko voice.) The astronauts then had to time their words between the pre-recorded voices, and the actors playing the apes had to mime the actions. In regard to the staging, McCarthy said, "It was mainly impressionistic, relying on use of geometric shapes, platforms, and key bits of constructed set (e.g. the prison cage). Most of the world/magic was established through creative use of lighting and sound effects."

The show – planned to run for around 90 minutes – opened with the liftoff of a space mission crewed by two astronauts, going by the names of either Taylor and Brent, Bob and Jeff, or Brad and Danny (and sometimes Mike). The names were fluid and prone to constant change, dependent upon the actors playing the parts or the time and location of a given performance (Taylor and Brent were soon dropped completely as sounding too American).

The astronauts encounter difficulties, enter a time warp and crash-land in London in the year 3085 (the same year in which the TV series was set). All this occurs within the first few minutes! Our heroes survive and soon meet a beautiful but mute, human-looking female (whose name varied between Pela, Pila, and Pilah). They are then captured by an army of gorilla soldiers – well... two gorillas, actually – and strike up a conversation, with neither side seemingly surprised by the other's appearance.

Scene two shifts the action to the London-based Ape City, where Urko, watched by Zaius, is giving a *Beneath the Planet of the Apes*, Ursus-like speech to an off-stage crowd. Following the speech, the captured astronauts are presented for inspection and quickly caged, deemed too valuable to execute.

Scene three introduces the friendly chimpanzee Galen, who quickly makes his sympathies known. By the end of act one, he has helped the astronauts to escape, but has himself been captured.

Act two opens with Galen on trial (similar to in the TV show's pilot episode), and it's fair to say that things are not going his way. The trial is interrupted by a sighting of the escaped astronauts, and Urko halts the proceedings to oversee their recapture personally. The astronauts have re-acquainted themselves with the mute girl, whose sole purpose seems to be to provide eye-candy for the dads in the audience. They get into a fight with some gorillas and manage to overpower them (Yeah, right, go on...I dare you! Get down to your local zoo and try to overpower a gorilla, and let me know how that works out for you!), then arm themselves in preparation for an attempt to rescue Galen.

It's right around this point that the stage show descends into pure pantomime, with Urko and the astronauts creeping around the stage and the children in the audience being encouraged to point and shout, "He's behind you!" (Oh, no, he isn't!)

A stalemate leads to a *mano a mano* (*apo a apo?*) fist fight between Galen and Urko to determine who will walk free. Fortunately for Galen, the kids in the audience are on his side, and their vocal support and cheers are enough to ensure that our heroic chimp wins the day (uh oh... I sense another "WTF?!" coming on).

The fugitives retreat to the Forbidden Zone, find their repaired ship and, sans the girl but avec the chimp, escape. Sound of ship taking off. Urko is left alone, shaking his fist at the sky.

Hmmm.... reading that, I'm kind of glad my younger self never got to see it. A 14-year-old fat kid crying with embarrassment would not have been a pretty sight!

In 2010, McCarthy discussed his involvement in the stage show with Hasslein Books. With his permission, the full script for the stage production can be downloaded at http://www.hassleinbooks.com/pdfs/stageshow_script.pdf.

In 2014, again with McCarthy's permission, the script was adapted by Bill Hollweg, a co-founder of BrokenSea Audio Productions (and an avid *POTA* fan) as a full-cast "radio play," complete with music and special effects. Hollweg had enjoyed McCarthy's script and seized his chance to be a part of simian history. "Rich Handley sent me an email mentioning this might make a cool audio drama," Hollweg told me[8], "and put me in touch with Mike McCarthy to get his blessing. Thankfully, one of my partners in audio-drama-making crime at BrokenSea, Lothar Tuppan, had time to mix the show from a script I had adapted from Mike's original script from the '70s."

Adapted? Hollweg explained:

> The only real changes were some character names – Plato, Orak, and Nero (instead of Gorilla #1, Gorilla #2, Gorilla #3). As this is an *audio* drama – and from having made over 100 myself – I find that it makes it easier for the listener to keep track of side characters when they are named. Any other changes were mainly stage directions that were originally intended to be visual but did not translate at all well in an audio drama. So an added 'over here' to a character's lines, or an 'UFFFF' when someone falls or gets on a horse... *anything* to help audibly describe the movement and the choreography of a scene.

Hollweg sent his changes to McCarthy and received his blessing on them all. His adaptation is available as a two-part, free MP3 download at the BrokenSea website: http://brokensea.com/potauk.

Some of BrokenSea's artistic choices may not be to everyone's taste, but having listened to the show, I find it matches perfectly with how I imagine the play would have been presented and performed back in the 1970s. Whether that's a good thing or not, I'll let listeners decide for themselves, but Hollweg's audio drama stands as the closest any of us are likely to get to experiencing the production, given that no recording of the actual stage show has yet surfaced.[9]

As juvenile as the stage production may have been, it was successful enough to warrant having two entirely separate full companies perform the show simultaneously in two different venues: one in London, at the Theatre Royal in Stratford, and the other in Great Yarmouth, at the Windmill Theatre. The Great Yarmouth show was co-produced by Bill Kenwright, who went on to become a successful and famous West End Theatre producer with shows all over the world. Kenwright told me he remembers very little about his time on *Planet of the Apes*, other than that "It was a particularly hot summer! Consequently, business was poor. However, I have wonderful recollections of

---

[8] Via e-mail correspondence conducted in November 2015. All Hollweg quotes come from that conversation.

[9] A brief video of one arena-show rodeo *has* survived, however, thanks to *Apes* fan Derek Tait, who recorded a performance at Plymouth Hoe in 1978: https://www.youtube.com/watch?v=xJ6gmxvGqVs.

apes standing outside the Windmill Theatre, or walking along the seafront at Great Yarmouth, handing out show leaflets."[10]

Both shows performed well and had a decent run, but with the TV series now off the air, audience numbers soon diminished as interest inevitably faded. "The TV audience was very important for us," McCarthy recalled. "Most of our audience came from that. Public interest was waning a bit, and it reached a natural end."

The last gasp for the *Planet of the Apes* stage show came in 1978 with a limited run in the British seaside resort of Cleethorpes. This was also directed by Mike McCarthy, but it was only ever booked for a two-week run.

Following his stint on *Planet of the Apes*, McCarthy went on to work as a director with a number of different theatre companies up and down the country. He eventually set up his own company, Popular Productions, worked as a freelance director-producer, and completed an M.A. degree in European cultural planning. In 2006, he set up a new company, Lakin McCarthy Entertainment, which has taken him back into mainstream entertainment. He is now a producer and promoter of live entertainment.

McCarthy is the unsung hero of the live *Planet of the Apes* appearances. Without his generosity in sharing his script, and his willingness to spare the time to answer an endless barrage of geeky questions, this offshoot of the *Apes* universe would have remained little more than rumor.

Rory Lister, who had played one of the astronauts in some of the arena shows, had gotten on so well with Mike Caulfield that, in 1976, he found himself invited to portray an astronaut once again, this time in the stage production of *Planet of the Apes*, which he gladly accepted. Looking back on those days, Lister recalled:

> Mike told me that there would be two shows per day, Monday to Saturday, one in the morning and one in the afternoon. On arrival at Great Yarmouth, Mike met me and we went together to meet the rest of the cast. I am afraid that after such a long time, I have forgotten most of their names. However, four I do remember: Mike Dalton (the other astronaut), Fortunato Evangalista (Galen), Dave Downes (Gorilla – he was a professional stuntman), and Angela Daniels (Pila the slave girl) from the TV show *Sale of the Century*.

Lister said he remembers the shows running smoothly, everything going well, and fans always waiting by the stage door for autographs, but one incident

[10] *Simian Scrolls* issue #18. Summer 2015:
http://pota.goatley.com/scrolls/simianscrolls_18.pdf.

stood out: "This one time, the soundtrack (the apes all mimed because the heavy masks made their own voices sound muffled) failed one afternoon as Galen was talking with the astronauts. Undaunted, Fortunato carried on in his own voice, which had a very strong Italian accent. The audience didn't seem to mind, though!" Lister looks back on it all with great affection, he told me, and is glad to have been a part of it. In fact, everyone involved who was asked the question seems glad to have been a part of it.

So it's easy for a 14-year-old boy to be dismissive of and dismayed by the "just for kids" mentality of much of what came at the tail end of the wave of '70s apemania. A lot of those toys, comics, and cartoon shows – and, yes, the U.K. live performances – no doubt contributed to diminishing the public's perception of the *Apes* franchise as one not worthy of adult attention.

But as an adult, one can look back and appreciate that for any shortcomings there may have been, the live *Planet of the Apes* shows were put together by people with a passion for the material – people who, to this day, remain proud of what they achieved. Yes, these live appearances were juvenile and yes, they were simplistic, but… in every way that they were ever intended to be, they were a resounding success.

The 800-Pound Gorilla in the Room: Tim Burton's Reimagining

by Rich Handley

In many families, there's one person who doesn't fit in with the rest. This individual makes decisions others question, is viewed as a disappointing black mark on the family name, and is no longer welcome at holiday gatherings. The mere mention of this drunk uncle, antisocial cousin, or paroled offspring is enough to make eyes roll, blood pressures rise, and fists clench, as barely submerged resentment comes boiling back to the surface amidst disdainful comments about wasted potential and disrespect for elders.

For *Planet of the Apes*, that black sheep is Tim Burton's contribution to the franchise. When the filmmaker's "reimagining" of the 1968 classic hit theaters in 2001, fandom was abuzz with anticipation about what Burton might be able to do for the mythos. The writer-director had adeptly demonstrated, with such wonderful films as *Beetlejuice*, *Batman*, *Edward Scissorhands*, *The Nightmare Before Christmas*, *Ed Wood*, and *Sleepy Hollow*, that he could be remarkably imaginative, innovative, and visually bold, and it was intriguing to anticipate how he might use those strengths to the apes' advantage. Tim Burton re-making a film about human-size apes dominating over mankind in a paranoid, post-apocalyptic future? God, yes. The director could do amazing things with a camera and had a flair for the bizarre – surely he would do the family proud.

Then the movie opened in theaters.

Angry complaints echoed in lobbies as viewers exited the first showings feeling betrayed by a loved one, cursing Burton for besmirching the clan's good name, and muttering in disgust about how upset *Apes* patriarchs Pierre Boulle, Rod Serling, and Michael Wilson would be had they lived long enough to see what he'd done to the family business. As often happens with such schisms in the bloodline, those who took a more forgiving stance by defending the film's positives found themselves mocked or dismissed as well, lumped in with the bad apple who had caused such familial strife.

For better or for worse, though, the 2001 *Planet of the Apes* film is part of the franchise – the sixth entry in an ever-growing list of movies that now number nine. As the outcast of the *Apes* lineage, Burton's remake had some undeniable problems in terms of writing, acting, directing, tone, make-up choices, and excessive homages, and a lot of the criticism it has received has been justifiable. But is the movie as bad as people make it out to be? Is it deserving of its place as the family pariah?

Despite its negatives, the Burton film also sported a (mostly) stellar cast, several standout characters, dazzling visuals, and an ambitious (if not entirely realized) premise. What's more, it spawned a brief line of spinoff novels and comic books that were a surprising diamond in the rough, far exceeding the quality of the movie itself.

When one considers the *Planet of the Apes* films we almost had instead, one thing is clear: it could have been a lot worse. That's admittedly not a ringing endorsement, but perhaps, 15 years since the film's theatrical release, enough time has passed (and enough anger has subsided) that it's time to reevaluate and reexamine the reimagining to reassess whether any redeeming qualities might warrant reconsideration.

Origin of the Species

It was a long and winding road that led to Burton's door, and it started in 1988, when writer-director Adam Rifkin was invited in to pitch ideas for the first new *Apes* film since 1973's *Battle for the Planet of the Apes*.

Among those proposals was *Return to the Planet of the Apes*, in which a descendant of Heston's George Taylor (Rifkin's script ignored *Beneath the Planet of the Apes*' Earth-melting conclusion) leads a human revolution against the Ape Empire, a government modeled after ancient Rome. The simian civilization is plagued by a civil war between rival gorilla and chimpanzee factions (only three orangutans live in the Empire, serving as its highest court judges), and the villain of the story is General Izan, a cruel, decadent gorilla who has ruled the Empire with an iron fist for 20 years, ever since assassinating the leaders of both factions.

Rifkin's screenplay features a human lead named Duke, the orphaned son of Taylor and Nova, who has been raised in a Forbidden Zone community near the ruins of New York City. Izan executed Taylor when Duke was three years old – Nova had already died by that point – and the boy has since been raised by Cornelius, who is now in exile. Duke journeys to Ape City to kill Izan and avenge his father. Captured in the process, Duke is slated for execution, along with Wynora, the leader of the Simiantarian Liberation Movement (subtlety of nomenclature has never really been an *Apes* strongpoint), and the two are forced to fight a massive gladiator called The Machine.

By story's end, the giant warrior slays Izan, while Duke and Wynora are set free, and Izan's son Pax brings peaceful reforms to the Empire (how could he not, given his name?).

With makeup legend Rick Baker – a veteran of ape prosthetics with such films as *Greystoke: The Legend of Tarzan*, *Gorillas in the Mist*, and *Mighty Joe Young* under this belt – slated to design the simian makeup, Danny Elfman hired to compose the film's score, and both Charlie Sheen and Tom Cruise vying for the starring role of Duke, the film was a go until mere days before pre-production was set to begin. New studio executives demanded multiple rewrites, however, and the project was abandoned.

While the premise may sound intriguing in synopsized form, Rifkin's screenplay is rather uninspired, and fans might very well have been just as put off by it (particularly the discarding of *Beneath*'s events) as they would eventually be with Burton's final product. In any case, the fact that a new *Apes* film had been promised, only to be yanked away at the last moment, did not bode well for future efforts.

This was but the first stinging disappointment to those hoping, at last, to be able to watch a new entry in the *Apes* film franchise. Director Peter Jackson, with spouse and writing partner Fran Walsh, pitched a treatment in 1992 – not a reboot, but rather a sixth installment of the classic series, set during a Renaissance period in simian history sometime after *Battle for the Planet of the Apes*. Intriguingly, Walsh and Jackson had intended to cast Roddy McDowall as an elderly, grey-haired chimp modeled after Leonardo da Vinci.

Little is known about the story, as their script has never surfaced, but McDowall's involvement alone should have been reason enough to throw boatloads of money at it. Sadly, this concept stalled due to a change in Fox honchos from Joe Roth to Tom Jacobson, who reportedly disliked Jackson's concept and, astounding though it may be, was entirely unaware of McDowall's importance to the *Apes* saga as the actor who gave life to Cornelius, Caesar, and Galen, three of its most beloved characters.

Now, it may sound absurd that a film studio would put such an uninformed person in charge of *Apes'* rebirth, but it's not unprecedented. *Superman Lives*, Kevin Smith's un-filmed 1996 script, was assigned to producer Jon Peters, who told Smith that Superman could not wear his usual suit or fly, had to fight a giant spider (later a polar bear), and had to have bodyguards at the Fortress of Solitude. As anyone even remotely familiar with the world and character of Superman would know, these requests were absurdly off the mark. Plus, Peters had no idea who Kal-El (Superman's real name) was, which is all anyone needs to know to understand why he was wrong for the job. Smith did turn in a script, but it was ultimately jettisoned by the newly signed-on director – Tim Burton.

After Peter A. Chernin (a producer, in recent years, of *Rise of the Planet of the Apes*, *Dawn of the Planet of the Apes*, and *War for the Planet of the Apes*) assumed the role of Fox chairman, Oliver Stone was brought in to executive-produce and co-write another *Apes* reboot in 1993. With such thought-provoking films as *Platoon*, *Wall Street*, *Born on the Fourth of July*, *The Doors*, *JFK*, and *Natural Born Killers* under his belt, Stone – a storyteller who has never shied away from shining a light on human ugliness in order to convey a dark message – would seem to have been an ideal fit.

However, Stone has also been quoted, in Paul A. Woods' *The Planet of the Apes Chronicles* (Plexus Publishing, 2001), as deeming the original five-movie series "awful," so it's doubtful that he would have done any justice at all to the apes had his film been made. A writer and/or producer need not be a die-hard fan of a franchise in order to create a good film, but when one comes into it with actual *contempt* for the source material, that is not a recipe for success.

Stone's project utilized a script by Terry Hayes titled *Return of the Apes*, involving an ancient simian civilization and prophetic Biblical codes. Hayes' credits include such post-apocalyptic films as *Mad Max 2: The Road Warrior* and *Mad Max Beyond Thunderdome*, so he wasn't a bad choice to write it, and ancient simians and religious undertones would certainly fit the *Apes* mold.

Sounds promising, right? Unfortunately, Hayes' screenplay falters in living up to that promise and does not read *at all* like a *Planet of the Apes* tale.

The plot revolves around a Harvard professor, Doctor Billie Rae Diamond, who is working to cure a rapid-aging disease affecting human pregnancies, and whose research predicts mankind will be extinct within six months. Her lab assistant, Will Robinson (an apparent homage to Bill Mumy's character from *Lost in Space*, and a predecessor to James Franco's similarly named, also-curing-an-illness lab scientist Will Rodman, from *Rise of the Planet of the Apes*), realizes the disease is due to a mutation in mitochondrial DNA.

The two scientists use floatation tanks to travel 100,000 years into the past (presumably, the screenwriter had recently watched Ken Russell's 1980 film *Altered States*) to locate the first modern human and change the course of evolution by eliminating the malady from human DNA.[1] There, they encounter the Seven Tribes, a group of prehistoric early-human clans populating a region called Middle Earth.[2] Diamond and Robinson find the first modern human, an orphan girl called Aiv (pronounced "Eve," because of course that's her name), and keep her (and, thus, humanity) safe... or something. The scientists remain stranded in the past (hence, the *Lost in Space* reference), raising both Aiv and Diamond's infant son together.[3]

There is a society of talking apes in the script, led by Lord Drak, a hugely muscled military commander stereotype, but really, there's precious little to tie this rather incomprehensible story to *Planet of the Apes* – which, remember, is exactly what Oliver Stone wanted. It's difficult to imagine that it's what *the fans* would have wanted, though.

Don Murphy, Stone's partner on the project, summed up the concept for *Sci-Fi Universe* in 1994 in a rather telling quote:[4]

---

[1] Hey, don't ask me – *I* didn't write the thing.

[2] Yes, Middle Earth, as in *Lord of the Rings*. There are even characters named Aragorn, Ghan Nazgul, and Strider, utterly guaranteeing that the J.R.R. Tolkien estate would have gone into full lawsuit mode had they gotten wind of any of this.

[3] According to David Hughes' *Tales from Development Hell: The Greatest Movies Never Made?* (Titan Books, 2012), Diamond's son is named Adam, a rather obvious counterpart to Eve. The name Adam does not appear in the version of the script posted at http://www.simplyscripts.com, but it's possible that Hughes found the name in an iteration not publicly available.

[4] Williams, David E. "Oliver's Apes." *Sci-Fi Universe* (July 1994). Archived at http://pota.goatley.com/magazines/sci-fi-universe-1994-06-07.pdf.

The first films were set in a future in which mankind has destroyed himself, but ours is actually set in *Quest for Fire* times, the dawn of man. It has very Biblical, mythic overtones. It isn't the sixth movie in the series – or a remake of the first one – but a reinvention of the concept of the *Planet of the Apes* using nineties technology and a completely new story... It's going to be *Gorillas in the Mist* meets *The Terminator* – a humongous rethinking of the entire concept.

I know there are lots of fans of the original film series out there, and that they will be offended – but if you watch most of those films, they're dated. We are not making the reinvented *Planet of the Apes* to appeal to the hundred or thousand people who cannot get enough of the *Apes* marathons [on TV], we're going to make it so it appeals to the forty million people who want to see what could easily be the next *Jurassic Park*.

Not exactly the kind of thing you'd want to hear from someone helming an *Apes* reboot.

The movie would have starred Arnold Schwarzenegger and possibly Sir Ben Kingsley, while Sam Raimi, Chuck Russell, and Phillip Noyce were all considered as potential directors.[5] First Rick Baker and then Stan Winston, both eminently talented at their craft, were approached to design the ape prosthetics, but in the end it didn't matter. Like prior attempts, this one faltered as well, after Hayes was reportedly fired for refusing to make the film overtly kid-friendly by having the lead human teach apes how to play baseball – a rather silly demand on the studio's behalf, yet an indication of Hayes' integrity. Given the screenplay's weaknesses, it may have been a mercy killing. Say what you will about Burton's *Apes* film, but at least it wasn't *Gorillas in the Mist* meets *The Terminator* and Major League Baseball in the vein of *Quest for Fire* and *Jurassic Park*, nor was it drowning in misplaced *Lord of the Rings* references.

Next brought on board were director Chris Columbus and screenwriter Sam Hamm. Hamm's script, simply titled *Planet of the Apes*, is similar to Hayes' attempt, with another plague threatening humanity (this time with Area 51 scientist Susan Landis working to cure it), though the action takes place on Orbis Terrae, a planet orbiting Alpha Centauri. Schwarzenegger was still attached to the project, but Columbus dropped out in 1995 after Fox rejected Hamm's screenplay.

The ape-ruled Orbis Terrae is home to a human population left savage and mute by a plague. Lord Zaius and the Orang Council keep gorillas and chimps oppressed, and maintain a secret stronghold called Olympus Base, from which

---

[5] I'd pay good money to see a Raimi-directed *Planet of the Apes* film. Fox, take note.

they monitor Earth transmissions in order to steal human religion, science, and art as their own. When Earth's nations begin developing space programs, the orangutans send a spacecraft to spread the plague to our world, hoping to eliminate mankind's threat. Tracking the vessel to its point of origin, Landis and four other astronauts visit Orbis Terrae to find a cure, but instead end up as hunted animals. Ultimately, Landis and fellow scientist Alexander Troy return home, only to discover that, as in Boulle's novel (and in Burton's final product), apes have taken over Earth in their absence.

Due to the story's premise of simians aping human culture, the humor in this version is pretty similar to that of the short-lived animated series *Return to the Planet of the Apes*, with ape-y versions of Earth proper nouns galore. These include ape journalist Barbaria (Barbara Walters), fast-food restaurant Banana King (Burger King), perfume company Calvinius (Calvin Klein), actor Macaque Cullcin (Macaulay Culkin), pornographic publication *Apehouse* (*Penthouse*), and oh so painfully more. Granted, the cartoon did not delve into simian porn, given that it was aimed at single-digit-aged children on Saturday mornings in the 1970s, but it did mention playwright William Apespeare and a painting called the *Apea Lisa*, so Banana King and Macaque Cullcin would have fit right in.

The following year, James Cameron stepped in as producer. This could have been great for the franchise, given his work on such science-fiction classics as *Aliens*, *The Abyss*, *The Terminator*, and *T2: Judgment Day*. Cameron invited Roland Emmerich to direct, but the latter turned down the offer. This *is* great for the franchise, given the long string of mediocre, one-note, form-over-substance blockbuster fluff pieces that Emmerich has written and directed throughout his career, such as *Independence Day*, *Godzilla*, *The Day After Tomorrow*, *10,000 BC*, and *2012*. The thought of Emmerich writing, directing, producing, or even attending a matinee showing of a *Planet of the Apes* film should give any fan the shivers. Thankfully, it didn't happen. Burton's effort was William Apespeare compared to what Emmerich likely would have delivered.

Peter Jackson returned to pitch his same idea as before, but despite Fox's enthusiasm for Jackson's ideas, the director declined the job due to concerns that Schwarzenegger's and Cameron's interests might conflict with his own. Given Jackson's later work on the *Lord of the Rings* saga and, particularly, *King Kong*, as well as his determination to honor the classic films by featuring McDowall in a prominent role, it's a tragic loss that he was never given the chance to bring his simian vision to life.

The apes continued to navigate the twists and turns of Hollywood Boulevard, with such actors as Patrick Swayze, Harrison Ford, and Kevin Costner rumored for lead roles. Michael Bay was among those considered to direct (suddenly, Emmerich doesn't seem so bad an option), but Peter Hyams was Cameron's next choice.

An anonymous leak in 1998, which may well have been a hoax, claimed that Cameron's movie would be a continuation of the classic films – specifically, an altered-timeline revisit of the 1968 movie featuring an insane descendant of Caesar and an advanced Ape City more akin to that from Boulle's source novel. Reportedly, Heston would have returned to the role of Taylor as the leader of a community of intelligent human savages. Again, though, take all of this with an Alpha Omega Bomb-sized grain of salt, given the anonymous nature of the leak. In any case, when Fox rejected Hyams, both Cameron and Schwarzenegger walked away, and it was back to square one.

Enter William Broyles Jr., a veteran screenwriter of several notable films (*Apollo 13*, *Cast Away*, and *Entrapment*, with *Unfaithful* and *The Polar Express* soon to follow), who was promised a great deal of creative control as he penned a *Planet of the Apes* reboot titled *The Visitor*. Broyles' first draft, dated 24 September, 1999, bore the subtitle "Episode 1 of The Chronicles of Ashlar," and followed a previously submitted 20-page document, "Annals of the Planet Ashlar," dated 4 August of that same year, in which the author outlined many details of the alien world's atmosphere, mythology, culture, geography, and history. Between the latter title and the screenplay's subtitle, as well as the enormous amount of background details he came up with, it's clear that Broyles had a huge landscape in mind, one that went well beyond a single film. It's fascinating to consider what might have been had he been able to pursue it.

Richard D. Zanuck, who helmed the original *Apes* film in 1968 as 20th Century Fox's head of production, returned to the franchise as the producer of *The Visitor*, which by this time had been renamed, simply, *Planet of the Apes*. Several directors were approached, including Andrew Kevin Walker, Frank Darabont, Graham Yost and, again, Michael Bay, before Burton finally signed on in February 2000 – and then went to work changing Broyles' screenplay, much to the writer's exasperation. (Think about that for a moment: Fox had *The Walking Dead*'s Frank Darabont in mind... but instead chose to proceed with Tim Burton. Talk about missed opportunities.) Once at the helm, Burton brought Baker and Elfman back into the fold to oversee makeup work and compose the soundtrack, respectively.

Many actors were considered, and some of the most intriguing options were those not chosen. Matt Damon, Ben Affleck, and Leonardo DiCaprio were all considered for the lead as astronaut Leo Davidson, but the job went to Mark Wahlberg. Given Wahlberg's narcoleptic blank-stare approach to the role, it seems a crime that one of the others wasn't hired instead, as Damon, Affleck, and DiCaprio are all gifted actors who might have breathed some life into the rather stiff Davidson character. Wahlberg has turned in a few solid performances over the years, most notably in *Boogie Nights* and *The Perfect Storm* (both of which were recent hits at the time, and no doubt played a role in his hiring), but as *Apes*' latest astronaut, he turned in a wooden performance that can best be summed up as "dead in space." And handsome.

If looks could kill, Mark Wahlberg's Leo Davidson and Estella Warren's Daena might have blown fans away. Unfortunately, looks don't count for much when it comes to weak performances.

The other primary and secondary roles went to Tim Roth as General Thade (*Dawn of the Planet of the Apes*' Gary Oldman was also considered for this character), Helena Bonham Carter as Ari, the late Michael Clarke Duncan as Attar, Paul Giamatti as Limbo, Cary-Hiroyuki Tagawa as Krull, David Warner as Ari's father Sandar, Kris Kristofferson as Karubi, and Estella Warren (a fellow advocate of the blank-stare acting method) as Daena. Heston signed on as Thade's gun-fearing father Zaius (an ironic, if ham-fisted, nod to the classic films' Doctor Zaius, as well as to Heston's five-term stint as president of the National Rifle Association), while Linda "Nova" Harrison appeared in a "blink and you'll miss it" cameo as a non-speaking human in Limbo's slave wagon.

Marky-Mark and the Monkey Bunch

Burton's film is not a straightforward remake of the original. In fact, it isn't really a remake at all, given that it features different characters facing different challenges in a different plot in a different era and on a different planet. As such, Burton coined the term "reimagining" to describe the approach his movie (an amalgam of elements from Boulle's novel, the films, and even the TV series and cartoon) would take.

Like most incarnations of the franchise, the movie tells a tale of sapient apes inheriting the world from humanity. Like the Heston classic, it focuses on a lone astronaut trying to survive in an upside-down world. Like the TV show, it features talking humans acting in a subservient capacity to simian society as abused slaves. Like the animated series, it contains a prophecy of a space traveler and revered religious figure arriving from the past. And like Boulle's novel, it takes place on an alien planet (one with twin suns and moons, something a lot of viewers apparently missed, considering the number of reviewers who misinterpreted the film as taking place on a future Earth) and ends with a surprise twist following the astronaut's return home (the same twist as in the book, actually, but entirely out of context and thus incomprehensible).

The film opens in 2029 aboard the space station USAF *Oberon* – an immediate clue that this is a new timeline separate from the prior films, since Caesar's 1991 rebellion and the subsequent nuclear war cannot have taken place. Captain Leo Davidson, a cocky, Hollywoodized Air Force pilot, is assigned to help scientists train genetically bred chimpanzees, gorillas, and orangutans. This includes having them pilot space pods for use during dangerous missions (think *Project X*, but without a likable main star like Matthew Broderick), and really serves no purpose, story-wise, other than to set up the ending. Davidson often butts heads with Grace Alexander, the station's chief medical officer, who dislikes how Leo teases his ape charges. (More on her later.)

When chimp pilot Pericles is lost in space aboard one of the station's pods, Davidson heads out in another pod to rescue him and ends up caught in an electromagnetic storm – a quantum time storm, according to the novel *Planet of the Apes: Fall* – that propels him to an alien world.[6] Leo emerges from the crash as a tribe of primitive humans, led by grizzled chieftain Karubi, run past him, pursued by screeching, leaping ape hunters in a scene that is visually very impressive yet reminds viewers how much more effective a similar scene was in the 1968 original, minus all the screeching and leaping.

Captured by the apes, Davidson is delivered to sarcastic orangutan slave trader Limbo, who sells him to a chimpanzee human-rights activist named Ari, the daughter of Senator Sandar and this film's Doctor Zira analogue. A fellow slave, Daena, is attracted to the off-worlder and grows jealous of Ari's seeming romantic interest in the man – an odd plot development, given their different species, and an ironic callback to Zira's revulsion at kissing the "so damned ugly" Taylor. Daena is played by the breathtaking Estella Warren, a champion synchronized swimmer[7] and former fashion model whose limited repertoire as an actor (which basically amounts to substituting sultry pouting for emoting) becomes regrettably obvious during any scenes she shares with the likes of Bonham Carter or Giamatti.

Assigned as a servant in Sandar's employ, Davidson escapes that same night, taking with him Daena and a few other entirely forgettable human slaves, as well as Ari and her gorilla protector, the disgraced General Krull. Forced to ally with them is Limbo, whom the ape soldiers mistakenly assume has aided their cause. Together, this motley band travels to the fabled city of Calima, which Davidson believes will enable him to find a means of returning home. Unbeknownst to the rebellious astronaut, word of his arrival has inspired neighboring human tribes, who travel to meet him there.

Meanwhile, General Thade, an ambitious chimpanzee military leader (an intriguing reversal, actually, given chimps' tendency to be pacifistic in every *Apes* incarnation that preceded the 2001 film) tracks Davidson and his comrades across the land. Thade hates humans with a passion, and is determined to learn the secrets of Calima and prevent the "spaceman" (as he calls Leo in a scene shown in a pre-release trailer but not in the movie itself) from fomenting insurrection among local humans. At Thade's side is a hulking gorilla named Attar, who is fiercely loyal to the general and could probably

---

[6] The planet is called Ashlar in Broyles' screenplay, though the name is never mentioned in the final film. According to Dark Horse Comics' movie adaptation, the Ashlar scenes take place in the year 5021.

[7] Seriously. Warren almost competed in the 1996 Summer Olympics, in fact. She may not be much of an actor, but she's apparently quite an athlete.

bench-press the *Oberon* with two hairy fingers while simultaneously doing push-ups with his other arm and peeling an entire banana tree with each foot.

The general is in love with Ari (or more likely in lust, given the ease with which he later brands and discards her) and takes her decision to follow Davidson as a personal betrayal. He convinces Sandar that his daughter has been abducted and uses the incident to convince the senator to grant him dictatorial powers.

Charlton Heston, who appeared as the gun-fearing Zaius as a nod to the original films, shares a scene with Thade (Tim Roth), one of *Planet of the Apes'* most fascinating villains.

Davidson arrives at Calima and is stunned to discover that it's his old space station, lying decrepit in the desert. Accessing the computer (which works just fine after a devastating crash and three thousand years' of sand erosion), he realizes that the *Oberon* crew must have followed his pod into the anomaly to rescue him, only to be propelled to Ashlar as well, arriving millennia before Davidson due to the EM storm's strange properties... or something. It's never really made clear. The crew, long since dead, had fallen victim to a mutiny staged by an ape named Semos, who led his fellow simians away from the station to a strange new land, where they established a society of their own.

Thade's forces attack at Calima — so named for the scorched remains of a sign mounted near the ape trainees' former cages, labeled "Caution: Live Animals" (which should have come as a jaw-dropping surprise to exactly no one who had ever watched *Star Trek: The Motion Picture*). Davidson ignites the station's remaining fuel, thanks to a nuclear power source that has conveniently survived the millennia, which injures the first wave of the ape army, enabling the assembled human tribes to rise up against their oppressors.

In the heat of battle, Attar kills Krull, his former commander, and Thade nearly slays the spaceman, but a second pod descends, carrying Pericles, who has only just arrived due to the EM storm's strange properties... or something. When the chimp gives Davidson a happy hug, the warring apes immediately lower their weapons, perceiving the space-suited newcomer to be the return of their beloved Semos[8], and his gesture a sign that apes and humans should take a cue from John Lennon and imagine all the people living life in peace.

Limbo wastes no time in transitioning from slavery to the drug trade, selling aspirin to human children while sporting a facial expression that screams out, "Your mom couldn't pick you up today from school. Climb into this van and I'll drive you home. Want some candy?"

Thade tries to murder Pericles, which the other apes deem blasphemous, causing Attar to brand his friend and commander a traitor. The general gets himself locked in a compartment aboard the *Oberon*, and Davidson uses Pericles' pod to lift off and return to Earth, only to find that in his absence, it, too, has fallen under ape control. How does he know this? Because of the simian police officers arriving to apprehend him after he crashes in Washington, D.C., in front of what should be the Lincoln Memorial, but instead bears the snarling face of Thade, giving rise to an endless stream of "Ape Lincoln" jokes.

Sackcloth and Ashlars

Despite its non sequitur of an ending, Burton's *Planet of the Apes* reboot actually had a lot going for it when the movie went into production. Truly, whatever flaws it had, the film did not suffer from a lack of creative talent. It had that in spades: a skilled director, a veteran screenwriter, a brilliant composer, a master makeup artist, and a solid actor lineup (Wahlberg and Warren notwithstanding). Plus, it had a storyline far more akin to *Planet of the Apes* than what either Rifkin, Hayes, or Hamm had turned in. The DNA was strong and *should* have resulted in a solid final product. So what went wrong?

---

[8] Oddly, none of the apes seem to notice that Pericles, as a non-evolved, 20th-Century chimp, cannot speak English and is the size of a child compared to their human-like stature. Either the religion of Ashlar portrays Semos as a diminutive simpleton, or else simian faith is as blind as human faith tends to be.

Pretty much all of the above, actually.

Despite his powerhouse list of credits, Burton proved ill-suited to *Planet of the Apes*, his usual larger-than-life aesthetic getting in the way of storytelling (although, giving credit where it's due, his version of Ape City is wonderfully designed – if apes ever built cities, they would probably extend vertically as well as horizontally). Broyles' script, meanwhile, after being ripped apart by Burton and the studio, ended up a hodge-podge of clichés, weak dialogue, and unnecessary homages to the original films that were often cringe-inducing in their non-subtlety – "Take your stinking paws off me, you damn dirty human!" comes to mind. The soundtrack, somewhat effective but oddly redundant, was not one of Elfman's best. And as for Baker's prosthetics work, it was uneven, with male apes looking fantastically realistic, yet female chimps (especially Bonham Carter's Ari) bizarrely resembling post-facial-surgery Michael Jackson.

One of the film's greatest strengths was simultaneously one of its biggest missteps: namely, casting. On the positive side, Roth, Bonham Carter, and Giamatti all turned in the stellar performances one would expect actors of their caliber to deliver, making Thade, Ari, and Limbo the three standout characters by a wide margin, while Duncan, Tagawa, Warner, and especially Shadix all did their best to make their minor roles jump off the screen as well. The movie's simian characters were more intriguing than the story they were allowed to tell, and the actors playing them helped to elevate the material.

Alas, the same cannot be said of the human characters, not one of whom was remotely interesting – and it's a major problem when the actors portraying the two human leads seem entirely incapable of showing emotion. Warren and Wahlberg both sleepwalked through every scene, preventing the audience from connecting with either Davidson or Daena, apart from admiring their tightly clothed, perfectly formed physiques. Some of the fault lies in the fact that neither character was given any interesting dialogue to deliver, but a chunk of the blame also falls on the shoulders of the actors and director for failing to make the most of the lackluster script.

During the second season of the British science-fiction comedy *Red Dwarf*, in an episode titled "Thanks for the Memory," Arnold Rimmer takes a bite of a fried-egg sandwich made by his bunkmate, Dave Lister, which he fully expects to be revolting but, in fact, turns out to be delicious. Amazed at how much he enjoys it, Rimmer exclaims:

> I could never invent a sandwich like this, Lister. You see, all the ingredients are wrong. The fried eggs: wrong. The chutney: wrong. The chili sauce: all

wrong. But put them together and somehow it works. It becomes right. It's you – this sandwich, Lister, is *you*... All your ingredients are wrong. You're slobby, you've got no sense of discipline, you're the only man ever to get his money back from the Odor Eater people, but people *like* you, don't you see? That's why you're a fried-egg-chili-chutney sandwich.

Tim Burton's *Planet of the Apes* film is the polar opposite of a fried-egg-chili-chutney sandwich, whatever that might be. The ingredients are mostly right, yet put them all together, and somehow it's just not as tasty as it looks like it should be.

Throwing the Ape Out With the Bathwater

Burton's reimagining brought in $362 million worldwide at the box office, with a $100 million budget, so it clearly made money – and it does have its ardent defenders. Film.com writer Eric D. Snider gave it a glowing review back when the film hit theaters, noting:

> I can't think of a better person to have directed this film than Tim Burton. His touch is sly and whimsical. This is a serious science-fiction adventure, but Burton is still cognizant of the fact that monkeys are funny. *Planet of the Apes* takes itself just seriously enough to warrant respect and attention, but not so seriously it chokes on itself. It also avoids the preachiness that infested the original... Burton creates an amazingly believable world. Rick Baker's makeup effects and Colleen Atwood's costumes are shockingly good.[9]

Still, by and large, despite its financial success, the film has been soundly trashed by critics and fans alike. *TV Guide* reviewer Maitland McDonagh wrote, back in 2001:

> Whatever the faults of the first *Planet* and its sequels, they were all about something; this film is pure, empty (if gorgeous) spectacle, and the decision to loosen the tongues of the ape planet's humans (they were mute in the original) undermines the contrast that lies at the heart of the story's power: civilized apes vs. beast-like men.[10]

It's a sentiment that noted film critic Roger Ebert apparently shared, as he wrote:

> The movie is great-looking. Rick Baker's makeup is convincing even in the extreme closeups, and his apes sparkle with personality and presence. The sets and locations give us a proper sense of alien awe, and there's one neat long shot of the ape city-mountain that looks, when you squint a little, like Xanadu from *Citizen Kane*. There are lines inviting laughs ("Extremism in

[9] http://www.ericdsnider.com/movies/planet-of-the-apes/
[10] http://www.tvguide.com/movies/planet-of-the-apes/review/135178/

the defense of apes is no vice") and others unwisely inviting groans ("If you show me the way out of here, I promise I'll show you something that will change your life forever")...

Planet of the Apes is the kind of movie that you enjoy at times, admire at times, even really like at times, but is it necessary?

Given how famous and familiar Franklin J. Schaffner's 1968 film is, Tim Burton had some kind of an obligation to either top it or sidestep it. Instead, he pays homage. He calls this version a "reimaging," and so it is, but a reinvention might have been better. Burton's work can show a wild and crazed imagination, but here he seems reined in. He's made a film that's respectful to the original, and respectable in itself, but that's not enough. Ten years from now, it will be the 1968 version that people are still renting.[11]

And in 2016, during the Television Critics Association's summer press tour, Dana Gould, creator of IFC's horror-comedy *Stan Against Evil*, took potshots at the film. "Unlike the *real* Tim Burton," Gould quipped, his series' photography director, also named Tim Burton, "knows what a second act is... Oh, yeah, I said it. Only a genius could make *Planet of the Apes*. It's hard to take that premise and make it boring."[12]

Although there is some undeniable truth to Snider's words (despite his having confused monkeys and apes), it would be difficult to argue with Ebert, McDonagh, Gould, or the multitudes of other detractors who have found fault with Burton's product. At press time, the film has only a 45 percent critics rating at RottenTomatoes.com,[13] and an even lower score – 27 percent – among moviegoers. By comparison, the 1968 *Apes* film has 90 percent and 87 percent ratings, respectively, while 2014's *Dawn of the Planet of the Apes* currently boasts ratings of 90 percent and 88 percent. Regardless of what one might think of RottenTomatoes' scoring system, that's a stark difference.

The film may look damn pretty and sport some excellent performances, and it arguably turned out better than the aborted attempts would likely have been (other than Jackson's, which sounds like it could have been amazing). But the inescapable truth is that it failed to find a proper audience, which is why no sequels have followed, why the movie's bizarre and controversial ending has

---

[11] http://www.rogerebert.com/reviews/planet-of-the-apes-2001

[12] Nakamura, Reid. "Dana Gould Rips Director Tim Burton for His 'Boring' Film *Planet of the Apes*." The Wrap, 31 July, 2016: http://www.thewrap.com/dana-gould-rips-planet-of-the-apes-director-tim-burton-boring/.

[13] https://www.rottentomatoes.com/m/1108704-planet_of_the_apes/

never been revisited, and why Fox chose to reboot the franchise again in 2011 with the far more successful *Rise of the Planet of the Apes*.

And yet...

Burton's reimagining introduced some wonderful tie-in lore to the *Apes* mythos in the form of novels and comic books that *far* surpassed the movie on which they are based. The biggest tragedy, when it comes to this film, is not that it failed to thrill fandom, or that it failed to result in theatrical sequels – it's that many fans have largely overlooked these spinoff tales, either dismissing them without reading them due to the presumption of guilt by association, or never having known they even existed. As a result, they've missed out on some eminently enjoyable *Planet of the Apes* continuations.

Dark Horse Comics published a short-lived series of comic books set a few decades after the film's events, showing the aftermath of Davidson's departure and the effect he had on Ape City. The comic featured an older, imprisoned Attar; teased the whereabouts of Ari, missing for many years at the story's opening; and introduced a compelling cast of new characters, including Thade's power-hungry granddaughter, Minister Shiva.

The comic, penned by Ian Edginton and Dan Abnett (both major *Apes* fans, which showed), had everything the film lacked: interesting human characters about whom readers could actually care, strong storytelling, and a vision that went beyond just "Let's reboot *Planet of the Apes* and try to out-clever the classic films' creators," which seems to have been Burton's primary motivation. Unfettered by poor acting and directing choices, the comic did something remarkable and unexpected: it took the world of the 2001 film, applied the 1968 version's approach, and thus made the reboot far more like *Planet of the Apes* than the movie itself managed to do. And yet, the series lasted for only nine issues before dying a quiet death without resolving its ongoing plotlines.

In the first volume of this essay anthology, *The Sacred Scrolls: Comics on the Planet of the Apes*, writer Lou Tambone, in his essay titled "Dark Horse Goes Ape: Is There a Soul in There?", lamented the missed opportunity the comic's premature ending represented:

> It's difficult to avoid becoming wrapped up in the stories they created in this run. They took what Burton started and put some real thought into expanding that universe in a smooth way – minus the movie's substantial acting, writing, and directing deficiencies – while keeping the overall *Planet of the Apes* mythos intact. That's quite an accomplishment, which makes

the cancellation that much more depressing. Imagine where it could have all gone?[14]

Tambone's essay provides an in-depth discussion of the comics, so there's no need to cover that same ground here. Suffice it to say that they're well worth reading and deserve an honored spot in any *Apes* comics collection – right alongside four novels released in 2002 by HarperCollins: *Force* and *Resistance*, by John Whitman, and *The Fall* and *Colony*, by William T. Quick.

Whitman's two novels, as well as two planned but unpublished sequels (*Rule*, by J.E. Bright, and *Extinction*, by Whitman),[15] were aimed at young-adult readers – but don't mistake that as meaning they're not worth reading if you're past your teens, because they are. Like the comics, these novels greatly expanded on Ashlar's history and society, making it clear just how mesmerizing Burton's film *could* have been if handled properly.

Whitman's novels detailed the backgrounds of Ari, Daena, Attar, and Thade years before the movie, revealing what their lives were like as they were growing up, and establishing motivations for the characters' on-screen attitudes and actions. Readers met Daena's mother Sarai, a human clan leader with a vision of forging better inter-species relations between her people and the apes. Sarai's tragic, violent death, in Bright's unpublished *Rule*, would have instilled in Daena a deep-seated hatred and distrust for her simian masters.

It's a shame that the third and fourth novels never hit shelves. The authors explored the close friendship that existed between Ari and Attar before her troublemaking ways conflicted with his military and religious discipline. Ari also shared an unlikely bond with Sarai, lending some much-needed depth to Daena's on-screen anger at the chimp.

---

[14] http://sequart.org/books/41/the-sacred-scrolls-comics-on-the-planet-of-the-apes/.

[15] I'm lucky to have been able to read *Rule*, which Bright completed, as well as Whitman's notes for what would have become *Extinction* had not low sales and the film's lukewarm reception resulted in the cancelation of not only those two novels and Dark Horse's comics, but also additional installments in Quick's saga.

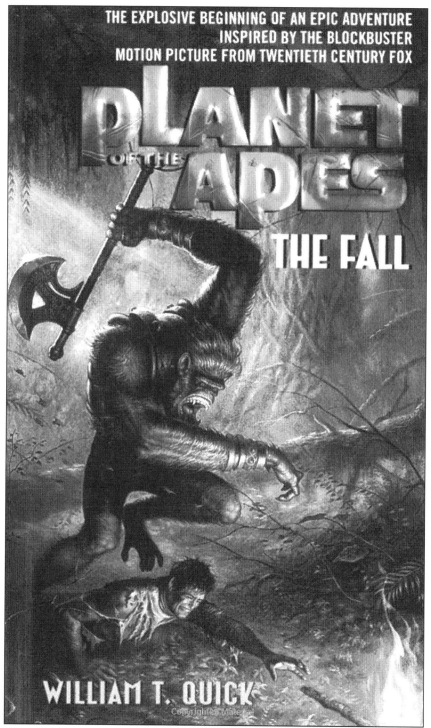

William T. Quick's *Planet of the Apes: The Fall*, the best spinoff novel to arise from Tim Burton's reimagining, offered readers their first look at Semos.

Of particular interest, the authors explained the nature of Thade's falling-out with Krull, leading to the latter's disgrace. According to the books, after Krull rebuked Thade for expending excess time and military resources tracking humans through the jungle, the chimp conspired with a religious leader, Pontifex Timon, to arrange for Krull to be exiled, then replaced him as general. Watching Krull's film scenes after reading the books lends the gorilla greater relatability than Burton's film alone allowed.

But the true diamonds in the Burtonverse rough are Quick's *The Fall* and *Colony*. Set thousands of years before the movie opens, following the crash of the *Oberon*, these two novels establish the events that transpire as the humans work to survive on a hostile alien world, by genetically engineering the station's ape population to make them sufficiently intelligent to serve as a defense and labor force, thus enabling the crew to survive under direly harsh conditions. Most importantly, Quick reveals the origins of a character mentioned several times in the film but never shown: the ape savior known as Semos.

The story of Semos is riveting, as the author approaches his ape uprising similarly to how the filmmakers presented Caesar's rebellion arc in *Conquest of the Planet of the Apes*. When we meet the young, red-gold-furred chimpanzee – the son of Pericles, Davidson's smiling chimp pilot from the movie, it turns out – he is named Jonathan Benavides and is being raised by a benevolent human *Oberon* crewmember, Molly Benavides (an analog to Caesar's foster-father Armando), along with her son David. David, meanwhile, is Leo's son, born of an affair between Wahlberg's character and Molly before the astronaut vanished into the spatial anomaly and bored millions of theater-goers.

The bond between young David and Jonathan is wonderfully written. The two are not just friends; they consider themselves brothers, regardless of their different species, and are as close as any two siblings can be, watching out for and supporting each other at all times. So when Jonathan comes to recognize, as a teen, how his people are effectively humans' slaves, it is doubly tragic. His betrayal and slaughter of humanity, under his self-chosen new name of Semos (an anagram of Moses), puts him at deadly odds with the brother he greatly loves, leaving David with no choice but to attempt to assassinate him. It's the stuff of which great literature is made, and would have provided a powerful follow-up film.

In addition, *The Fall* greatly fleshes out the character of Grace Alexander, whose genetic alteration of three species for the purpose of creating a slave-labor underclass raises a number of questions regarding mankind's inherent repugnance and the ethics of science – which are, after all, the bread and butter of *Planet of the Apes*. *Colony* continues the story by bringing the conflict into the next generation, as Semos' sons help their aging father forge a floundering ape society on a planet that is not only inhospitable, but inhabited by dinosaurs of various shapes and sizes, some of them quite intelligent and all of them incredibly dangerous (it's a lot better than it sounds in synopsis).

Obsessed with procuring safety for apekind, Semos is neither a good father nor a good husband, often neglecting his family and putting his people's needs first. Burton's film portrays him as both a villain and a savior, depending on one's perspective (human or ape). Quick puts both aspects into sharp focus, contrasting Semos' actions with those of his nemesis (Grace) and his brother (David), and the result is a fascinating and heartbreaking read. Ignoring the existence of these books out of distaste for Tim Burton's remake means missing out on two of the better-written and -conceived *Apes* tales out there. The best thing one can say about *The Fall* and *Colony* (and it's also true of *Force, Resistance*, and Dark Horse's comics line) is that they don't come off merely as extensions of the Burton movie. They come off as *Planet of the Apes*.

Alas, the same cannot be said of UbiSoft's 2001 *Planet of the Apes* video game for the PC and Sony PlayStation. The game, as well as a side-scrolling version for Nintendo's Game Boy Color and Game Boy Advance platforms, was conceived in 1998 to coincide with what was, at the time, James Cameron's planned film. Ultimately, the two games were released to coincide with Tim Burton's reboot. The plot, characters, and aesthetic of Burton's version in no way connected to those of the games, however, as they were based largely on the characters and premise of Boulle's novel, with the apes inhabiting a technically advanced society, yet utilized the classic films' costuming and style.

Plagued by poor gameplay, a plodding pace, and non-player-friendly controls, the games received weak reviews and are just not interesting enough to devote a great deal of discussion to here. Suffice it to say that it's ironic that the least impressive tie-in to Burton's reimagining is the one product that actually has nothing to do with the film.

The Forest for the Trees

It's all too easy to dismiss an entire franchise because the first outing fails to entice. One needn't delve much further into Jim Varney's Ernest P. Worrell stories if *Ernest Goes to Camp* and *Ernest Saves Christmas* aren't one's cup of tea, as the other movies in that series aren't likely to get much better. But every now and then, a sequel or prequel comes along that is actually better than the story that spawned it. *The Godfather: Part II, Terminator 2, Aliens, The Empire Strikes Back, The Dark Knight,* and *Star Trek II: The Wrath of Khan* are all widely praised as surpassing their predecessors, for instance.

Still, these examples followed up prior films that were eminently enjoyable,[16] so even though the sequels were better, it's not as if viewers were writing off the entire meal out of disgust over the first helping. But what about series in which the first film is widely lambasted, as Burton's *Planet of the Apes* tends to be? Writing off the *Star Wars* prequels after watching *The Phantom Menace* would mean never seeing the far-superior *Revenge of the Sith*. Skipping the *Evil Dead* sequels due to the first movie's low budget would mean never experiencing the genius insanity of *Evil Dead II* and *Army of Darkness*. Walking away from the James Bond films after finding *Dr. No* dated would mean missing out on brilliant follow-ups *From Russia With Love, Goldfinger,* and *Thunderball*.

As such, the chances of any comics or novels based on Tim Burton's *Planet of the Apes* reboot succeeding were practically nil. These tie-in tales had the cards stacked against them from the outset, which is unfortunate, since they not only elevated Burton's film to something greater than it was on its own, but were excellent in their own right. This, in fact, might be the best reason for not throwing out the ape with the bathwater: had the movie never been made, then neither would Quick's and Whitman's novels, or Edginton's and Abnett's comics, have been published.

Tim Burton's reimagining lacked the solid writing of Boulle's source novel, the depth and cutting social commentary of the classic films, the prevailing friendship theme of the TV series, and the staying power of the current batch of movies. Spawned from a tumultuous chain of events culminating in a rapidly revolving door of writers, directors, and producers, it suffers from questionable decisions and a lack of proper vision. But it's not the abject failure it's often made out to be. There is much to enjoy about it, from the fine performances of many in its cast to the wonderful makeup and set design, to the introduction of characters like Ari, Limbo, and Thade, and especially to the surprisingly high quality of its ancillary spinoff materials.

It's the 800-pound gorilla in the room... but it's still part of the family.

---

[16] Yes, even *Star Trek II*, which followed *Star Trek: The Motion Picture*. I am not afraid to admit that I love the first *Star Trek* movie. So there.

Caesar: A Tale of Two Kings

by Edward Gross

Back in the 1960s, during the so-called Silver Age, DC Comics came up with a concept that allowed them to essentially reboot a number of their Golden Age superheroes who, for one reason or another, had gone out of vogue. For instance, the Flash, whose secret identity had been Jay Garrick in the 1940s and '50s, was replaced by the Barry Allen version of the character, while '40s and early '50s Green Lantern Alan Scott was superseded by Hal Jordan. With those successes, the character reboots continued.

The imaginative notion the writers came up with was that there were parallel Earths existing on different dimensional planes, on which events would unfold similarly yet with significant differences.[1] It's that sort of conceit that one could apply to the *Planet of the Apes* films, both the classic 1968-'73 series (*POTA* Prime, as I think of it) and the most recent re-imagination (which we'll call *POTA* 2)[2] that began with 2011's *Rise of the Planet of the Apes,* continued with 2014's *Dawn of the Planet of the Apes*, and will go forward with 2017's *War for the Planet of the Apes*. Doing so allows both timelines to carry on without one negating the other.

---

[1] Physicists and science-fiction writers have, of course, explored the same notion since long before DC Comics applied the idea to its superhero mythology.

[2] Technically, *POTA* 2 would be Tim Burton's 2001 remake, but that film is outside the scope of this essay.

While *POTA* 2 is beginning the journey that will result in a world with similarities to the one on which Charlton Heston's George Taylor arrives in the original timeline, the journey to get there is already markedly different from what came before. This is particularly true in the case of the character of Caesar, the de facto chimpanzee hero of both series.

In each instance, we have an evolved ape born into an extraordinary situation. In *POTA* Prime, this situation is that in *Escape from the Planet of the Apes*, three chimpanzees, Doctors Cornelius, Zira, and Milo, have arrived in the present from Earth's future, unwittingly there to serve their pre-destined roles of launching a series of events that will result in the dominance of simians and the fall of humanity. In *POTA* 2, *Rise* presents us with the chimpanzee known as Bright Eyes[3], taken from the jungle and used for experimentation that genetically alters her so that when she gives birth, it is to a child already pre-evolved beyond any other ape on the planet. This is similar to the offspring of Cornelius and Zira, whose genetics separates him from all other apes. So right from the moment of their births, the future saviors of simian culture, both called Caesar (the Prime version was initially named Milo in tribute to the good doctor), are an ape apart.

The similarities don't end there. Both are orphaned as infants, unwittingly setting them on their ultimate paths. In *POTA* Prime, the three talking apes (Milo is killed by a modern-day gorilla shortly after they arrive) are initially embraced by the public and the media in a way that would make the Kardashians jealous, but thanks largely to the efforts of the U.S. President's scientific adviser, Doctor Otto Hasslein, it isn't long before the tide turns against them. Gradually recognized as a potential threat to the future of humanity and of the planet itself (the destruction of which, while under sedation, Zira reveals she witnessed from the confines of their space capsule some 2,000 years later), the parents are killed. It is only through Zira's exchanging of her baby with that of a present-day circus chimpanzee that their child lives on.

In *POTA* 2, Caesar's survival in some ways seems even more unlikely. His mother, the aforementioned Bright Eyes, is experimented on at Gen-Sys Laboratories with an anti-Alzheimer's cure called ALZ-112, an artificially created

---

[3] "Bright Eyes" is the nickname that Zira gives George Taylor in the original *Planet of the Apes* film. In fact, many of the names in *Rise* and *Dawn* pay homage to the classic films, further illustrating the mirroring between the *POTA* Prime and *POTA* 2 timelines. See later footnotes for additional examples.

retrovirus that has the desired effect of increasing her intelligence. But while scientist Will Rodman[4] is pitching the drug to investors, Bright Eyes goes on a rampage and is killed by security. Will's superior, Steven Jacobs[5], ends the project and calls for all of the chimps involved in the experiments to be euthanized. But Rodman soon discovers that Bright Eyes became wild not due to an adverse reaction to the drug, but because she was protecting her previously undiscovered newborn child.

Thanks to the efforts of chimp handler Robert Franklin,[6] Will agrees to take the infant home rather than have it put to death. Very quickly, it becomes obvious that the baby, named Caesar by Will's Alzheimer-suffering father, Charles, is extraordinary. In a series of scenes quickly covering the next three years, we watch the evolution of Caesar 2, demonstrating an intelligence far beyond that of a same-aged human counterpart. We also gain a sense of kindness and compassion about him that is a direct influence of being raised among humans, and good ones at that.

Despite the fact that we don't get to watch Caesar-Prime grow up, from the moment we meet him, we know that there's an innate goodness to him, instilled by Armando, the circus owner whose compassion for animals – and belief that the progeny of Cornelius and Zira might do a better job at managing the planet than humans have – allowed for his survival in the first place. Both Caesars grew up in a state of innocence, oblivious to the realities of the world and the fate that had been inflicted upon their kind. Indeed, it's in leaving the security of their respective environments that they each head down the path toward leadership and revolution.

In *POTA* Prime, specifically the opening of *Conquest of the Planet of the Apes*, we are immediately brought up to speed on the apes' status in human society: there is a well-established master-slave hierarchy in place, one foretold by Cornelius in *Escape*. Some years earlier, astronauts had brought back a virus from space that infected dogs and cats, leading to both species' extinction. Humans, longing for pets, turned to apes – whose inherent intelligence made it obvious that a few basic tricks could be taught – but their pets eventually

---

[4] The name "Rodman" provides several homages (whether intentional or not) to the original film series. The first *Apes* screenplay was written by Rodman (Rod) Serling. Actor Roddy MacDowall portrayed not only Cornelius and Caesar, but also TV series character Galen. Finally, the name is a partial anagram of "Armando."

[5] Named after *Planet of the Apes* producer Arthur P. Jacobs

[6] Named after Franklin J. Schaffner, the 1968 film's director

became their slaves. It is into *this* environment that Armando brings the young Caesar, ostensibly to promote his circus, but in reality to allow his adopted "son" to gain a fuller understanding of the world at large in general, and of his own people in particular.

For Caesar, it's a terrible awakening; the idealism of his world is very quickly stripped away, with things only going from bad to worse when he shouts out in defense of a chimpanzee being abused by the police and then slips away in fear, leaving Armando to fend for himself as he tries to convince the officers that his ape did not actually speak. Although Armando does manage to get away from the crowd and is reunited with Caesar, he relates to him that he will turn himself over to the authorities to try and clear up the situation, and that they will meet at a certain point. *But*, in a worst-case scenario, if Armando does *not* show up, then Caesar's only hope for survival will be to merge himself into the city's ape population.

Much of young Caesar 2's view of the world was shaped by what he could see out of his window in *Rise of the Planet of the Apes*.

The Caesar of *POTA* 2 also brings his fate unto himself by his own actions. In his case, he's still living at Will's home when he witnesses, from the window of his attic bedroom, Charles (who had gained back his wherewithal thanks to ALZ-112, but has now slipped back into dementia) in an altercation with an overbearing neighbor, Douglas Hunsiker. Caesar comes to Charles' defense, pummeling the other man and biting off his finger, but as a result is, due to court order, sent to an ape sanctuary. There, for the first time, he must live among his own kind. And while this sanctuary may not represent the same magnitude of inhumanity as the slavery presented in *POTA* Prime, it quickly becomes apparent that most of the handlers there are cruel to the apes and are more than happy to accept payments to let Gen-Sys experiment on them, thus turning them into the same sort of product as the slaves in *Conquest*.

This is the point at which both Caesars must adapt to their situations. For Caesar Prime, it means, as instructed by Armando, becoming part of ape society, passing himself off as a slave and being "employed" by Governor Breck, which affords him a closer look at the cruel ways in which most humans treat apes – the seeming sole exception being Breck's right-hand man, MacDonald. Initially, Caesar has no great plan as he attempts to figure out how to slip away and reunite with Armando. It's a similar situation with Caesar 2, who starts off in the sanctuary very peacefully (albeit frightened), attempting to take in this life that's so very different from the one he's used to while waiting to go home. But there are key events that drive both of them to change things up.

Caesar Prime is carrying out the menial duties assigned to him when he discovers that Armando has died while in custody, having thrown himself out a window in an effort to save Caesar rather than admit the truth about him. What follows for Caesar is actually seeded by an earlier moment when Breck comments to his team that if every ape who disobeyed an order were sent back to Ape Management for reconditioning, the place would be overrun in short order. There's a gleam in Caesar's eye even then which takes on greater meaning when, in coming to realize that there is strength in numbers, he starts triggering little acts of revolution in other apes for the purpose of forcing their reconditioning and, in turn, resulting in great numbers of apes amassing in Apes Management at the same time. Simultaneously, he begins meeting with other apes to get them to help him stockpile the tools of revolution, including guns, kerosene, knives, and more. Humanity has betrayed him, everything he's ever believed in, and his people, and the time to strike back is coming.

Caesar 2 also experiences a sense of betrayal, though in this case it comes from Will, who visits him at the sanctuary for what Caesar believes will be the long-awaited opportunity to return home. He quickly finds that this is *not* the case. Once Will has gone, a devastated Caesar throws himself against the wall of his cage and immediately starts wiping away an image he had drawn on the wall of the window from which he used to look out into the world from his room at home. It is at *this* moment that he truly accepts his fate, when he decides to go from victim to victor and refuses to let *anything* stand in his way.

His approach in taking command is to first show all of the other apes that *he* is the alpha. To do so, he befriends the gorilla, Buck[7], by waiting until the humans are gone for the night, and then freeing him from his cage and allowing him to roam around in the sanctuary's main pen in a way he's never been allowed to before. With Buck on his side, Caesar 2 takes down the sanctuary's current ape leader, Rocket[8]. In many ways, this is a start of the revolution and allows Caesar 2 to gain numbers. But whereas Caesar Prime seems to have some sort of telepathic connection – at one point, he compares himself to an Emperor Moth, "which can communicate with another over a distance of 80 miles" – Caesar 2 begins by revealing himself to be more evolved than the others, and then using ALZ-113 (a more virulent form of the retrovirus, which he has stolen from Will's house after sneaking out of the sanctuary) to increase their intelligence.

There actually comes a moment in both universes when the tide of seeming inevitable revolution *could* have been stemmed – when the Caesars could have been stopped in their tracks and humanity, in turn, would have been spared. In *POTA* Prime, it comes after Governor Breck has been told that Caesar is, indeed, the child of Cornelius and Zira, and that Breck's greatest fear has come to pass. In the meantime, MacDonald, who has shown compassion for the apes all along, is the one person to whom Caesar *does* reveal himself (prior to his being forced, via electric shock torture, to speak for Breck). As a stunned MacDonald stands before him, Caesar pretty much details *exactly* what he's planning, adding that the only course left to his people is revolution. While MacDonald claims this is an effort doomed to failure, Caesar emphasizes that if so, then there will be a second attempt and, if necessary, a third.

The conversation is interrupted by the sound of arriving police. After an instant's hesitation – a *crucial* instant – MacDonald makes the decision to let Caesar go. Not long afterwards, the ape is captured and MacDonald holds humanity's fate in his hands a *second* time when he manipulates the shock table's power so it only *seems* like Caesar has been electrocuted after he has spoken (Breck having shown a modicum of compassion rather than torturing

---

[7] Named after Buck Kartalian, who portrayed gorillas in *Planet of the Apes* and *Conquest of the Planet of the Apes*

[8] Named after *Planet of the Apes* set designer Norman Rockett

him further). When it's only the technician left in the area, Caesar silently arises from the table, kills the man, and sets off on his threatened revolution.

Caesar 2, likewise, could have been stopped, but wasn't. There is one pivotal scene when the apes have all been cognitively awakened in the sanctuary (which has begun to happen at Gen-Sys as well, through Jacobs' insisted-upon experimentation). When the abusive worker Dodge Landon[9] confronts him with an electric prod, it is at this moment that Caesar decides to strike back, quickly getting the upper hand on Landon as the other apes watch. And it is during this confrontation that he speaks his first word: "No!" (then chillingly repeats it over and over again). During all of this, the much kinder Rodney has taken position from above, armed with a tranquilizer rifle that we'd seen him use on Caesar and Rocket during an earlier confrontation. In shock over what he's seeing transpire, he never takes the shot, thus allowing Caesar 2 the opportunity to continue and paving the way for all that follows.

There are two significant moments in these sequences. First, the apes turn their anger toward Rodney and start to assault him, but Caesar 2 stops them and gently escorts him into a cage for his own protection. It's a moment mirroring *Conquest*, when apes attempt to attack MacDonald but Caesar Prime stops them from doing so. More importantly for Caesar 2, when Landon makes a move a few minutes later, Caesar ends up killing him – the first human that he has slain – and we see the emotional toll this instantly takes on him. Obviously, there is no blood lust in him; he is just determined to do what he needs to.

Caesar 2 leads all of the apes – and there are a lot of them – out of the sanctuary. Their first step is to infiltrate the city, where they invade Gen-Sys, freeing all of the apes who have been experimented on there. These include the scarred Koba (who does not look like there's a genial bone in his bonobo body) and Cornelia[10], a female ape who had been removed from the sanctuary for experimentation, which has a profound impact on Caesar 2 (though since most of her scenes were left on the cutting-room floor, the audience has no idea why). After freeing numerous apes from the San Diego Zoo, they confront police in the city, which gradually leads to the Golden Gate Bridge and a tense standoff and subsequent battle, which sees the apes fleeing into the Muir Woods redwood forest.

---

[9] Named, of course, after two of Taylor's shipmates in the 1968 film
[10] Named in homage to Caesar Prime's father and son, both called Cornelius

Before they do so, there is an interesting moment when Jacobs, the man behind Gen-Sys, is dangling from the edge of the bridge in a downed police helicopter (on which he had previously pointed out the "leader," Caesar, to sharpshooters). He actually reaches out to the chimp for help, but Caesar refuses to give it. The temptation is to kill this man, but his moral conscience won't allow him to. Of course, he has no problem with that task falling to Koba, who is more than happy to give the copter enough of a kick to send it down to the water below.

Caesar Prime had to mask his abilities, often behind a chain leash – not unlike the one worn by Caesar 2.

The mirrors to *Conquest* are all there. In *POTA* Prime, Caesar (whose parents initially lived in a zoo after traveling through time in *Escape*) bands together with various apes in the city and marches toward Ape Management. They're confronted by an armed militia, whom they ambush on a foot bridge. Next, armed with even more weapons, they attack Ape Management, where the apes within are *already* beginning to get jumpy and aggressive, their instinct telling that that *something* is happening. By the time Caesar Prime and the other apes arrive, things are ready to explode – and they pretty much do, as the apes take over amidst much bloodshed.

A distinct difference between this and the events in *POTA* 2 is that, with the exception of MacDonald, there is *no* hesitation on Caesar's part. The apes kill the human handlers without remorse (especially in the uncut version of *Conquest*) and Caesar does nothing to stop it.[11] Indeed, his rage is so deep that he himself comes *this* close to killing Breck when told just why the man hates apes as much as he does (humans hating apes is like hating the dark side of themselves, the governor explains), but he restrains himself. Barely. Mostly so that Breck will live long enough to see what's unfolding.

And what *is* unfolding is presumably indicative of what is happening around the world as apes, after years of abuse and tightly contained resentment, are finally allowing those feelings to rupture onto the surface. We see a city in flames, apes in control, and humans on the receiving end of their fury. We also see, in Caesar Prime (and this is almost the exact opposite of Caesar 2), a ruthless leader of the revolution who clearly embraces all that his actions have wrought. In an impassioned speech, he lays out the situation exactly as it is, stating that from this day forward, apes will rule supreme and humans will be *their* servants... *if* they're lucky enough to survive. If you go with the film's original ending, before it received a re-edited, more hopeful conclusion, there is *nothing* conciliatory about Caesar. Even MacDonald kneels before the angry mob. This is an Emperor Ape who has ascended above humans and makes it clear that neither he nor any other ape will be subservient again.

(Of course, the theatrical ending has Caesar offering something of an olive branch – that humans will be treated humanely – but that's the bullshit ending.

---

[11] The novelization of *Conquest* introduces an Ape Management employee named Morris, whom Caesar considers the least cruel of all handlers, and who is brutally beaten to death during the apes' raid on the complex. Caesar regrets that so kind a human would meet so horrible a death, but feels unable to prevent it.

After everything the character has been through, he would *not* be so quick to change his tone or mission. The change is summed up best by this: in the theatrical cut Breck lives, while in the original he is bludgeoned to death by armed gorillas who receive the go-ahead from Caesar.)

Caesar 2, conversely, has fought a violent battle with humans on the Golden Gate Bridge, and seems to have found solace in the Muir Woods. Even when Will shows up and offers to protect him if Caesar comes home, the ape looks at his followers, turns back to Will, brings him in close and, in the first words he's spoken to his "father," comments, "Caesar *is* home." It's a stunning moment for Will, and an uplifting one for the audience as Caesar – despite what it will ultimately mean for humans – has gone through the journey of a lifetime, from pet to surrogate son to leader. An unanswered question the more peaceful ending brings with it is this: what's to stop the police, or even the military, from entering the forest to take them out?

The other question pertaining to both Caesars is how their revolution microcosms will ultimately lead to the complete downfall of humanity. In *Conquest,* as noted above, we're left with the impression that Caesar's actions are having a telepathic domino effect, with revolution after revolution being staged around the world. In the case of *Rise*, the ALZ-113 retrovirus turns out to be deadly to humans – and extremely contagious. The first victim of this second vaccine is Franklin, who, before dying, infects Will's neighbor who lost a finger to Caesar. Hunsiker, who turns out to be an airline pilot in the movie's final scene, displays the first symptoms of the virus while about to board an airplane. What audiences are then shown, through an animated graphic over the closing credits, is that the pilot infects the passengers on his plane, who in turn spreads the infection to many others. In quick order, we see that the spread of that virus is having a global impact.

Sometime Later...

So what *is* the aftermath of revolution? You knock down a statue of Saddam Hussein and you think it's over? That you've won? Obviously, that's *not* the case. There has to be a plan... unless circumstances remove all sense of planning from your hands.

In the case of both *POTA* Prime and *POTA* 2, the scenario picks up years later, the former being represented by the fifth film in its series, *Battle for the Planet of the Apes,* the latter by the second film in *its* series, *Dawn of the Planet of the Apes*. What we learn is that in the case of *POTA* Prime, the war with the apes has led to an off-camera nuclear confrontation that has decimated much of the planet, wiping out (insofar as we can tell) the vast majority of human life. In *POTA* 2, the virus – now dubbed the Simian Flu – has done the job for the apes, killing most of mankind. The resulting societies, in both cases, serve as a reflection of their respective Caesars.

In *Battle*, we see that Caesar Prime has largely held on to his conciliatory tone from *Conquest*'s theatrical conclusion. There is no question that apes are in command and that surviving humans are subservient to them, but he has carried out his promise to treat them humanely, a philosophy echoed by other chimpanzees and the orangutans. The gorillas – led by the head of the military, General Aldo – are another story. Their hatred for humans runs deep, and it is only through Caesar's leadership, and the support of most of his people, that any notion of a coup on the gorillas' part is held at bay. Initially.

Caesar 2's simian society is markedly more idyllic – though the apes soon find themselves preparing for the inevitable war with humans.

Life has changed for Caesar Prime. He is married to the chimp Lisa (introduced in *Conquest*) and they're the parents of young teen Cornelius, a seemingly well-adjusted prince. We also learn that Breck and MacDonald are dead, but the latter's brother serves as one of Caesar's closest advisers. This, in itself, says *a lot* about Caesar Prime, most notably that he is not consumed with hatred for humans; that he recognizes the wisdom in *some* of them, and that he encourages their involvement in building this society and forging a common future... so long as they're following the simian lead. Also advising him is Virgil, a brilliant orangutan who is able to speak frankly with him in a way that few others would.

Apes and humans in Prime continuity live in what can best be described as tree houses (due to the film's low budget), and the system of government – with Caesar most assuredly at the top – is demonstrated by the Council, which is attended by all three ape species, but not humans.

In *POTA* 2, the circumstances are markedly different, but with several similarities. Caesar and his fellow apes – who communicate more through sign language than words – have found peace in the aftermath of their original break for freedom, and their population has grown a great deal in their tree-house village. This is a strictly apes-only culture, borne not out of some sort of anti-species bigotry (though one could easily see that being the case if circumstances were different), but because, as established early on in the film, there has been no sign of humans for the past two years. The virus has wiped them out, and out of those ashes has come peace.

The apes adore and revere Caesar 2, including his orangutan advisor Maurice,[12] a Virgil analog introduced in *Rise*. Even the most aggressive of the chimps, Koba, has become like a brother to Caesar, going so far as to save him from a bear early on in *Dawn*. This truly is an idyllic society, yet with all of that, there is an element of melancholy about Caesar, a sense of loss he still has for humanity, though whether that's limited to the Rodmans is unknown. From what we're able to surmise about Caesar, the loss of life – ape or man – is something that he always carries with him, and to have a species seemingly driven to extinction gives him *no* pleasure.

Caesar 2's mate is Cornelia, the character (very) briefly established in *Rise*, and they are the parents of a teenage son named Blue Eyes,[13] as well as the newly born Milo.[14] Whereas Cornelius, in *Battle*, is a well-adjusted prince with a close bond with his father, Blue Eyes comes across more as an obstinate teenager who chafes under Caesar's guidance and is extremely susceptible to outside influences. Their relationship seems tentative at best, much to his father's frustration. Caesar's primary driving force is maintaining the family –

---

[12] Named after actor Maurice Evans, who portrayed Zaius in the original films

[13] The nickname that Zira gives astronaut Bill Hudson in *Return to the Planet of the Apes*, providing a surprising film homage to the animated series

[14] A reference not only to *Escape*'s Doctor Milo, but also to Caesar Prime's original birth name

both immediate and extended – that he has built throughout the past decade. Nothing else seems to matter to him.

The contrast to Caesar Prime is that whereas in *Conquest* his focus is on freeing his people, in *Battle* it is decidedly on the future and his Pollyannaish view of a world that will live on for eternity now that apes are at the helm. Humans, as far as he sees it, should feel lucky he came along to save them from themselves. But it is actually MacDonald who wants him to recognize the full picture, to know the truth about Earth's destiny – a truth from which Armando apparently kept him insulated. To do so, they will have to go into the Forbidden City, the nuclear-mangled remains of Los Angeles. There, deep underground, are information archives which should have survived the blasts, within which lies information that Caesar will want to hear from the recorded mouths of his parents, Cornelius and Zira.

Finding such a possibility too tempting to ignore, Caesar agrees to travel into the city with MacDonald and Virgil. There, they do unearth the archives – still operational – through which his parents provide details of the future, most notably the fact that in the end, Earth will literally be destroyed in a war begun by ape aggression. It's a moment of disillusionment for Caesar; in some ways, it strikes him with a profound sense of failure, in that it is *his* people who will ultimately doom the world. As such, it's a heavy burden for him to carry, one that, by coming into conflict with what he has spent years believing, instills within him a determination to avoid that future if possible.

His hope is challenged when the trio find themselves subject to a hunt by humans in the city, scarred from radiation and led by Governor Kolp (one of Breck's associates from *Conquest*), who wants to capture them. Barely escaping, they make their way back home. As it turns out, Caesar's search for answers may have awakened a force that previously didn't know the apes had survived, starting them on the road to a more dismal possibility. Indeed, at one point, the audience sees humans handling the Alpha-Omega Bomb that will one day serve as the tool of the word's destruction, in *POTA* Prime's second entry, *Beneath the Planet of the Apes*.

That particular paradigm is flipped in *POTA 2,* as it's actually the humans who inadvertently come into contact with the apes by traveling from the human ruins to ape territory. It begins when a man named Carver encounters Blue Eyes and Rocket's son, Ash. Panicking, he shoots Ash, causing the apes to call out for help. Instantly, Carver and a fellow human, Malcolm[15], are surrounded by apes. Though stunned to see humans – and furious to learn that one of his own has been shot in this first encounter – Caesar demands that they leave, which they do, terrified.

What immediately becomes apparent is Caesar's internal struggle. On the one hand, he views this as an unfortunate series of events, but he's simultaneously under pressure – particularly from Koba – to deliver a message to the humans. That is precisely what he does, as he and hundreds of apes on horseback travel to the ruins of San Francisco, where surviving humans, all genetically immune to the virus, are living. Stunned to hear Caesar speak, the humans are told to stay in their territory and the apes will stay in their own. It's an impressive, though purposely non-violent, show of force.

What should have been the end of the situation is anything but. The humans are desperate. They are almost out of electrical power and need access to a hydroelectric dam in ape territory. While human leader Dreyfuss wants to use their armory to take what they need, Malcolm is adamant that he be allowed three days to convince Caesar to let them work on getting the dam operational again. Heading back, he is violently brought before Caesar, who, in the hope of greater peace, gives permission for Malcolm and his family – son Alexander and second wife Ellie – as well as Carver and a couple of others, to proceed, provided they hand over their guns. Koba is outraged by this, his seeds of discontent instantly obvious where humans are concerned.

Caesar's faith is frayed when Milo, playing around, inadvertently discovers Carver's hidden gun, and all hell breaks loose, with Caesar demanding that the humans leave. It is only after Ellie administers antibiotics to the ailing Cornelia (who fell ill following childbirth), that Caesar relents and allows them one more day to work on the dam – provided Carver be taken away from the area. This illustrates just how badly Caesar wants there to be trust between the species; despite evidence to the contrary, there is a possibility of peace between them. It's a characteristic that joins the two Caesars.

In both *POTA* Prime and *POTA 2,* we see the Caesars having to fight back against strong oppositional forces, with Aldo's and Koba's hatred for humans pushing against their leaders' hope for that peace. In the case of Caesar Prime,

---

[15] The first name of *Conquest*'s MacDonald – who serves the same function in *Conquest* as Malcom does in *Dawn* – according to Mr. Comics' *Revolution on the Planet of the Apes* miniseries

there is actually cause to Aldo's desire for a militant response. He tolerates humans in their community because Caesar has told him to, but the Forbidden City humans, he believes, threaten them all. And, indeed, they *are* mapping out an attack of ape territory, with Kolp hoping for a bit of comeuppance for what Caesar Prime had triggered years earlier.

From all appearances, Koba believes he's right as well: while Malcolm and the others are working on the dam, Koba and a pair of his followers go to the city, where they watch humans test-firing armaments, and he is stunned to see the size of their armory. When he reports this to Caesar, he's in a state of disbelief that the humans are still there, causing him to accuse Caesar of loving humans more than apes, and even more than his own sons.

Surrounded at that moment by his people, Caesar weighs out his response before essentially beating the hell out of Koba and nearly killing him, then releasing him at the last possible second and gasping, "Ape no kill ape." It's an important moment for him; with humans back in the picture, he recognizes Koba's instant hatred and the path down which it could lead them. It's as though he knows, on one level, that the greater good would be served without Koba, but he can't bring himself to cross that line, especially knowing Koba's history of abuse at humans' hands. To do so would be to violate the very notion of the apes as one family that he has been attempting to instill.

In the world of *POTA* Prime, gorilla dissent is what Caesar is forced to deal with, epitomized by the fact that when he holds a Council meeting following the experience in the Forbidden City, he invites several humans to attend, MacDonald among them, and Aldo leads his troops out in protest. It later becomes even more obvious that Aldo's hatred is not limited to humans, as he shares with his soldiers a plan to kill Caesar – a plan overheard by young Cornelius, who suffers injuries at the gorilla's hands that eventually lead to his death. Immobilized as he sits vigil at his dying son's bedside, Caesar is oblivious to the fact that Aldo is having humans locked in the corral as he assumes power. From there, the gorillas break into the armory to steal weapons and prepare for battle with the mutated humans. Following Cornelius's death, Virgil informs him of what's been happening and Caesar immediately confronts Aldo, though that confrontation is interrupted by an attack by the mutants, leading to the film's titular battle.

POTA 2 sees things take a decidedly different turn. The work on the dam is a success, and power is restored. It is possibly the most significant moment in Caesar's interactions with the humans as, with light ablaze at a nearby gas station and music blaring from its sound system, he moves over to Malcolm, then offers his hand and a single word: "Trust." The human returns the gesture, driving home the point that Caesar's faith has been justified.

Unfortunately, as was the case with Aldo, Koba is making moves against his king. To begin with, he and his followers kill several humans in San Francisco and take their weapons, then Koba murders Carver, whom the bonobo frames in death as an attempted assassin of Caesar. In actuality, during an evening celebration of the newly brokered peace, Koba sets the apes' homes ablaze and shoots Caesar, leaving him for dead and claiming it was the humans who did it. At Maurice's suggestion, Malcolm and his family run for safety.

There is a significant moment with Carver right before his death that plays into Caesar's philosophy of trust. Carver, one of the most bigoted humans we have met insofar as the apes are concerned, hears the music and is genuinely excited — not just because of what that restoration of electricity means to the human community, but because he recognizes that Caesar was *right*. For Carver, it's a truly transformative moment and a direct reflection of the kind of leader that Caesar is.

What follows, on a much grander scale than in *POTA* Prime, is a battle between the apes and the humans, as Koba quickly assumes power and leads an all-out attack on the humans in Caesar's name. The battle swiftly moves into the city, where Koba feeds his bloodlust, along the way seducing Blue Eyes with promises to avenge his father's death.

While the battle rages in the city, Malcolm, Ellie, and Alexander find the still living Caesar and nurse him back to health. Blue Eyes is eventually rejoined with Caesar, having been brought to Will Rodman's old house by Malcolm, and recognizes that Koba has lied to him — to everyone. After seeing the horrors unleashed by Koba, including the murder of Ash, Blue Eyes comes to realize that what he had viewed as a weakness in his father, where humans are concerned, is actually a source of strength.

In both universes, the films eventually culminate in one-on-one confrontations between the Caesars and their opponents. In *POTA* Prime, following the defeat of Kolp's forces, it occurs during the final sequence between Caesar and Aldo, the former having been pushed too far by the latter and realizing that Cornelius's death is a direct result of the gorilla's actions. Caesar stalks him up a tree where, while attempting to stab the chimp with a sword, Aldo falls to his death.

In *POTA* 2, the still-mending Caesar arrives in the city and sees the horror of what Koba has wrought, including the imprisonment of humans and apes who are loyal to Caesar. They, too, end up in battle, in this case on a partially constructed tower that the humans have rigged with explosives to fight back the apes. It's a savage battle, but one in which Caesar proves victorious – though he initially tries to prevent Koba from falling to his death after the latter throws Caesar's words back in his own face: "Ape no kill ape." But looking around at the dead and wounded apes around them while holding onto the flailing Koba's hand, Caesar decides, "You are not ape," and lets him go for the greater good.

In the end, both Caesars and their people face very different futures. With *POTA* Prime, after Aldo and the mutants have been defeated, Caesar orders the humans freed from the corral, but there is a general lack of gratitude. MacDonald tells him, "If you mean to free us, Caesar, then free us. We are not your children." He demands that they be equals, living together in peace and love. "Love?" Caesar mocks. "The human way is death," to which Virgil offers a simple question: "Aldo wasn't human... was he?" *Those* words, combined with everything Caesar learned in the city and from what he has endured, prove the most enlightening.

In response, a new beginning of simian and human co-existence emerges, and it's the path on which Caesar will lead them. Will it be successful? A hint of that answer comes some six hundred years later, when the orangutan Lawgiver is providing lessons to human and ape children, who sit side by side in an outdoor classroom-like setting. It is a markedly different vision of the Lawgiver than we've heard of earlier in the *POTA* Prime series, whose most famous words were "Beware the beast, Man...." It would seem that Caesar's leadership in that timeline has had the most profound effect possible, as he has quite literally altered the destiny of planet Earth and its people – whatever species they may represent.

Caesar 2, sadly, doesn't seem to have the same opportunity. As he relays to Blue Eyes, apes believe that they're better than humans, but they're more alike than they think. And in the end, despite the fact that Koba has been disposed of[16], the future of Caesar and his people in this timeline looks to be far grimmer.

---

[16] Or *has* he? In a post-credits sequence, an ape's screeching can be heard, indicating that Koba may have survived his fall (just as Aldo certainly should have,

Yes, the enemy is gone, but countless humans have been slaughtered and, making things even worse, as the ape army attacked the city, the humans managed to make contact with a military vessel and gave them their coordinates. Translation: a military response is coming.

Malcolm warns Caesar to flee or there will be war, but the chimp replies that war has already begun, started by the apes – and the humans will *not* forgive them. For a moment, both he and Malcolm had thought they had a chance to change the course of ape and human history, but now that chance has dissipated, to be replaced by an unknown future.

Two Caesars and two timelines, joined by a common approach to leadership with visions of a greater tomorrow for their people. The circumstances of each may vary, as do the results of those ambitions, but in the end, they represent two of the genre's most significant heroes, each charting the destiny of the planet of the apes.

given the very short distance he falls in *Battle for the Planet of the Apes*). As of press time, it is unknown whether Koba will return in *War for the Planet of the Apes*.

Dawn of the Rising War

by Joseph F. Berenato

War is coming.

Barring any unforeseen delays or extinction-level events, 14 July 2017 will see the release of *War for the Planet of the Apes*, the third film of the new saga and the eighth[1] *Apes* film overall.

Like the previous two – *Rise of the Planet of the Apes* and *Dawn of the Planet of the Apes* – *War* does not *necessarily* tie in with the original pentalogy,[2] but instead follows a brand-new timeline.[3]

There is no virus that wipes out cats and dogs (though there *is* a virus, of course). Apekind is not domesticated and used as house servants, though it *is* used. And there are no time-travelling Ape-o-nauts serving as portents of a future in which mankind is doomed to fall from nuclear annihilation... though annihilation does loom on the horizon.

At least, that's as much as we know from the trailer for *War*.

---

[1] Yeah, I said eighth. I don't care what Rich Handley says; *that* film doesn't count.

[2] More on that later

[3] Which also ignores the film by Tim Burton, lending further credence to my belief that it is nothing more than a mass hallucination, like *Batman and Robin* or *Star Trek Into Darkness*. LALALA THEY DON'T EXIST LALALA

"I Did Not Start This War..."

In the upcoming third installment, humankind and apekind are in all-out war for survival and, presumably, mastery of the planet. Talking apes fight hairless apes. Gorillas fight guerillas.

But how did it get to that point?

In the original pentalogy, apes revolted because of the way that humans were treating them, starting with Aldo,[4] the first ape to say "no." Change the name from Aldo to Caesar, and that's more or less exactly what happens in the current trilogy.

Rise of the Planet of the Apes tells the story of Caesar (Andy Serkis), a young chimpanzee born of a mother who had been treated with ALZ-112, a neurological reparative drug designed as a cure for Alzheimer's. The architect of that drug, Will Rodman (James Franco), designed ALZ-112 in the hopes of helping his father, Charles (Jon Lithgow). An unintended side-effect, however, was that it granted young Caesar incredible intelligence, creating a being more capable of complex thought and emotion than any of his ape brethren (or any humans his age, for that matter).

One of those emotions, unfortunately, is anger. When Caesar sees a neighbor, Douglas Hunsiker, get into an argument with Charles, the chimpanzee leaps to the rescue and attacks said neighbor. That, even more unfortunately, leads to Caesar's incarceration in an ape preserve, where cruel caretakers mistreat apes on the regular.

This galvanizes Caesar once again to leap to the rescue, but in a different way – he escapes one night to steal the latest version of the drug, ALZ-113, from Will's house to use on his fellow apes at the preserve. These smarter apes then all break out and head to Gen-Sys Laboratories, the pharmaceutical giant responsible for the drug's production and home to a bevy of other incarcerated apes.

All apes now freed, they head over the Golden Gate Bridge and land in Muir Woods National Monument, there to live out the rest of their days in peace and harmony.

Okay, not really.

---

[4] At least, according to Cornelius and Zira. The first ape to say "no" was actually Lisa.

Without the encumberance of humanity, ape society has been allowed to flourish.

An unintended side-effect of ALZ-113[5] is that, unfortunately, the virus it uses to spread through the system is fatal to humans. The end of the film shows the trail of the virus – which will come to be known as Simian Flu – over the face of the planet, implying that it will lead to humanity's extinction.

Fast-forward ten years or so to the start of *Dawn of the Planet of the Apes*. Apekind has been living as a community of equals under the benevolent rule of Caesar. Man has not been seen for at least ten winters, until a group show up in the forest and are chased out... after shooting an ape child.

As it happens, there is an entire society of human survivors living in San Francisco, and they've made their way into ape country in the hopes of firing up an old hydroelectric dam. Caesar agrees to let them proceed with their work, which foments dissention in the ranks – chiefly with Koba (Toby Kebbell), Caesar's right-hand bonobo. A power struggle follows, and, in the ensuing chaos, apes attack the human settlement, setting the stage for the next installment in the saga.[6]

---

[5] Will Rodman's work has a lot of unintended side-effects, it seems. He probably should have been fired years ago.

[6] Yes, of course this is all a gross over-simplification of the first two films, but it is (hopefully) enough to pique your interest and get you to sit down and watch them.

"I Offered You Peace. I Showed You Mercy."

Caesar, much like his counterpart in the original pentalogy,[7] does not seek out war with humans after the initial conflict more than a decade prior. Even then, that was not an attack on all of humankind, but instead on those who had directly wronged the apes in his newfound family. Caesar worked with the humans because he understood their work and the necessity thereof, and continued to let them into ape territory even after the shooting. He believed that the humans have just as much of a right to exist as the apes, so long as one does not infringe on the other.

The humans, on the other hand, don't see things quite the same. They view the apes' existence as a threat to their sovereign dominion over the planet… which isn't all that dissimilar a view to the one that landed them there in the first place.

"All of Human History Has Led to this Moment."

Humanity's treatment of apes, good-intentioned or otherwise, is essentially what led to their near-extinction. Never mind that various species of monkey and ape have entered their own stone age, perhaps as far back as 4,300 years ago.[8] Never mind that some apes have learned how to communicate in sign language, and exhibit IQs near 90 (with the average human score being 100)[9] – even without the help of ALZ-113.

From trapping them and taking them out of their homes to placing them in circuses or zoos or conducting medical experiments on them, humans have regularly used apes to suit their own ends. This issue was touched upon, of course, in the original pentalogy – with humankind being the subject of exploitation and experimentation in the first film, and apekind the subject in subsequent installments – but it lies at the center of *Rise* and, to a slightly lesser extent, *Dawn of the Planet of the Apes*.[10]

All of this is true in the *Planet of the Apes* universe, and all of it is true in ours, as well, with the motion picture industry being no exception. Apes have been used in films for decades, alongside the likes of Clint Eastwood and Ronald Reagan, mostly in the role of comic sidekick. This has not, however, been the

---

[7] See the essay immediately preceding this one for more on that.
[8] Barras, Colin. "Chimpanzees and monkeys have entered the Stone Age." BBC.com/Earth. 18 August 2015.
[9] Weyman, Erin. "Six Talking Apes." Smithsonian.com. 11 August 2011.
[10] More on that later, too.

norm with ape-based films of any kind,[11] and the most recent *Planet of the Apes* films made it a point not to use an actual ape anywhere in the filming – not even in the background.

"The Irony Is We Created You."

While John Chambers's makeup work for the original *Planet of the Apes* film is legendary – and was aped quite nicely by Rick Baker for the 2001 redux[12] – *Rise of the Planet of the Apes* (and its subsequent sequels) went in a different direction entirely. Off the table immediately was the possibility of using actual animals in the film, and with good reason. At a panel for the film at the 2011 San Diego Comic Con International, director Rupert Wyatt addressed that exact issue. Said Wyatt, "We wanted to tell our story without using live apes for any number of reasons. It would be a cruel irony to tell the story of the exploited and repressed and use live apes to do so."[13]

Given the nature of the story – actual apes fresh from the jungle, laboratory, or preserve – the use of humans in ape makeup also seemed counter-intuitive. That left only one viable alternative: computer-generated imagery (CGI). For that, Wyatt turned to the folks at Weta Workshop, which gained prominence with *Avatar*, the *Lord of the Rings* trilogy, and, perhaps most applicable here, 2005's *King Kong*. Both of those last two have one thing in common: Andy Serkis, who portrays Caesar in the current films.

Serkis is hailed as the king of motion-capture animation because of his work in those projects (as well as his subsequent work in *The Hobbit: An Unexpected Journey, Star Wars: Episode VII – The Force Awakens*, and the modern *Apes* films). In particular, his portrayal of Gollum/Smeagol in the *Lords of the Rings* films garnered so much attention that critics began to discuss whether such motion-capture work makes one eligible for an Academy Award (the actor isn't *technically* on screen, but the work and facial expressions are unique to said actor).[14] Given this background – both the previous work with Weta and the acting chops to go along with it – Serkis was a natural choice for Caesar.

---

[11] Bellotto, Adam. "Makin' Monkeys: The Evolution of Primate Special Effects." Filmschoolrejects.com. 10 July 2014.

[12] LALALA IT'S NOT REAL LALALA

[13] Evry, Max. "PETA Actually Likes *Rise of the Planet of the Apes*." MTV.com. 4 August 2011.

[14] Poole, Oliver. "Can Gollum get the precious Oscar nod?" *The Telegraph*. 10 February 2003.

Andy Serkis's transformation into Caesar is nothing short of cinematic sorcery, thanks to the innovative work of Weta Workshop.

Weta's previous work with *King Kong* and *Avatar* made them no stranger to creating believable animal fur and complex facial expressions, but *Rise* presented all new challenges. "This is the first live-action film that has its main character as a thoughtful, feeling, self-aware animal," Wyatt said in a 2011 featurette.[15]

Given Caesar's prominence in the film — as well as that of his CGI simian cohorts — the special effects department had to make sure that the titular apes were believable. The same featurette included interviews with various members of Weta's staff, who weighed in on the process.

In addition to correct skeletal structure and physiology, other considerations were taken into account. "The creatures really do have the correct anatomical layers. They have muscles and fat and skin, [to] make them as realistic as possible," said Simon Clutterbuck, Weta's creature supervisor.[16]

---

[15] Billington, Alex. "Watch: Incredible Weta Featurette for *Rise of the Planet of the Apes*." <u>FirstShowing.Net</u>. 3 August 2011.

[16] Ibid

Additionally, Gino Acevedo, Weta's texture/creature art director, noted, "We had to put in all the very fine wrinkles in all the characters."[17] This helped to ensure that close-ups of the characters yielded believable-looking flesh, be it on the hands, on the face, or around the eyes.

Weta's lead texture artist, Kevin Norris, described how it all took shape. "At the same time, the model department [are] doing the groom, laying out the fur, and handing that off to shaders as well," he said, "so that they can apply hair that then goes to the shots department, where everything comes together."[18] Tack on ape-movement training classes, and the end result is a host of living, breathing chimpanzees, orangutans, gorillas, and bonobo with a chip on his shoulder, each one as realistic and believable as their non-CGI human co-stars.

And not a single, actual ape was used, anywhere.

This attention to detail, and the commitment not only to *not* use apes but also to show that the overall effect can be even more believable without them, earned praise for *Rise of the Planet of the Apes* from a number of circles. In 2011, People for the Ethical Treatment of Animals (PETA) awarded *Rise* the Proggy Award for the Most-Animal Friendly Feature Film. Said Lisa Lange, PETA's senior vice president:

> *Rise of the Planet of the Apes* reminds viewers that animals are feeling beings who deserve compassion, and its stunning use of CGI shows that there's no need to subject apes to the stress of filmmaking. Rupert Wyatt's methods back up PETA's message that apes should be protected and respected.[19]

This is one of the central themes of the recent films, and they show us precisely what happens when humanity does precisely the opposite.

"Nature Has Been Punishing Us Ever Since."

Animal experimentation, and the ethical quandaries it brings, has been a central theme of the entire *Planet of the Apes* franchise, dating all the way back to the novel that started it all: Pierre Boulle's 1963 novel *La Planète de Singes*. There, astronaut Ulysse Mérou is shown various experimentation procedures performed by apes on humans because of the similarities in physiology between humans and their simian counterparts.

---

[17] Ibid

[18] Ibid

[19] Evry. "PETA Actually Likes…"

The scene is much for the same for George Taylor (Charlton Heston) in 1968's *Planet of the Apes* film, when he sees the aftermath of a lobotomy performed on his shipmate Landon.

These scenes, along with their clinical coolness, are designed to evoke horror in the audience, and they do. Look at the savage apes, operating under the guise of science, committing terrible acts on intelligent beings. What manner of evil beasts are these, who claim to be civilized but allow such monstrosities?

Humans, of course, in a subversively obviously allegorical kind of way.

The third film – *Escape from the Planet of the Apes* – saw humans for the first time cast in the same light, as their treatment of Cornelius and Zira wasn't dissimilar to the way apes treated humans previously. The fourth – *Conquest of the Planet of the Apes* – saw humans treating apes every bit as savagely as apes would one day treat their once-oppressors.

If these were ancillary themes in the original pentalogy, the current soon-to-be-trilogy has shifted them front and center.

From the very start of *Rise of the Planet of the Apes*, we see chimpanzees taken out of the wild and delivered to a laboratory for testing. We don't know exactly what kind of tests they undergo, except for Bright Eyes, who was the recipient of ALZ-112. Later in the film, we meet Koba for the first time, and we know immediately that this isn't his first time in a laboratory. It's never exactly described in the movie precisely what kind of experimentation he underwent (though we do learn in *Dawn of the Planet of the Apes* that he spent most of his life in a laboratory[20]), but given the scarring on his body and his attitude toward humans, it was clearly enough to make him go bananas.[21]

It is specifically Will Rodman's work that will be the undoing of humanity, though he rides on the shoulders of all those who came before him. Yes, his work created a super-intelligent civilization of apes. Yes, his work created a super-virus with a mortality rate of close to 100 percent, which has brought mankind to the brink of extinction. He did eventually start to recommend scientific caution – after unethically injecting an experimental drug into his own

---

[20] *Dawn of the Planet of the Apes: Firestorm*, by Greg Keyes, reveals what Koba endured, and it isn't pretty. Those who have read that novel have no trouble understanding the bonobo's hostility toward humanity.

[21] I'm sorry. I'm so sorry.

father and keeping a genius chimpanzee secret for years – but it was too little, too late.[22]

One thing that Will didn't take into account was how the ALZ-113 virus might react in humans versus in chimps. Just because there were no illness side effects in apes did not and should not have meant that it would be safe for humans. But Will Rodman, of course, isn't the only researcher guilty of this. While the audience can look at Will's folly and wonder how he could have made such a glaring oversight, the truth is that it was used in the film to mirror actual research.

"Macaques are infected with HIV and AIDS – regardless of primates' inability to develop HIV," said Humane Research Australia chief executive Helen Marston. In praise of *Dawn*, the group observed that "drugs react differently in humans than they do in other animals… yet primates are still used for research into human ailments."[23]

Without a 100 percent match in physiology in genetic make-up, there's no way to predict with absolute certainty how a drug or virus will react in different species. While science has yet to breed an extinction-level virus in our world, for the humans in *Rise* and *Dawn*, it's too late.

This fear of such a virus, of course, makes these films all the more topical. What resonated with audiences in 1968 was the now-famous ending, wherein we learned that it was Earth all along, and humanity had somehow destroyed itself in a nuclear holocaust. Fear of nuclear war is still present, naturally, but it isn't as much at the forefront of the collective consciousness as it was almost fifty years ago.

Novels like Stephen King's *The Stand*, films like *Outbreak*, and television shows like *The Walking Dead* all speak to an innate fear of that which we simply cannot combat – tiny microscopic germs. This fear isn't without historical precedent, either. The Black Death took 200 million lives in Europe and Asia.[24] The Flu Pandemic of 1918 infected a third of the planet and killed anywhere between 20 and 50 million people.[25] Avian influenza, Ebola, and Zika regularly strike fear into travellers.

---

[22] Literally any time *before* Franklin the lab guy was infected with the superflu would have been a better time.

[23] Quinn, Kari. "Humane Research Australia hails cruelty message in *Dawn of the Planet of the Apes*." *The Sydney Morning Herald*. 10 July 2014.

[24] "De-Coding the Black Death." BBC.com. 3 October 2001.

[25] "1918 Flu Pandemic." History.com.

It is only logical that filmmakers decided to take a similar track with the Simian Flu, tapping into more modern fears as to how society crumbles.

"This Is Our Last Stand."

Enter *War for the Planet of the Apes*.

Society has crumbled. Ape society has risen. Pockets of humanity, with a genetic immunity to Simian Flu, survive — besides the colony in San Francisco, there is another one to the north that is coming to aide them against the ape encroachment. Nuclear reactors have burned out or gone critical, which may or may not lead to the burial of the Statue of Liberty, and may or may not beget a race of subterranean mutants. The *Icarus* — not coincidentally, also the name of the ship with Taylor, Landon, and Dodge in the 1968 film — is still presumed lost in space, and may well be on its way to the year 3978.[26]

Apes, under the vengeful guidance of Koba, have attacked the human settlement. Though Caesar was able to wrest control back, stop the skirmish, and dispose of the interloper, war is still coming, and it cannot be avoided.

And that's about as much as we knew, until the trailer for the latest film dropped on 9 December 2016... and we didn't learn much from that, either.

What is left of the U.S. Army, led by the Colonel (Woody Harrelson), has answered the distress call sent at the end of *Dawn* and is embroiled in conflict. About them, *War* director Matt Reeves said, "The troops he leads are a particularly hardened splinter unit called the Alpha Omega. That's a little reference to *Beneath the Planet of the Apes*. Alpha and Omega is the beginning and the end, and they feel that's what they represent for humanity."[27] (Keen-eyed viewers may recall that the Alpha-Omega Bomb from *Beneath* was also responsible for the complete destruction of the planet.)

---

[26] Like I said at the beginning, though these films don't *necessarily* follow the original timeline, they *do* drop enough hints to lead us to believe that the events of the 1968 film are at the inevitable end of this saga. Many online arguments — too numerous to cite here — posit that *these* films culminate there, and the arrival of Cornelius, Zira and Milo into the 20th century, the consequent birth of Caesar, and the apparent harmonious living between apes and man in *Battle for the Planet of the Apes* suggest a *new* timeline started by the arrival of the time-travelling Ape-o-nauts.

[27] Williams, Owen. "War For The Planet Of The Apes: exclusive trailer breakdown with director Matt Reeves." *Empire Online*. 9 December 2016. Any further referenced commentary from Reeves originates from this article.

If nothing else, *War* offers more apes on horseback, which is always a joy to watch.

They are in a bitter conflict with the apes, who have retreated into the woods, according to Reeves, to regain a sense of parity with the humans. Some apes, however – those previously loyal to Koba – have turned traitor and have allied themselves with mankind. Things may not be all what they seem with the conflict, which leaves a mystery for Caesar to solve – as well as a war to win.

"This is part of the mystery," Reeves said, "where Caesar's revenge story becomes a grand detective story."

What that means is anyone's guess, of course.

"If We Lose..."

One of the most confusing aspects of the upcoming film – and, indeed, of its immediate predecessor *Dawn* – is that it's often difficult to know who to cheer for. The natural inclination, of course, is to root for Caesar, the main character. But to do so means that one is thus cheering for humans to lose, and consign them to the eventual fate as seen in the 1968 film.

Logically, of course, we as moviegoers know this is where it will end up. We *know* that the apes will win. We *know* that humanity is going to be subjugated. We know that humans must lose.

And so, as traitorous to our species as it may be, we cheer for the apes. We want Caesar to win. It's the only possible outcome.

"It Will Be a Planet of Apes."

It's right there in the title.

A Novel Approach to *Planet of the Apes*

by Steven J. Roby

It's a good memory, though I can't say for sure that it's an accurate one. But I think it happened like this...

I watched *Conquest of the Planet of the Apes* in a theater. It was the first *Apes* movie I saw. Still buzzing with the excitement of a 10-year-old fanboy, and waiting for Dad to pick us up, I went into a nearby bookstore and found the novelization of *Beneath the Planet of the Apes*. And that was that: I was hooked on *Planet of the Apes*, on screen and in print. During the next few years, I tracked down Pierre Boulle's original novel in a British paperback edition (under the unfortunate title *Monkey Planet*), as well as the novelizations of the other three *Apes* movies, the four books based on the TV series, the three books based on the animated TV series... and, eventually, books based on the more recent versions of the series. Even the Tim Burton version... though I have to admit the Burton tie-ins might still have been sitting on the shelf, unread, if the opportunity to write this article hadn't come up. (Gee, thanks, guys.)

A Bit About Novelizations

There have been movie and television novelizations and tie-ins just about as long as there have been movies and TV. Randall D. Larson's 1995 book *Films Into Books: An Analytical Bibliography of Film Novelizations, Movie, and TV Tie-ins* lists novelizations going as far back as *Metropolis* (1926) and *King Kong*

(1933). Even now, when you can own a copy of the movie and see it on your own big, high-definition screen whenever you want to, novelizations are still written and published. The cynical take is that they're just quickly churned-out merchandise to help promote a movie and make a few extra bucks – and that's probably true, sometimes. But a novel can do things movies can't. In the case of older films, books can present scenes that would have been impossible to realize before the age of computer-generated imagery (CGI). And they can do a better job of presenting the internal life and thoughts of the characters. For example, W.J. Stuart's novelization of *Forbidden Planet* breaks the story into chapters that present a single character's perspective.

But novelizations can be interesting for other reasons, too – sometimes, there are intriguing differences between the film and the novel. An author may be working from an early draft of the screenplay; scenes may have been dropped from the final cut of the movie; and the novelist may have the freedom to make changes to the story, whether to plug plot holes, add to the page count, or improve characterization. Isaac Asimov made significant changes in his take on *Fantastic Journey*. Ellis Weiner made *Howard the Duck* funny and entertaining. (No, really. I read the novel first, then saw the movie. I would have been better off just doing the first.) One of the Ellery Queen mystery novels was an adaptation of a Sherlock Holmes film that presented the movie's story as a book within a book: Ellery reads what is supposedly a lost manuscript by Watson, involving Jack the Ripper, and does his own follow-up investigation. Depending on the writer, the subject matter, and the licencing folks, there's a lot of interesting things that can be done in a novelization.

Meanwhile, in academia, novelizations are becoming an area of study. Adaptations have been a popular subject for some time, usually in terms of films and other media adapted from proper literary novels. But now scholars like Thomas Van Parys are building up a literature of novelization studies. For example, from his "The Study of Novelisation: A Typology and Secondary Bibliography" (2011):[1]

> Here I make a plea for more attention to novelisations, not to demand respectability for these novels *per se* (for bad writing is unfortunately the rule rather than the exception), but to show its significance and ubiquity as a cultural and literary practice.

---

[1] http://www.academia.edu/5655316/
The Study of Novelisation A Typology and Secondary Bibliography

More usefully, and less condescendingly, from the abstract of his 2011 Ph.D. thesis, titled "Read the Novel: Science-Fiction Film to Novelization":

> The third part presents close readings of four case studies [...] from three particular angles, namely fidelity, description and point of view.

Fidelity, description, and point of view are useful points to consider when evaluating novelizations. Differences between a film and its novelization are always interesting, because they provide a look at what could have been, whether because they're based on an earlier draft, or include deleted scenes, or because the author had the rare freedom to make a few changes. Description is an issue, since the author is translating a visual form into words. Some go to great effort to describe what's on the screen, including characters' appearances, settings, and so on; others take for granted that the reader already knows what James T. Kirk or Luke Skywalker looks like, and just get on with things.

As for point of view, novels are internal and often follow a particular character's perspective. How do you manage that when you're working with a film, which has the camera's freedom to cut from character to character, scene to scene? Stuart's *Forbidden Planet* shows a writer taking a carefully thought-out approach to the matter. But in many of the *Planet of the Apes* films, we're often following a single lead, like George Taylor or John Brent or Caesar or Leo Davidson. It's not as much of a challenge.

Deborah Allison, in a 2007 paper looking at Ron Goulart's novelization of *Capricorn One*, says:

> Novelisations can thus be seen to give rise to three main areas of interest. As historical documents they can be of use when considering a film's developmental process. They also provide alternative readings of the film script and may, by extension, help to enrich a viewer's retrospective relationship with the film itself. Thirdly, they offer an avenue for exploring the differing narrational forms and capabilities of the two media.[2]

I made those points above, but now I've got someone with a doctorate in film studies backing me up. Clearly, you're not wasting your time reading this. (Coincidentally, I've read Goulart's novelization but never got around to seeing the movie.)

The point of all this is that novelizations aren't – or, at least, don't have to be – just ephemeral bits of marketing that disappear when the movies fade from the screen. There are solid reasons for reading (and even enjoying) them.

---

[2] http://journal.media-culture.org.au/0705/07-allison.php

So, on to the *Planet of the Apes* novelizations. You're a *Planet of the Apes* fan – well, you're reading this – and you've seen all the movies. You may not have read the books. Some have been out of print for decades. Let's look at what you may have missed.

Conspiracy of the Planet of the Apes

There's no novelization of the first film, *Planet of the Apes*, because it was based on Pierre Boulle's novel. Still, when Francis Ford Coppola produced his film *Bram Stoker's Dracula*, in addition to Stoker's actual novel *Dracula* being reissued, the film was novelized as *Bram Stoker's Dracula* by Fred Saberhagen. Philip K. Dick was offered a sizable paycheck to novelize *Blade Runner* if he'd let his original novel, *Do Androids Dream of Electric Sheep*, go out of print. He declined, so another writer, Les Martin, was hired to adapt it as a young-adult novelization.

But the film *Planet of the Apes* is very different from the novel *La Planète des Singes*, and in 2011 we finally got something to put in the novelization slot. Sort of. Andrew E.C. Gaska's illustrated novel *Conspiracy of the Planet of the Apes*[3] is, essentially, a novelization of the scenes we didn't see. Instead of focusing on Charlton Heston's character, Taylor, the novel focuses on what happens to his fellow astronaut, John Landon, and also features a number of characters in Ape City and elsewhere.

Gaska's novel fills in a lot of the missing pieces of the story, not only showing what happened during the first film from other perspectives, but also putting pieces in place for *Beneath the Planet of the Apes* and *Escape from the Planet of the Apes*. It also spends a lot of time providing a backstory for Landon and the mission on which he and Taylor were sent.

Some problems will come to mind for anyone who knows the movies: we know (or assume) that Taylor is the only talking human the apes encounter, and Landon ends up lobotomized well before the end of the story. Gaska finds ways to work within those limitations. (Spoilers!) Landon interacts with apes who have secrets to keep already. When he speaks, they're not about to go public. But Gaska also throws in an unexpected complication. The telepathic bomb-worshipping mutants from *Beneath* have made contact with him.

---

[3] Published in 2011 by BLAM! Ventures and Archaia Publishing, and written in collaboration with Christian Berntsen, Erik Matthews, and Rich Handley

Andrew E.C. Gaska's illustrated novel fills in the blanks of the 1968 film, giving us scenes not witnessed on screen.

The mutants control the astronaut occasionally, using him as their eyes in Ape City, as they try to determine whether they're at risk of being attacked by the apes' armed forces. And they know that he'll be useless as a spy if his ability to talk is discovered, so they keep him from talking most of the time. It's a neat bit of plotting, and certainly less contrived than having two astronauts with injuries that conveniently keep them quiet.

Landon is partly kept under control through reveries, trips back into his past on Earth and during previous space missions. We get a number of flashbacks, some providing good and suspenseful stories in their own right. These flashbacks are consistent with the movies, right down to the chronology and the culture of Earth circa 1970. Not only that, Gaska writes as though the book were published back then, in a pulpy style that leads nicely into the next read. This is one to read whether you're interested in novelizations or not.

Beneath the Planet of the Apes

In later years, *Beneath the Planet of the Apes* became one of my favourite *Apes* movies, though it spends a lot of time replaying beats from the first film. But it was completely new territory when I read the novelization. *Conquest* was all I'd seen at that point.

Michael Avallone's *Beneath the Planet of the Apes*[4] was published by Bantam, making it the only one of the four original novelizations not published by the much smaller Award Books. Ironically, though Award is long gone and forgotten, the writers of their books are much better known today than the almost-forgotten Avallone. He may be remembered by many readers of this book, though – in addition to a lot of private-eye pulp, Avallone wrote tie-in novels based on *The Man from U.N.C.L.E.*, *Hawaii Five-O*, and other franchises. Under his own name and several pseudonyms, he's known to have written more than 200 novels.

Bill Pronzini profiles Avallone in his book *Gun in Cheek: A Study of "Alternative" Crime Fiction*,[5] a collection of so-bad-they're-great quotes from old pulp private-eye stories. He cites a series of "Noonisms," lines from Avallone's Ed Noon PI stories, and adds that there are Noonisms in all of Avallone's books. One of Pronzini's examples: "My stunned intellect, the one that found death in his own backyard with him standing only feet away, hard to

---

[4] Keith Laumer was first hired to novelize *Beneath*, according to Randall D. Larson's *Films into Books: An Analytical Bibliography of Film Novelizations, Movie and TV Tie-Ins*. When Laumer backed out, Avallone was offered the job.
[5] Coward, McCann & Geoghegan, 1982

swallow in a hurry, found the answer." You can find some similarly unique prose in *Beneath the Planet of the Apes*.

> It was terrifying.
>
> And he had no idea where Nova was. Or what they might have done to her. Whoever *They* were.
>
> *They!*
>
> In his torn-apart and beleaguered intellect, he was no longer able to make any judgments or solve any mental problems. His entire universe of consciousness and stable thinking was awry; he had lost all sense of rhythm, balance and common sense.
>
> He was only hurtingly aware of one great truth.
>
> He had fled from the mockery of the Great Apes into something perhaps twice as alien, a dozen times more hazardous. A hopeless morass of terror, horror and who knew what else?
>
> Meaning—he had jumped from the frying pan directly into the fire.
>
> As perhaps—Taylor had?
>
> It was too early to tell. Too early to tell anything.

The repetition, the use of lots of adjectives and adverbs, the sentence fragments, they all appear throughout the book. Not that I had any issues with the writing when I first read the novel, some forty-odd years ago. It's not dull, anyway.

Avallone sticks closely to the film, with some minor changes due to writing from the screenplay rather than the finished product. For example, the cell in which Brent and Taylor finally meet is described very differently from what's on screen, but what happens there is pretty much the same. If you've seen the final shooting draft available on the Internet (for example, at *Hunter's Planet of the Apes Archive*[6]), that's what you get in the novelization. There are a couple of "meanwhile, back at Ape City" short segments with Cornelius and Zira, in the last few chapters, but they don't add much at all. It's only my knowledge of the series that had me hoping Avallone might lead up to their escape, but he couldn't – he didn't know it was coming, after all.

Overall, it's a quick, pulpy read that stays extremely faithful to the final shooting draft and, consequently, to the film itself. If you read novelizations for what they add to the story, you won't be too happy with this one. But if you enjoy over-the-top pulpy writing and haven't encountered Avallone before, this could be the beginning of a beautiful literary friendship.

---

[6] http://pota.goatley.com/scripts.html

Escape From the Planet of the Apes

The series takes one step backward and three steps forward with its writers for the remaining 1970s novelizations. Going from a major paperback publisher to a small (and now long–defunct) organization like Award Books isn't exactly progress, but Award was able to find some good writers whose careers were taking off. For *Escape*, they got Jerry Pournelle, now a well-known science-fiction writer and, for quite a few years, an influential columnist in computer magazines. As Pournelle wrote on his Chaos Manor blog in 2012:

> Many years ago – early 1972 I think – I was asked to write the novelization of the film *Escape from the Planet of the Apes*. This was while we were writing *Mote in God's Eye* but before we sold it so I needed money to live on, and I was offered a couple of thousand dollars to do this as a work assignment – that is, my name would be on the book, but all rights to the novel were owned by the publisher. I did it in a couple of weeks – Alan Dean Foster who had done a number of film novelizations gave me some invaluable tips on how to do it – and shipped it off.[7]

Pournelle's and Larry Niven's *The Mote in God's Eye* went on to become a very popular sci-fi novel, nominated for the field's major awards, and Pournelle's career took off. As a result, his *Escape* novelization is basically a footnote in his career. But for something bashed out quickly for money, it's a good, solid read.

If you like novelizations that add a lot to the movie, introducing new characters or expanding on characters not fully explored on film, adding new scenes to provide more context and suspense, this is for you. Interestingly, Pournelle doesn't focus as much on Cornelius and Zira early on, but builds up a suspenseful military/political thriller framework. Much of the book is told from the perspective of military personnel, the President of the United States, and his scientific advisor, Doctor Hasslein (identified on-screen as Otto Hasslein but called Victor in the novel), who are concerned with the national security issues raised first by an unexpected spacecraft landing and then by the ramifications not only of intelligent, talking apes but the future from which they escaped. The sympathetic scientists Lewis Dixon and Stephanie "Stevie" Branton also get a lot more development. Certainly, there's some of that in the movie, but in the novel, the apes are almost supporting characters until the later chapters.

---

[7] http://www.jerrypournelle.com/chaosmanor/recovering-novelizations-and-a-billion-dollar-bond/

Pournelle builds more suspense around the revelations about the war that destroys the Earth, Zira's pregnancy, and other key events. He follows the film's storyline closely, but by expanding the role of a few characters and exploring their perspectives, he makes the story more effective. *Escape* has never been my favorite of the movies, but the novelization makes up for its weaknesses. And it probably doesn't need saying, but Pournelle's prose is much better – if also much more straightforward – than Avallone's. The novelization of *Escape* is a good, solid expansion of the film, and worth a read.

Conquest of the Planet of the Apes

Conquest was the first *Apes* movie I saw, and the first issue I found of Marvel's *Planet of the Apes* magazine contained part of its *Conquest* comic-book adaptation. (Apparently, there's a book about *Planet of the Apes* comics. Sounds interesting, doesn't it?)[8]

I enjoyed the two recent movies, *Rise of the Planet of the Apes* and *Dawn of the Planet of the Apes*, and I thought, as fun as the old movies were, they didn't have this kind of intensity. Well, it had been a few years since I had last watched *Conquest*. Like a repo man's life, *Conquest* is always intense.

As with Pournelle, John Jakes was at a pivotal point in his writing career when the chance came along to do this novelization. He'd been writing fantasy and science-fiction stories and novels throughout the years, but could have been headed for relative obscurity like Avallone. Jakes was probably best known, at least among genre fans, for his Conan-like Brak the Barbarian tales and his comedic take on sword and sorcery, *Mention My Name in Atlantis*. But less than a year after *Conquest* was released, Jakes was the bestselling writer of the historical fiction series *The Kent Family Chronicles*, followed by a number of other hits. By 1978, instead of adapting movies to book form, he saw his books being filmed for television.

So I truly wish that Jakes' novelization could have been a bit better. Instead of Pournelle's clear and flowing prose, echoes of Avallone's pulpiness appear occasionally. Fortunately, the clunkier bits appear early on and the book eventually picks up.

---

[8] Handley, Rich, and Berenato, Joseph F. *The Sacred Scrolls: Comics on the Planet of the Apes* (Sequart, 2015): http://sequart.org/books/41/the-sacred-scrolls-comics-on-the-planet-of-the-apes/.

Like the other writers, Jakes was working with the screenplay, not the finished film. In this case, that makes the book more interesting. There were some changes made along the way, as can be seen in the unrated version of *Conquest* now available on Blu-ray. The book follows the grimmer, bloodier path taken by the screenplay and the unrated version. Jakes starts with the script's opening (not found in either version of the film), in which guards chase and kill a rogue ape who turns out to have been viciously abused. The story doesn't lighten up from there.

You can get everything you need from *Beneath* by seeing the movie, and everything you need from *Escape* by reading the novelization. For *Conquest*, I'd suggest both. Jakes includes a lot of scenes that should have made it into the film. We see much more of Armando's interrogation in the book, which helps make more sense of his final scene and gives a bit more characterization to Governor Breck and his staff. More importantly, we see more of Caesar's planning and setup for the revolution, which comes too quickly in the movie.

What the movie does is visually pound home the story's brutality. The uprising is suspenseful, violent, and appalling. Jakes does his best to capture it in prose, but it really needs to be seen to be fully experienced. Even though the theatrical version has a toned-down ending, it's still pretty bleak. Like many solid novelizations, Jakes's *Conquest of the Planet of the Apes* fills in the story's gap, adds little bits of backstory beyond those in the screenplay (like Armando's memories of the bookstore owner), and makes you want to see the movie. It's 95 cents well spent.

Battle for the Planet of the Apes

The last of the original *Apes* films rounds out the circle, showing the beginning of what would become the Ape City of *Planet of the Apes* and the Forbidden Zone of *Beneath the Planet of the Apes*. It tries to find a little hope after *Conquest*, but it still has its share of violence and death. It just... feels a bit more cartoonish and, for me, at least, a lot less suspenseful. It's not aided by what seems to be a low budget. Fortunately, novelizations don't have to worry about budgets.

David Gerrold was in the early phase of what has been a long and successful career in science fiction. He started out by selling the classic "The Trouble With Tribbles" to *Star Trek*, and not long before he novelized *Battle*, he'd published two classic nonfiction books about *Star Trek*. Gerrold discussed his journey into the world of the apes in his *Starlog* column in 1977[9]. Award Books shared an office building with the science-fiction magazine *Galaxy*, and Award asked them for help in finding another writer to pen the latest novelization. Gerrold's name came up and he was interested in the job, with one proviso: that he could be an ape in the movie. Gerrold's article says nothing more about the novelization, but goes into detail about his part as a dead chimpanzee during the battle sequence.

Battle sometimes feels like a tug-of-war between another *Conquest*-style story of brutality and a more kid-friendly story of hope and youngsters and goofy mutants and big, dumb gorillas. The book retains a bit of that feel. On the one hand, Gerrold hews closely to the screenplay, which contains a number of elements that didn't make it to the final film, and which would have made it darker yet: the inclusion of the Alpha-Omega Bomb from *Beneath*, confirming that Kolp's people are the ancestors of the people of the Forbidden Zone; a sequence in which Kolp corners Caesar with a flamethrower, taunting and wounding him; and a much bloodier end to the mutant invasion, with almost every mutant invader hunted down and killed by the gorillas. There's also a romantic, if slightly creepy, subplot for Kolp with his aide, Alma.

Gerrold's style in this one sometimes reads like it was aimed at younger readers. That may have been by editorial mandate; the book is also noticeably shorter than the two previous books. When Gerrold writes from Aldo's perspective early on, he's being faithful to Aldo's less-than-stellar thinking abilities, but still, this is a lot of exclamation marks:

> "Aaargh!" he snarled. He hated the school! He hated writing! It was a useless waste of time—it was an occupation fit only for men! And for the weaker apes, chimpanzees and orangutans! "Effete intellectuals," he fumed; they weren't much better than humans!

Kicking off Kolp's invasion, Gerrold starts a paragraph with the words "Explosion of action!" So... letting his prose draw a bit of attention to itself, certainly more than Pournelle did, though with more deliberation and control than Avallone.

And so ends the original era of *Planet of the Apes* movie novelizations. One interesting trend, particularly in the last two, is that the literary versions are darker. The films of *Conquest* and *Battle* ended up with changes to make their endings less bleak, less grimly violent, but those endings remain in the books.

---

[9] Gerrold, David. "State of the Art." *Starlog* #7 (August 1977): http://pota.goatley.com/misc/starlog-june-1977-gerrold.pdf.

There would be seven TV novelizations published during the next few years, as discussed elsewhere in this volume,[10] but that was the end of the movies. For that millennium, at least.

Planet of the Apes (2001)

Back in the early 1970s, when I was reading the above novelizations for the first time, I was also discovering *2001: A Space Odyssey*. We went to see it at the drive-in a few years earlier, but my dad was so bored that we drove right back out. I remember calculating that I would turn the impossibly old age of 38 in that far-off, futuristic year.

And it came to pass that the future arrived and I reached that ancient age of 38... and I had a new *Planet of the Apes* movie to see. I saw it during its theatrical run and didn't watch it again until very recently. It turns out, except for the last five minutes or so, it's not that bad a movie. Most of my antipathy comes from the ending. Tim Burton made no effort to be consistent at all with the previous movies, but they weren't particularly faithful to Pierre Boulle's original novel. So why not go for a drastic reboot? Why not give the audience something it hadn't seen already?

For the most part, despite a few too many inside jokes and references, that's what it does. It relies much too heavily on coincidence, Helena Bonham Carter's character perceives some special intelligence in Mark Wahlberg's character that I never saw, some relationships are only very thinly sketched out, and the tone lurches from serious to comedic and back again. But there are several good actors in the cast; the sets, design, makeup, and costuming are all quite good; and the story moves at a decent pace.

Then there's that ending. The twist at the end of the original movie is meant to blow your mind, but also to snap everything into a new focus. Suddenly, you see the whole picture. Burton's twist explains nothing, arises logically from nothing – it just induces a massive "WTF?" reaction.

So there's one good thing about the novelization: it doesn't have that twist ending. The book's author, William T. Quick, said in a 2002 interview in *Simian Scrolls* issue #5[11] that Burton kept things close to his vest while making the film, and that Quick didn't get that scene in the screenplay from which he worked. He said he added that scene to the manuscript for a second edition that never

---

[10] See the essays by John Roche and Zaki Hasan.
[11] http://pota.goatley.com/cgi-bin/pdfview.pl?uri=scrolls/simianscrolls_05.pdf

saw print. John Whitman's novelization for young readers also failed to include the surprise ending, as did Dark Horse Comics' adaptation.[12]

Quick was a reasonably well established science-fiction writer when Harper Collins hired him to novelize the movie. He has a mix of books under his own name, as well as ghostwritten works, and currently writes a political blog called Daily Pundit.[13]

To be honest, my expectations were low (based on memories of my first time seeing the film), and they were lowered further by my first exposure to Quick's text. From page 1:

> A blizzard of stars rushed in, vast beyond comprehension, pouring from the cup of time into the eye of eternity.

That is a remarkable mix of nested metaphors. Pouring a blizzard (of stars) from a cup (of time) into an eye (of eternity)? Quick uses a lot of metaphors and similes throughout the book, but rarely as strained as this one. Then there's the last paragraph on page 1:

> Across the buttons... a long, hairy finger! Tap. Tap-tap. Tappity-tappity-tap! Digital patterns, a web, a path across the stars. Tap-*tap*!

Fortunately, Quick drops the sound effects. There's still an undeniably pulpy tinge to a lot of the prose, but after a few pages it starts to feel like a deliberate stylistic choice. At times, the narrative point of view is a bit shaky, going from omniscient third person to a particular character's third-person perspective, and sometimes moving from one to another to another in a single paragraph, but most of the action follows the viewpoint of Mark Wahlberg's character, Leo Davidson.

As the book progresses, closely following the film, I found myself drawn in, less distracted by Quick's style. The constant references to apes as monkeys grow tiresome, but that may well be a result of staying close to Davidson's perspective, as he does that throughout the movie.

There are a few very small scenes that don't appear in the final film but may be in the screenplay. The main differences are at the end. The twist is missing, of course; the book ends with Davidson taking off into space and entering the wormhole. But the battle and the final confrontation between Thade and Davidson play out a little differently – not significantly enough that fans really need to experience both, but it's noticeable. Quick also brings the

---

[12] Also published was an illustrated chilren's tie-in book titled *Planet of the Apes: Leo's Logbook—A Captain's Days in Captivity*, by Benjamin Athens.
[13] http://www.dailypundit.com

whole Davidson/Daena/Ari romantic triangle a bit more out in the open, and he uses the characters' names. In the movie, I didn't get most of their names. There was the blonde, the guy played by Kris Kristofferson, the slave trader, Thade's main gorilla buddy, Ari's gorilla buddy... you get the idea. Now I know I was watching Daena, Karubi, Limbo, Attar, Krull, and so on.

Overall, revisiting the movie and reading the novelization turned out to be a more pleasant experience than I anticipated. Ending aside, the novelization doesn't change enough or add enough to be essential, nor is its prose style a key selling point. But now I'm interested in reading Quick's original tie-in novels to see where he goes with them and find out whether his prose is stronger when he has a bit more time to work.

Rise of the Planet of the Apes

A few years later and another reboot, one apparently aimed at the modern viewership. Forget the futuristic science-fiction elements, focus on the here and now, and make it the beginning of a new apocalypse. It's *Planet of the Apes* for the *Walking Dead* generation, remaking elements of *Escape* and *Conquest* in a new way. But it wasn't novelized.

Dawn of the Planet of the Apes: Firestorm

The success of *Rise* may have been a surprise, but *Dawn* was expected to be a hit. Building anticipation, a novel set between *Rise* and *Dawn*, titled *Dawn of the Planet of the Apes: Firestorm*, appeared two months before the film's premiere, filling the long story gap between the two movies. It was published by Titan, a U.K.-based publisher of media-related books and magazines, and written by J. Gregory Keyes. Keyes has written a number of original fantasy novels; his tie-in credentials go back twenty years to a trilogy of *Babylon 5* novels about the Psi Corps, followed by books based on *Star Wars* and the *Elder Scrolls* video games.

Firestorm explores, in detail, a key difference between the original movies and the new continuity. We didn't see a *Conquest of the Planet of the Apes*, just the fall of a single city. The new continuity explains how the events in one city spread throughout the world, by way of a viral outbreak. It's a perfect fit for the 21st Century. If anything, *Firestorm* runs the risk of seeming too familiar, too much like all the outbreak movies and TV series in recent years.

Firestorm, by Greg Keyes, fills in the blanks between *Rise* and *Dawn of the Planet of the Apes*.

Rise of the Planet of the Apes ends with the virus beginning to spread among the human population and the apes fleeing to the forest. *Firestorm* picks up very shortly thereafter.

In San Francisco, a reporter, a politician, and an emergency room doctor find themselves dealing with a strange new plague. In the woods, Caesar and his band try to figure out how to live in their new home. Also in the woods, a primatologist (a friend of the reporter) and a mercenary with experience poaching apes are working with a corporate army looking for the apes. The human side of the story tells a good outbreak conspiracy story, while the ape side focuses on Caesar's fellow apes becoming more intelligent and aware of their increasing intelligence.

In addition to switching between the perspectives of its large cast of characters, Keyes builds characters' backstories through flashbacks and conversations. Malakai, the poacher, and Koba, the one-eyed bonobo from the films, get the most attention. They're both capable of good, but they're also both damaged. Malakai has had terrors inflicted on him, become dehumanized, and committed terrible acts himself. Koba has been victimized but wants, at times, to do some victimizing himself. Malakai starts to become more human through working with Clancy, the primatologist, and encountering the apes. Koba, meanwhile, seems to deal with his damage through his bond with Caesar, earning the latter's trust.

There's one main human link between *Firestorm* and *Dawn*: Dreyfus, played in the film by Gary Oldman. As *Firestorm* begins, he's a retired police chief running for mayor. He's well characterized and clearly a younger version of the man he is in the film.

As the story progresses, the body count rises. Not every character introduced here is dead by the end of the book, but many are. Nor do they all die of the plague. The rapid spread of the outbreak leads to a lot of violence. Civilization hasn't quite collapsed by the end of the novel, but it's not hard to see that the state of San Francisco in the film is coming soon.

It's pretty clear what happens in the ten years between *Rise* and *Dawn*, and there's no shortage of outbreak stories, but this is a well written, strongly characterized novel that has the unique point of showing the apes begin to become a society of intelligent beings. It's a strong setup for *Rise*, but also an enjoyable novel in its own right.

Dawn of the Planet of the Apes

Alex Irvine, like his predecessors, has a track record with both his own original fiction and a number of novelizations and tie-ins. He's written books in the *Transformers* and *Supernatural* universes, and has penned several comics-related tie-ins as well.

Irvine's novelization of *Dawn* follows the movie closely. It doesn't add many new scenes, but it fills the pages by focusing much more on the thoughts of the viewpoint characters, humans and apes alike. Considering how little dialogue there is in long stretches of the movie, this goes a long way to make up for the lack of visuals.

Irvine also goes into some detail explaining exactly what it is that Malcolm and the others are doing during the scenes involving the dam. The use of technical detail slows the scenes down but also increases the suspense, by making the risks more clear.

The climactic battle between Caesar and Koba seems to be a little different from the filmed version, but a leap-for-leap, blow-for-blow description might be a bit much on the page. Irvine captures the suspense well, especially when writing from the perspective of Caesar, recovering from a gunshot wound but still having to get to the top of the tower to confront Koba and fight him.

Like Keyes, Irvine has a clean, professional prose style that doesn't draw attention to itself. He does a bit of descriptive writing where needed and manages the shifts between character viewpoints effectively. Irvine meets the challenge of putting in words an intensely visual story, and does a solid job of capturing the story and its characters. In the film, a number of supporting characters are quickly drawn in broad strokes with little dialogue to give them more than a dimension or two. Characters like Malcolm's son, Alexander, are more fully drawn in the book, through their own viewpoint scenes and those of the others around them. There's also a line or two about Dreyfus that may be there to connect to his characterization in *Firestorm*.

There's one noticeable addition, one scene completely absent from the film: the epilogue. The military help arrives by sea. They see the apes. Caesar and the apes see them and roar a challenge. "It rolled out across the city just lit by dawn, and they waited for the humans to choose." It's a more overt cliffhanger. The next film seems likely to pick up where this left off, not leaving room for a *Firestorm* to fill in the blanks[14], but a novel set outside the San Francisco area, providing backstory for the new human characters in *War for the Planet of the Apes*, could be a good approach. Another novelization seems like a safe bet, too.

Borrowing again from Van Parys, "Here I make a plea for more attention to novelisations." They broaden the film experience and they broaden the *Apes* fandom experience. At the very least, *Conspiracy of the Planet of the Apes* and *Dawn of the Planet of the Apes: Firestorm* each expand the mythos. The more straightforward novelizations provide alternate takes on some parts of the saga, complementing the often visually focused films by getting into the minds of the characters. They're part of the history of the *Apes* phenomenon.[15]

---

[14] Editors' note: Greg Keyes has, in fact, written a prequel novel to *War for the Planet of the Apes*, titled *Revelations*.

[15] And thanks to Titan Books, they will all soon be in print once again for the first time in decades – the four classic movie sequels, the 2001 film, and both TV shows – in a set of four omnibus editions.

Scoring the Simians: Music in the *Planet of the Apes* Saga

by Paul Simpson

> Jerry Goldsmith did one of the greatest scores on the planet when he wrote *Planet of the Apes*.
>
> – Michael Giacchino, composer of *Dawn of the Planet of the Apes*[1]

What sort of music does the name Jerry Goldsmith conjure up? Well, of course, if you're reading this book, chances are you're immediately going to think of his score for the first *Planet of the Apes* movie; after that, his work on *Star Trek: The Motion Picture* (a theme that was reused for *Star Trek: The Next Generation* on TV) might spring to mind. Or, perhaps, his music for *Patton* (which he composed in lieu of working on the second *Apes* feature). Maybe – and it's only a faint chance – you think of his music for *Escape from the Planet of the Apes* (though even he seemed to have forgotten about that when he was recording a commentary for the DVD of the first *Planet of the Apes* film!).

For the orchestral players who came in to record the score for that first *Apes* film back in the mid-1960s, Goldsmith was more commonly associated

---

[1] O'hara, Helen. "Film Studies 101: Michael Giacchino on Being a Composer." *Empire*, 30 May 2014: http://www.empireonline.com/movies/features/film-studies-101-michael-giacchino-composer/.

with lyrical themes, not atonality; tunes, not rhythms. True, he'd written some scores that were a bit more unusual – *The Satan Bug*, based on the Alistair MacLean novel, has more than its fair share of sound rather than tuneful themes – and his music for the 1962 film *Freud* used the 12-tone system to a certain extent. However, French horn players were expecting to be using their instruments in the standard way – not being asked to remove the mouthpiece, and blow into it from the other end; clarinettists expected to blow into their instruments, not simply click the keys. But that was the point. This wasn't the sort of score for which you put the LP on in the background to listen to – it wasn't a *Doctor Zhivago*, with epic music that would carry you away to a romantic place. It was part and parcel of creating a world that was very different (yet, in some ways, horribly similar) to our own.

Jerry Goldsmith went ape while conducting the *Planet of the Apes* soundtrack.

Jerry Goldsmith's commentary track on the first *Planet of the Apes* film also notes a key difference between the films made back then and the 21st-Century incarnations: the use of silence. Goldsmith explains that he and director Franklin J. Schaffner had discussions about which scenes required music, with the composer arguing strongly that there were key moments during the films which simply didn't need musical underpinning – the performances of the actors, and the situations in which they were told the audience everything they needed to know. It doesn't feel as if that conversation happened on the 2001 *Apes* film, or indeed on the most recent score by Michael Giacchino (though to be fair to Patrick Doyle, he notes, in the short documentary on the *Rise* home video release, that he too pulled the music back). When the music is there, it makes its point with dissonance and unusual rhythms, constantly changing time signatures so that the emphases come at odd points. There aren't grand melodies, just short motifs that move among the instruments.

Goldsmith's music for that first *Planet of the Apes* film is often described as setting the template for the scores that followed, both on large and small screens, but that isn't necessarily the case. Listen to the isolated soundtracks for the four movies that followed, as you can on the Blu-ray sets, and you realize that, just as the tones and the directors of the sequels changed, so did the music.

Some things did track, though. One of the elements most associated with the franchise as a whole, the ram's horn sound that epitomizes the apes in that vitally important hunt sequence in the first film, appears in different guises, most clearly in the Lalo Schifrin theme for the TV series – something emphasized by its inclusion on Intrada's set of music from the final two movies, where it somehow feels more like *Planet of the Apes* than either of those! The use of unusual percussion instruments is also common to many – but not all – who composed for the simian stories.

But the way things were different can be heard by listening to the score for *Beneath the Planet of the Apes*, penned by Leonard Rosenman. It's a much richer sound than Goldsmith's – it's been described as being "vertical" rather than "horizontal," which roughly means that more players were being used at the same time rather than having lots of them doing different things, effectively "crossing paths" with each other to create a diverse pattern. Rosenman had form in this area – he'd written one of the few science-fiction scores similar to *Planet of the Apes* with *Fantastic Voyage* (the miniaturized Raquel Welch movie that's been lovingly ripped off, er, homaged by so many small-screen shows since). When Goldsmith wasn't available, as Schaffner needed him for *Patton*, Rosenman was a logical choice, and while he didn't slavishly follow Goldsmith's lead, he did add in the weird percussion. (Not, it should be noted, that you'd know this if you'd bought the original "soundtrack album" back in the day. That was a reorchestrated, far more "normal" version.)

But what sets *Beneath* apart is "The Mass of the Holy Bomb," a version of the Christian Eucharistic rite reworked for the mutants' own perverse religion. If you want an idea of what Goldsmith might have done with this, have a listen to *The Omen* score. (If you've not heard this, go listen to it now. We'll wait.) That showed what one musical satanic mechanic could do... but Rosenman took a more traditional route. Apparently, writer Paul Dehn stated that he wanted the song to be similar to the Anglican hymn "All Things Bright and Beautiful" – one of the few times the writer's British nationality was evident – and that's what Rosenman gave him... with a twist.

The score of *Beneath* that was released a few years back contains the material that Rosenman recorded with the orchestra, not all of which made it to the final movie, and it's possible (should you so wish and, in the United Kingdom, if you're watching the film on Blu-ray) to line up the CD with the picture to determine how the scenes would have sounded. However, unlike in Goldsmith's and Doyle's scores, it seems as though the decision not to use the music didn't come from the composer, but from others during the rather hectic production of the movie.

Everything changed for the third film in the series, *Escape from the Planet of the Apes*. Since we were no longer on the planet of the apes – or at least on the planet with apes dominant – the music couldn't really reflect the harshness of life that existed there. Jerry Goldsmith returned to the saga and provided a score that, at least initially, seems much more on a par with the other material he and others were writing at the time. If you want to experience the whole thing, you've got to listen to the isolated score track – there's a 16-minute suite of music on one of the releases of his *Planet of the Apes* score, which is a reasonable representation of his work. Certainly the increased use of electronics is evident, particularly in the treatment of some of the physical instruments' output, but a lot of the time, it does feel as if it could be the underscore for a cop movie of the time – the use of a sitar dates it perhaps more than anything else.

Goldsmith wrote a mildly lyrical piece for Taylor and Nova in the first film (which he described, in the commentary, as the nearest they got to a love theme), but *Escape* did allow him to give Cornelius and Zira something more melodic than the humans had been permitted. As the movie goes on and the mood darkens, the pace of the music increases, and some of the fire that characterized sequences like the hunt in the first film is evident. However, I don't think anyone would call this one of Goldsmith's finest works.

One of the many budgetary constraints on the fourth film, *Conquest of the Planet of the Apes*, was in the music department. Rather than turn to someone with a large feature film resumé, the producers elected to use an up-and-coming composer, Tom Scott. Only 24 years old at the time, the jazz musician brought a fresh energy into his score – and it's worth seeking out the CD of this one, to ensure you get to hear his full music for the finale, a seven-minute cue that was one of the biggest casualties of the infamous reshuffling of the ending. In the theatrical movie, you may get a definite feeling of *déjà vu* (or *déjà écoute*), for rather than get Scott to record a revised version of his music, the producers went back to the first film and extracted some of Jerry Goldsmith's score. Scott's most famous piece is probably "Gotcha," the theme to 1970s cop show *Starsky and Hutch*, and there's a lot of that vibe to his music for the apes' near-future appearance, with a very jazzy feel – and no strings, unlike any of his predecessors. The brass players certainly earned their session fees for their work for the climactic part of the movie...

To an extent, the music came full circle for the final film in the original sequence, though it was Leonard Rosenman who came back to the series rather than Jerry Goldsmith for *Battle for the Planet of the Apes*. With the world now back – at least in part – under ape control, there's a return musically to the martial themes of the first two movies, with Rosenman moving away from the contemporary feel of the third and fourth films and readopting the more atonal, dissonant qualities of those scores. There's an almost clichéd element to the trumpets blaring away in the opening title sequence – "Colonel Hathi's March" from the contemporary animated version of *The Jungle Book* comes to mind every so often – but it's accompanied by such discord (and dis-chord) in the strings and woodwind that the harshness is clear from the start. There are some quieter moments, and you'll often find descriptions of the end music as being "optimistic" – though I always find the rising notes more disturbing than suggestive of a pleasant future.

And those rising notes are – consciously or otherwise – mimicked in the next great addition to the *Apes* mythos, the 1974 TV series. Lalo Schifrin, whose scores for *Dirty Harry* and *Mission: Impossible* defined so much of the screen musical landscape during the late 1960s and early 1970s, tapped into the zeitgeist that Goldsmith and Rosenman had created. That may sound like pseudo-claptrap, but is the easiest way of summing up the fact that the theme for the TV series (once you get past the "travelling through time" bit at the start) would work in any of the "harsh" movies (i.e. not *Escape*) – and some of the scoring for the episodes, particularly Schfirin's own, definitely feels as if it's channelling some of those elements. Schfirin had been approached to replace Goldsmith on *Beneath the Planet of the Apes* back in 1970, but wasn't able to fit the score into his schedule. He more than makes up for it with the TV show.

Like Goldsmith and Rosenman, Schfirin uses the lower registers on the piano in a percussive way; it's sometimes overlooked that the piano is a percussion instrument (you don't blow into it, or pluck strings – there are damn great hammers thumping into the wires), and it can be highly effective when used like that. The other composers who worked on the show followed suit – Earle Hagen's music for the episode *The Surgeon* is another that could be dropped into the movies without a major problem. If you're interested in how music scores for TV series are put together, then track down a set of the Intrada release from 2015 – Jeff Bond's booklet is a mine of information.

The following year's *Return to the Planet of the Apes* is often overlooked – many may say with good cause – but in addition to its rather catchy theme tune, it does have one key addition to the *Apes* saga: the song "I'm Going Humanoid Over You." Big-band jazz conductor and composer Dean Elliott provided the soundtrack for the 13-part animated series, with his score a little out of the ordinary for Saturday-morning fare (as was the series itself), and episode four provided an insight into ape music. "Never thought that I'd be acting humanoid. That ain't the simian thing to do," goes the Country-type song heard playing on a radio (the entire soundtrack can be found online easily enough), and no fan of the saga should go through life without experiencing this song. For North American readers, if you ever see references in British books to the Eurovision Song Contest, and you don't understand the quality of the music, then just listen to this and it'll put you in the right ballpark.

Now, while we're on the subjects of songs, let's take a little sidestep before we jump into the 21st-Century incarnations of the film franchise – because there was plenty of *Apes*-related music in the quarter-century or so between *Battle for the Planet of the Apes* and Tim Burton's reimagining in 2001 apart from that written for the two TV shows. Don't believe me? Well, so far there have been three large downloads of songs that have been inspired by the franchise, and quite a few of them derive from this period. Who, save in an effort to keep their sanity, can possibly resist the lure of the "Apes' Shuffle"? After all, it's got a pretty incredible pedigree – it comes from Jeff Wayne, the man whose best-known album reworked another science-fiction classic, H.G. Wells' *The War of the World*. Okay, it was from before he hit paydirt with "Forever Autumn" and the other classics from that, but the "Apes' Shuffle" is... well, it's different. It's a funky sound, with ape chattering in the background and a flute playing a counter-melody to the electronica.

What may surprise you more to learn is that this is actually a cover version: the original "Ape Shuffle" was arranged and conducted by Lalo Schifrin himself, although his original has more of an orchestral feel to it. Like many of these simian spinoffs, it can be found on YouTube thanks to someone uploading the original 45 rpm discs, but if you haven't been enticed by what we've said so far, maybe the brilliant description of it as "featuring a chimp vocalist apparently suffering from an asthma attack"[2] might tempt you? (Oh, and Jeff Wayne also produced a track called "The Ape Planet," which sounds like the music Barry Gray produced for the hillbillies episode of *Thunderbirds*!)

Being a little more serious for a moment, America wasn't the only place producing adaptations of Pierre Boulle's novel. Japan had its own version, a 26-part adventure called *Saru no gundan*, which appeared in 1974, around the same time that Roddy McDowall's Galen was leading Virdon and Burke around bits of Southern California. The series has had occasional releases in the United States – episodes were put together to form a TV movie called *Time of the Apes* (they're on YouTube, too), to which *MST3K* gave its usual reverential treatment. Others better versed in simianology can judge the show's merits, but its music certainly was very different from anything else in the *Apes* musical repertoire. It was written by Toshiaki Tsushima, a respected Japanese composer, and is very much in that country's idiom of the period – with electronics and percussion to the fore – so it's a much brighter sound than the down-low, bass-heavy scores that Western audiences would associate with *Apes*. A complete CD of the music has now been compiled for completists.

Apes weren't just appearing on large and small screens. A band called Electric Cowboy produced "Planet of the Apes... A Musical Trip." As the narrator – an ape called Gaylen (*sic*) – explains, "Sometimes it's difficult to hear from one planet to another, or from one mind to another." Sometimes it's difficult to comprehend exactly what the heck is going on in this album: think of one of those nature programmes like *Planet Earth* – you know, the ones narrated by David Attenborough (for U.K. readers) or Sigourney Weaver (for Americans) showing the creatures in their natural habitats. Then make that the planet of

---

[2] Rock Roots: The Irish Rock Music Archive. 5 October 2011: https://rockroots.wordpress.com/2011/10/05/ape-shuffle/.

the apes that is being examined... through a filter of 1970s Earth clichés. Even the promisingly titled "Live and Let Live," which you might hope will be a James Bond riff, bearing in mind *Live and Let Die*'s arrival in cinemas the previous year, turns out to be a lament that "your Mama doesn't like me because I'm covered in hair, your Daddy doesn't like me because I'm going nowhere..." Then again, any band that credits one of the instrumentalists as playing "good vibes" probably isn't taking the project too seriously.

That wasn't the first *Apes* cash-in record, by any means. A singer named Gary Knight came up with the unoriginally titled "Planet of the Apes" back in 1968, mere months after the movie came out. Starting portentously with a building fanfare, it ceases to be awe-inspiring the moment that Mr. Knight begins to sing. For some reason, he decided that a New Orleans Dixieland jazz style was the most appropriate manner in which to approach a dystopic tale of future devastation, misery, and slavery. Maybe the record executive who hailed Jerry Goldsmith's unavailability to write the score for *Beneath* had a point – there wasn't a marketable theme in the music for the original film. But was this really the best that could be done?

Talking of cash-in records leads us neatly to the Power Records albums. It may be a little unfair to bracket them with Gary Knight or Electric Cowboy, but they were similarly trading off the backs of the franchise's achievements – and, in their case, trying to extend it further. Four of their releases were adaptations of the movies (for some reason, *Conquest* wasn't included)... well, "adaptations" is probably too kind a word for the ten-minute versions. Not surprisingly, the music isn't drawn from the scores of the films – there's the occasional trumpet high call that sort of emulates the ram's horn motif from Goldsmith's original, but not much else. Power also produced new stories for the TV series characters[3], but once again the music was pretty generic.

Bar the occasional cover of Goldsmith's credit music for the first film on compilation albums, most music connected to the *Apes* saga in the latter part of the 20th Century concentrated more on the themes of the series in terms of its meaning and relevance to modern life than on the musical themes Goldsmith, Rosenman, *et al.*, had written. The next true musical adjunct came from the pen of Danny Elfman.

---

[3] "Battle of Two Worlds," "Dawn of the Tree People," "Mountain of the Delphi," and "Volcano"

Some directors come to a project with a composer apparently in tow – as Jerry Goldsmith had done with Franklin J. Schaffner. Put Tim Burton onto your film, and you're almost certain to get Danny Elfman. *Batman, Mars Attacks...* name any Burton movie (except *Sweeney Todd* for obvious reasons, and *Ed Wood* for less obvious ones) and the score will come from Elfman. He's one of those composers whose musical style is instantly recognizable through the "colors" that he uses in his scoring – whether it's a particular pattern of notes, or a certain sound that he asks his players to produce.

At the time, there were strong rumors that Fox was requesting changes to Elfman's score, and demanding that it be like a sci-fi version of Hans Zimmer's score for the recent Ridley Scott movie *Gladiator*. Elfman emphatically denied these rumors, noting that, as far as he knew, the studio was happy with what he produced. Interestingly, although Elfman maintained that his score would be very different from what Jerry Goldsmith composed for the original film – of which Burton's movie was a "reimagining" – it was built up in much the same way, with unusual percussion forming the core of the distinctive sound. However, whereas Goldsmith had picked the brains of one of his percussionists in the studio and revived instruments that had been used in the 1930s, such as the bass slide-whistle, Elfman recorded sessions with percussionists first and then wrote his score around them.

The music in Burton's movie is far more pervasive than in the original quintet of pictures, and there are times in this and the two later movies when you do sometimes wish that the orchestra could just shut up! It's a difference in the way that scores are viewed nowadays – the composer's job has increasingly become about telling the audience what they are meant to feel. As with computer-generated effects, a score is just one of the tools that a director can use when making his movie, and just as effects sometimes came to dominate the movies, so the music can sometimes do too much of the work, no longer reflecting what the audience is feeling but manipulating them into feeling it.

At the time, Elfman described his music as "a very big, aggressive, muscular, kind of a tribal, driving score"[4] which he based around three key scenes: the hunt scene early in the movie, a more tender moment between Mark Wahlberg's astronaut Leo Davidson and Helen Bonham Carter's ape Ari, and then the preparation for war at the end. It's a shame that there's not an

---

[4] Thaxton, Ford A. and Randall D. Larson. "Danny Elfman Revisits the Planet of the Apes." *Cinescape*, 2 August 2001.

isolated score for this one, as the CD had to be in stores at the same time as the movie, but music was being recorded right up to the last moment – which means that some of the tracks in the movie aren't on the album, and a number of items on the CD weren't intended for use in the film, although, ironically, having heard them, director Burton decided to track sections of "Ape Suite #2" into the final cut of the movie.

Burton's movie failed to kickstart a new sequence of *Apes* films, and although it was a decade before *Rise of the Planet of the Apes* hit cinemas, it was in development hell for five of those years. Once it was in full production, Scottish composer Patrick Doyle was brought on board; among his wealth of compositions were the scores for *Mary Shelley's Frankenstein* and *Harry Potter and the Goblet of Fire*. Just before joining the team on *Rise*, he also scored the first Marvel *Thor* movie. As is evident from the brief featurette on the *Rise*, home video release, Doyle enjoyed working on the project, and combined many different elements for the score, including getting his choir of African-American singers to chant the phrase "I've got a cookie for you," which he used as the rhythm for the scene in which Caesar releases the other apes. "You subconsciously think of certain rhythms of dialogue which can inform motifs and themes," he explained in the featurette. "It's all part of the artistic barrage you get from a film."

One key difference between this new version of the saga and its predecessors was the use of "real" apes – i.e. ones that couldn't speak. This meant that the music did have a larger role to play in communicating the emotions of the scenes, and Doyle felt that the music should tell the story. Although there are plenty of percussive elements to the score, there is also some beautiful melodic writing, and moments like the scenes on the Golden Gate Bridge when the two combine – something that didn't occur that often in previous movies.

With changes in the team responsible for the sequel, Doyle wasn't contracted to provide the score for *Dawn of the Planet of the Apes*, with the assignment going to Michael Giacchino, whose work was well known to genre audiences from the TV series *Lost*, as well as the big-screen reinventions of *Mission: Impossible* and *Star Trek*. He had worked with director Matt Reeves before on both *Let Me In* and *Cloverfield*. As with Danny Elfman's music, there are certain things that Giacchino brings to his scores which make them instantly recognizable, although they were comparatively muted in this soundtrack – fans of *Lost*, though, would probably find more similarities than those who just know his movie work. (If you're a lover of bad puns, then just check out the track titles – it's something that Giacchino does for the majority of his album releases – which include "Monkey See, Monkey Coup" and "Aped Crusaders.")

Dawn of the Planet of the Apes composer Michael Giacchino goes over the score with a tough critic. (Photo credit: ScoringSessions.com)

As the quote which opens this essay shows, Giacchino is a self-professed fan of Jerry Goldsmith's work, and there are many echoes of the score for the original movie, albeit ramped up. There are multiple different percussion instruments – including a piano fitted with screws between the wires so that when the hammer hits the wires, there's a weird additional vibration provided – with percussionist Emil Richards once again returning to assist an *Apes* composer as he did with Goldsmith 45 or so years earlier. There's no place for silence in this score, though: 115 minutes of music were recorded for the 131-minute-long movie!

Like Goldsmith and most of his other predecessors, Giacchino worked closely with his director, tweaking elements based on the input regarding character development he received – something that is vital when the music is there for such a large part of the movie. "You have to meld your minds because he has a story he wants to tell and my music has to tell the best version of that story," Giacchino explained to *Empire* magazine.[5] With Reeves returning for *War for the Planet of the Apes* in 2017, it would seem likely that Giacchino will get a chance to homage the master while still serving the fresh story for a second time.

The ideas behind Pierre Boulle's original novel and the 1968 movie continue to inspire musicians – if you've got the 2001 video game, you'll hear something very different, courtesy of Lionel Gaget and Raphaël Gesqua (closer to the Japanese soundtrack than any of the movies which inspired the game). But we've kept the best for last – a musical version which no true fan can ever miss: *The Simpsons'* "Stop the Planet of the Apes, I Want to Get Off! Starring Troy McClure"... "I hate every ape I see, from Chimpan-A to Chimpan-Zee," McClure/Taylor sings in this brilliant spoof of musical theatre and the franchise, before realizing that they "finally made a monkey of me." Will somebody please write the other 100 minutes of this stage show and get it on Broadway!

[5] O'hara, Helen. "Film Studies 101: Michael Giacchino on Being a Composer." *Empire*, 30 May 2014: http://www.empireonline.com/movies/features/film-studies-101-michael-giacchino-composer/.

Before, Beneath, Beyond, and Between the Covers of the Planet of the Apes: A Meditation on Precursors, Predecessors, Ripples, and Rip-offs

by Stephen R. Bissette

I. Apes Antecedents: Godfather of the Apes

Four thousand centuries have passed. The face of the world has changed. Our continent has been swallowed up by new seas; the glacial waters of the Pole descend as far as the shores of Africa. The only inhabitable regions girdle the globe between the two tropics. All our animal and vegetable species have been transformed during the Quinary period and the majority have ceased to exist. Humankind no longer exists.

On the other hand, several races of apes have been perfected, and among them, the Gorillas, having reached the highest degree of development, constitute the superior being. They live in societies, and their civilization, like their science, is highly advanced...

As the editors of the book in your hands well know, I've a soft spot in my post-(or is it pre-?) simian skull for the *Planet of the Apes* mythos. This obsession extends across the board, to the precursors, the original novel *La Planète des Singes / Planet of the Apes* (1963, a Swiftian novel still superior in many ways to all its multi-media incarnations and spinoffs) by Pierre Boulle, the movies, the comics, the knockoffs, and the successors. That obsession provides the meat of this contribution, beginning with a look back at the many predecessors to Boulle's classic novel.

Reconsidering the hardcore predecessors to the entire *Planet of the Apes* concept, it could (indeed, should) be argued that the historic precursor was another French author, one whose contribution to international science-fiction literature, and to the *Planet of the Apes* concept, has been too-long ignored and overlooked.[1]

Thanks to my long-time friend Jean-Marc Lofficier (and Black Coat Press publisher) and the legendary, incredibly prolific and productive Brian Stableford, English-speaking and -reading fans at long last gained access – *for the first time* – to the true predecessor and wellspring of all things *Planet of the Apes* in 2011. Fifteen years ago, this long-lost classic of the genre was rescued and reprinted as "Le Gorilloïde et Autres Contes de L'Avenir" (2001, Editions Apex), with an essay by Jean-Luc Buard on Haraucourt's legacy and science-fiction creations. Ever-attentive veteran sci-fi author, scholar, and translator Stableford took note, and thanks to Brian and his ongoing (and quite magnificent and sadly overlooked) run of translated editions of long-lost masterworks of French science-fiction, fantasy, and horror for Black Coat Press, we can now read "Le Gorilloïde" and eight other previously untranslated,

---

[1] Of course, the primary debt is to Brian Stableford, and to his publisher Jean-Marc Lofficier, but please allow me to note, with some pride, that my bringing much of the information revised and expanded for this publication to light originally on my blog Myrant in recent years has added some of the authors, artists, and creations discussed in this essay to the "official" *Planet of the Apes* literary chronology for online scholars of the mythos and franchises. See http://planetoftheapes.wikia.com/wiki/La_Planète_des_Singes, specifically footnoted material numbered 4, 5, 6, 9, and 10 (at the time of this publication), and please accept this fuller accounting as the first in-print published account of these predecessors.

undiscovered Haraucourt classics in English, in the collection *Illusions of Immortality*.

I thought this cause for celebration at the time, but the silence, thus far, has been deafening.

Haraucourt's story "Le Gorilloïde" was first published in 1904 in *Le Journal*, the Paris daily newspaper, and afterwards as the first (and, in his lifetime, *only*) self-standing volume of Haraucourt's science fiction as a chapbook in 1906. To provide a proper context for Haraucourt's accomplishment, it shall be necessary to wander a bit, if only to find our way. If you've never heard of the gentleman before – or never before in this particular context – allow me to introduce to you the once-famed, once-revered French poet, author, and scholar Edmond Haraucourt (born 18 October, 1856; died 17 November, 1941).

On his own website, Brian writes:

> Edmond Haraucourt (1856-1941) was amongst the pioneers of French scientific romance influenced by H. G. Wells, easily ranking alongside the better-known Maurice Renard and J.-H. Rosny Aîné.
>
> In this collection of nine ground-breaking science fiction stories, published beween 1888 and 1919, he describes the rise of the Antichrist, the cataclysmic consequences of the discovery of an immortality serum, a journey across the ruins of Paris in the Year 6983, the fall of the Moon upon the Earth, the last of the Great Wars that ends all life on Earth, and even a futuristic "Planet of the Apes" where evolved gorillas wonder, "Are Apes descended from Humans?"...[2]

Indeed!

It is impossible to read "Le Gorilloïde" for the first time and *not* be rocked by the realization that Pierre Boulle *had* to have read this story, or at least heard of it. Even in its format, Haraucourt's story seems prescient: it is structured, in three parts, as a lecture by one Professor Sffaty, interrupted by the reactions of his audience of "five hundred Gorillas of the noblest birth, the most illustrious apes in politics, finance and the various Institutes... assembled in the hall..."

Other than swapping around the *Planet of the Apes* cinematic pantheon of futuristic primate society's class rank to place the gorillas at the top of the sciences instead of the evolved orangutans and chimpanzees, here we are in the topsy-turvy imaginary future we know and love – only it's not Boulle's invention, it's Haraucourt's, circa January 1904 ("Le Gorilloïde" was originally serialized in three installments in *Le Journal* that month and year).

---

[2] http://www.philsp.com/stableford/translations/illusions_of_immortality.htm

There are other structural similarities that are striking: remember, too, Boulle also narrated his journey to the planet of the apes via a framing story, related by Jinn and Phyllis, a couple who find the account of the voyage (which comprises the novel) in a bottle; in the coda, Boulle reveals Jinn and Phyllis to be chimpanzees who simply disbelieve what they've read, since no lowly human would be capable of writing such a saga, much less experiencing it.[3]

That twist, too, was anticipated by Haraucourt, in a way.

This is the Holy Grail for *Apes* devotees. Haraucourt's story was published a full *59 years* before the original publication of Boulle's *La Planète des Singes* in France (from publisher René Julliard), and its U.S. publication as *Planet of the Apes* (Vanguard Press, June 1963); 60 years to the month before it was published in the United Kingdom under the title *Monkey Planet* by Secker & Warburg of London (and subsequent March 1964 American paperback debut via Signet/New American Library).

The rest of *Illusions of Immortality* is equally entertaining and astonishing, too. The other stories Stableford has translated are "Immortality" ("Immortalité, Conte Philosophique," originally published in 1888); "The Madonna" ("La Madone," 1890), "The Antichrist" ("L'Antéchrist," 1893, and of particular interest to me, prompting a complete overhaul of my ongoing revisions to the ever-growing essay on Christian horror literature and films[4]);

---

[3] Attentive fellow comics and media scholar Henry R. Kujawa adds, "It's actually a double-twist, since, just before the narrative returns to the framing sequence, the actual story's climax comes when the Astronaut, his wife & child succeed in escaping Apeworld, rendezvousing with his mothership, returning to Earth, and landing... only to be met by an army jeep, whose drive terrifies the woman when he takes off his helmet. 'It was a gorilla.' That scene, clearly, inspired the *opening* sequence of the 3rd movie." Henry R. Kujawa, 16 November 2012, posted on the comments thread at Myrant, "La Passion du Gorilloïde," archived at http://srbissette.com/secrets-of-the-planet-of-the-apes-continued/.

[4] My original 1999 essay on Christian Antichrist and apocalyptic horror films can still be read in print form in *S.R. Bissette's Blur Volume 1* (June 1999-March 2000) (2007, Black Coat Press), available at http://www.blackcoatpress.com/blur.htm and http://www.amazon.com/Blur-1-Stephen-R-Bissette/dp/1934543241 , or in digital form in the compilation volume *Horrors! Cults, Crimes & Creepers (The Best of Blur Book 2)* (2012, Crossroads Press & Macabre Ink Digital) available at http://store.crossroadpress.com/index.php?main_page=product_info&cPath=9_36 6_367&products_id=516 , https://nook.barnesandnoble.com/products/2940015674736/sample, or http://www.amazon.com/Horrors-Cults-Crimes-Creepers-Best-ebook/dp/B009B59WWM

"The End of the World" ("La Fin du Monde," 1893); "A Trip to Paris" ("La Traversée de Paris," 1904); "A Christmas Gift" ("Les Sabots de Noël," 1906); "Doctor Auguérand's Discovery" ("La Découverte du Docteur Auguérand," 1910); and "The Supreme Conflict" ("Le Conflit Supreme," 1919), with a full biographical introduction and notes throughout by Brian Stableford.

Illusions of Immortality is still a relatively new book (published by Black Coat Press in February 2012), but sad to note, like almost all of Black Coat Press's incredible sci-fi/fantasy/horror translated editions (two of which I've contributed artwork to, including a cover collaboration with Cayetano "Cat" Garza, Jr.), it's been ignored by whatever science-fiction fandom has become in the 21st Century, far from the notice of the very audience that would most treasure it. This is one of the most rewarding sci-fi rediscoveries of the year, to my eyes, and deserving of far, far greater attention and far, far more readers.[5]

I hereby declare Edmond Haraucourt the Grandfather of the *Planet of the Apes*.

II. Pulp Predecessors: Wellman, de Camp, and Miller

The apes talked among themselves in high, penetrating voices which sounded odd coming from those immense black chests. It was obviously an intelligent language, full of throaty consonants rather like coughing and retching sounds. They took turns riding and walking, studying the people with bright little eyes and jabbering away all the while.

Ruby Stern leaned over and whispered to Scherer: "What are these things, Emil? Gorillas?"

"I think so," answered the zoologist. "At least, I can't think of anything else they can be. They have longer thumbs and higher skulls than the apes of our time, and of course twentieth century gorillas didn't ordinarily walk erect the way these do, but a hell of a lot can happen in a million years..."

– Genus Homo by L. Sprague de Camp and P. Schuyler Miller (1941/1950)

We now need to backtrack to 1938, and a story not cited as yet by *Planet of the Apes* scholars and devotees.

---

[5] *Illusions of Immortality* is still available from the publisher at http://www.blackcoatpress.com/gorilloid.htm and via Amazon at http://www.amazon.com/Illusions-Immortality-Brian-Stableford/dp/1612270751 or for Kindle at http://www.amazon.com/Illusions-Immortality-Science-Fiction-ebook/dp/B008C1XJV6. Needless to say, this book scores my highest possible recommendation.

It could be argued that Pierre Boulle owed no debt to Manly Wade Wellman, but given the current 20th Century Fox cinematic reboot of the franchise, it's obvious that Boulle's current creative heirs (and the corporate franchise creative team now at the helm) owe a vast debt to Wellman's excellent short story "Pithecanthropus Rejectus," published in *Astounding Stories* (Vol. 20, No. 5, January 1938).

Wellman's "posthumous" contribution to the *Planet of the Apes* mythos predates even the de Camp and Miller novel *Genus Homo* (an acknowledged pulp science-fiction predecessor that I will get to momentarily). Wellman, it seems, was often conceptually ahead of his peers and his times. [6]

I originally read Wellman's story on a plane via the U.K. paperback *The Rivals of Frankenstein* (1977, Corgi), en route home from my first-ever UKAK[7] in 1985. Wellman's story was, in its day, a concise rethinking of a number of already-chestnut science-fiction novels, including H.G. Wells's *The Island of Dr. Moreau* (1896) and Gaston Leroux's now-forgotten *Balaoo* (1911, first published in *Le Matin*, 9 October to 18 December, 1911). *Balaoo*, in particular, was incredibly popular in its time, internationally renowned and widely imitated; Leroux, after all, was the author of *The Phantom of the Opera*. Leroux's seminal tale of a scientist hyper-evolving a primate via surgery was repeatedly filmed, starting with Victorin-Hippolyte Jasset's *Balaoo the Demon Baboon* (1913) and often "borrowed from." Official adaptations included *The Wizard* (1927) and − arriving in theaters years after the publication of

---

[6] The Manly Wade Wellman story has been reprinted in numerous anthologies. The story can be found in the anthologies *Science Fiction of the Thirties* (editor: Damon Knight; Bobbs-Merrill Company, 1976/Avon, 1977), *The Rivals of Frankenstein: A Gallery of Monsters* (editor: Michel Parry; Corgi, 1977/Barnes & Noble Books, 1980), *The Best Animal Stories of Science Fiction and Fantasy* (editor: Donald J. Sobol; Frederick Warne, 1979), and *The Mammoth Book of Frankenstein* (editor: Stephen Jones; Robinson, 1994/ Carroll & Graf, 1994). For current updates on this publishing history visit http://www.isfdb.org/cgi-bin/title.cgi?43973. For more on the role that "Pithecanthropus Rejectus" played in the context of Wellman's writings, and the role of cinema in Wellman's work, also see my article "Sherlock Holmes vs. The Red Planet, Part 1" in *Weng's Chop* #8 (Vol. 3, No. 2, September 2015; pp. 59-79), available at http://www.amazon.com/Wengs-Chop-Standard-Brian-Harris/dp/1518645291 (black-and-white edition) or http://www.amazon.com/Wengs-Chop-More-Expensive-Color/dp/1517340845 (color edition).

[7] I'm not sure what the heck UKAK stood for, but it was *the* annual British London comics convention in the 1980s and early 1990s.

Wellman's story – *Dr. Renault's Secret* (1942).

Movies derivative of *Balaoo*'s premise and trappings span from the Lon Chaney vehicle *A Blind Bargain* (1922) and the Universal "Paula Dupree the ape woman" films (starring Acquanetta and / or Vicky Lane) of the early 1940s on through the Mexican man / ape transplant horror films like Chano Urueta's seminal *El Monstruo Resucitado* (1953), Fernando Méndez's *Ladrón de Cadáveres* (1957), and René Cardona's *Las Luchadoras Contra el Medico Asesino / Doctor of Doom* (1962) and *La Horripilante Bestia Humana / Night of the Bloody Apes* (1969/1972). The ol' "surgically evolve an ape and / or transplant a man's brain into a gorilla" schtick was (and is) just everywhere. But they all owed and still owe a debt to H.G. Wells and Gaston Leroux – and Manly Wade Wellman knew that.

In Wellman's tale, his put-upon narrator is an ape named Congo who has been surgically altered to increase his intelligence and allow him to speak. He details his life with the scientist and the scientist's kind, caring wife, and the fact that he matured more quickly than the couple's own son, Sidney, who remained "a fat, blue-eyed baby that drooled and gurgled and barely crept upon the nursery linoleum, while I scurried easily hither and thither, scrambling up on tables and bedposts, and sometimes on the bureau." Congo's account notes his own ability to speak and his unhappiness with the patience and affection showered on Sidney while the scientist "acted grave – almost stern – where I was involved." Congo is also painfully aware of the ongoing surgeries necessary for his own rapid development, and how this further sets him apart from Sidney.

Sounding familiar? Replace surgical techniques with genetic and non-surgical enhancement of simian intelligence, and the first third of Wellman's "Pithecanthropus Rejectus" reads like a template for much of the 20th Century Fox franchise reboot, *Rise of the Planet of the Apes* (2011, by Rupert Wyatt, Rick Jaffa, and Amanda Silver), with often uncanny fidelity. The overall theme and thrust is also in accord with *Rise of the Planet of the Apes*, in many striking ways – in fact, I'd argue that Wellman was due a credit or at least an onscreen acknowledgement.

The narratives diverge significantly, however, when the scientist sells Congo to subsidize his future experiments. Congo is essentially recruited into show biz (shade of *Mighty Joe Young!*), but Wellman was a most literary man – and so, Congo is offered the part of Caliban in a production of William Shakespeare's *The Tempest* (and Congo himself is sharp enough to respond to the role, and recognize his affinity with Caliban's plight). Eventually, though, Congo contrives to realize his personal dream – his (ahem) "return to Africa," where he is violently rejected by the natural tribal apes and forced instead to return to civilization, totally aware of his complete misfit status and utter singularity as a sentient being: the tragedy of Frankenstein's monster, just as Mary Shelley conceived her monster. When Congo is reunited with his maker, the scientist informs Congo of his plan to surgically mass-produce more man-ape hybrids: "each a valuable property – each an advance in surgery and psychology over the last... In six or eight years there'll be a full hundred of you, or more advanced... I will lighten the labor of mankind..." At which point, Congo – just as Caesar does in *Rise* (as articulated in screenwriter Paul Dehn's original imaginary arc of the first *Planet of the Apes* movie series) – objects, and –

Go, read "Pithecanthropus Rejectus," then revisit (or enjoy for the first time) *Rise of the Planet of the Apes*. Also compare the original *Astounding Stories* illustration by William Elliott Dold, Jr. (1892-1967) for Wellman's "Pithecanthropus Rejectus" with Andy Serkis as Caesar (via Weta Digital CGI effects) in *Rise of the Planet of the Apes* – then tell me I'm wrong.

We must also reconsider L. Sprague de Camp's and P. Schuyler Miller's science-fiction novel *Genus Homo*, which *Planet of the Apes* fans and scholars *have* acknowledged as a literary predecessor to Boulle's novel for at least a decade. However, given the comic book precursors (cited below) that have since come to light, the role that *Genus Homo* may have played in the literary chronology that culminated in *Planet of the Apes* requires a proper assessment.

Given my high school sci-fi reading of the late 1960s and early 1970s, I (incorrectly) remembered it being a contemporary of the original Pierre Boulle novel – boy, was I wrong. I was surprised to find that it predated Boulle's satiric account of Ulysse Mérou's expedition to the Betelgeuse solar system by more than two decades.

Genus Homo was the prolific de Camp's first novel, and Miller's *only* novel; it originally saw print in *Super Science Novels* #7 (March 1941), and was subsequently published as a novel in 1950 by Fantasy Press.[8] The copy I read in

---

[8] Between the publication of *Genus Homo* in the 1941 pulp magazine and its revised novel publication, Aldous Huxley proffered his contribution to this family tree, *Ape and Essence* (1948). Others have written about Huxley's unusual book – written and published in the format of a discarded, rediscovered screenplay – which extrapolated a slightly different post-human simian Dystopia than *Genus Homo*. It was "...set in 2108 after a war has devastated most of the world and apes rule in

high school (borrowed, if memory serves, from my pal Alan Finn) and the one I reread as an adult were both the Berkley Books/Medallion paperback (1961, still predating *La Planète des Singes* by two years). Revisiting de Camp's and Miller's novel – which I highly recommend[9] – I must note that if the late DC Comics editor Julie Schwartz were still with us, I'd have been phoning Julie up in short order to talk to him about the book.[10] In fact, I'd be willing to bet cash on the barrelhead that it was the de Camp / Miller opus that Julie consciously riffed from for the *Strange Adventures* #45 story "The Gorilla World!" (more on this comic book story, and others, shortly).

The de Camp/Miller novel concerns a busload of folks passing through Pennsylvania who suffer a should-have-been-fatal accident only to Rip Van Winkle into the distant future. There's none of the "What planet are we on?"

---

place of man... [it] followed the attempts of a human biologist to make sense out of the upside-down world. When a group of researchers from New Zealand, the last bastion of human society untouched by the final war, arrived in post holocaust Los Angeles, Alfred 'Stagnant' Poole was captured by ruthless, de-evolved humans. He discovered their society had gone savagely wrong, with science being replaced by a type of devil worship. A baboon culture, on the other hand, living concurrently with the humans, was far more civilized and took steps to limit the humans' reproduction. Poole was shocked by all he saw, and returned to New Zealand with news that America was beyond all hope of salvation. Huxley's presentation, as the work of a misanthropic screenwriter, pokes fun not only at human folly but also the system of Hollywood..." (quoted from http://planetoftheapes.wikia.com/wiki/La_Planète_des_Singes). In this, it seems, Huxley was more prescient about Hollywood's interest in post-apocalyptic simian cultures than he himself imagined.

[9] *Genus Homo* is readily available in various editions (check http://www.abebooks.com/servlet/SearchResults?kn=Sprague&tn=Genus+Homo).

[10] I knew – and once worked for – Julie Schwartz during my freelance years with DC Comics; that gig was penciling a sequence for Robert Loren Fleming's and Keith Giffen's *Son of Ambush Bug* #5 (November 1986). I'd completely forgotten that my pages had a *Planet of the Apes* spin to it, via the DC universe's "gorilla" angle, until I checked online to double-check which issue I'd worked on: "The story is then interrupted by fill in pencils by artist Steve Bissette who takes the story in a completely different direction: Getting a phone call Ambush Bug learns that Cheeks is being held hostage and travels to the island that time forgot armed to the teeth with automatic weapons to fight the dinosaurs that live there. He ends up meeting Gorilla Grodd who tells him that Cheeks is somewhere on the island. Suddenly, Giganto bursts through the roof of the temple they are in revealing that he has Cheeks (Dressed up as Lois Lane) as his hostage. Ambush Bug wakes up and realizes that it was all a dream until he turns on the television and finds that everyone on TV are apes..." (http://dc.wikia.com/wiki/Son_of_Ambush_Bug_Vol_1_5). Small world!

folderol, since they *know* they've awakened to their native planet's future, where common lifeforms of the 1940s have either evolved into monstrous predators or gone extinct, and gorillas and baboons have hyper-evolved into the dominant sentient species. Could either de Camp or Miller have possibly known of (or even read) Haraucourt's 1904 short story?

The novel has its own rich energy, wit, and style, and the satiric digs at mankind via its extinction and all that has replaced it are still often delightful. That said, the pulpish sci-fi nature of de Camp's and Miller's opus is self-evident: the bus is buried when a tunnel caves in, trapping two dozen men and women on board (many of them scientists en route to a Columbus, Ohio, powwow) and perfectly preserving them all in one of those incredibly unlikely states of suspended animation upon which so much vintage futurist science fiction depended. This time, their million-year survival was initiated not only by the earthquake and premature burial, but also by an experimental hibernation "gas" that one of them thar scientists on board just happened to be carrying. Damn lucky, that.

Thanks to the biologist of the group, communication is established with the city-dwelling super-gorillas, opening the door for de Camp's and Miller's satire to kick in. Having based their culture on science, the gorillas have managed to eschew everything that resulted in the self-destruction of mankind. There's a passing reference to nuclear destruction – fleeting, vague, and entirely speculative – which seems unlikely in a 1941 piece of fiction; it must have been added for the post-Wold War II book edition (I've since tracked down the original *Super Science Novels* version, and will satisfy my own curiosity on this point during the winter months): "Had it been that something – atomic energy – unleashed and in the hands of uncontrollable men, which brought mankind smashing down in self-destruction and gave the world to these apes?"

In contrast to the *Planet of the Apes* movies, the gorillas (closer to what we now know of the real species) are a peaceful race; we are given considerable insights into the workings of the civilized gorilla culture. At one point, the gorilla hosts describe the evolved chimpanzees (the G'thong-smith) as

> a very clever lot, but nervous and quite irresponsible. Their history is full of strange stories of civil war, conspiracy, and murder. But they built some magnificent cities, with huge stone buildings. They look down on us because they say that we cannot make pictures and music, and cannot recite long pieces of writing as beautiful of theirs...

Thus, as in Boulle's novel and the subsequent film adaptations, divisions between the primate species and cultures are quite pronounced. It's the damned baboons (the Pfenmll) that are the war-mongering tribal culture! So, the humans pitch in to help the gorillas take on the baboon military-industrial complex (a monarchy, and savaged as such by the authors), culminating in some lively mayhem sure to please *Planet of the Apes* buffs. Even with the help of our human heroes, though, it takes more to turn the tide against the baboons – you see, the hyper-evolved primates aren't the only kingpin mammals supplanting now-extinct mankind: the first hyper-evolved mammals they spot are semi-civilized "ratoids" (that survive an encounter with an outsized "badgeroid" – there are also "squirreloids," "parrotoids," mutant armadillos, etc.), followed by their first encounter with "a race of civilized, man-sized beavers," and others. The rather metropolitan, outsized, super-intelligent beavers (!!!) save the day in the end.

Which makes me wonder, in retrospect, if my veteran writer-artist amigo Tim Truman hadn't read de Camp's and Miller's novel – after all, Tim concocted the *Time Beavers* graphic novel (1985, First Comics). But that's another story...

This does, however, bring us into the realm of comic books and graphic novels, at last. To my mind, the unacknowledged import of the de Camp/Miller novel is that it was the most likely wellspring for the seminal pre-Boulle comic book stories that anticipated so many particulars of *Planet of the Apes*.

III. Four-Color Forefathers: Binder, Infantino, Kirby, Dorfman, Ticci, and Giolitti

> "We can see other worlds existing in space – but are there other worlds in space that we can't see, perhaps close by in another dimension? Would it be a universe peopled by creatures resembling us – or would civilization there have advanced along a different path? There was only one way these intriguing questions could be answered – by crossing the barrier between the two worlds and see for oneself!"
>
> "Why, this world is exactly like Earth!"
>
> "Not exactly, Cora! That war memorial statue – the general is a gorilla!"
>
> – Otto Binder, splash page text (narrative caption and speech balloons) for "The Gorilla World!", Strange Adventures #45 (June 1954), page 1

"The Gorilla World!" appeared in *Strange Adventures* #45 (June 1954). My coverless copy of this venerable DC "gorilla cover" gem is well-worn and well-read. I've had it for more than 40 years! This DC science-fiction corker may be just one of almost countless DC comics sporting apes and gorillas to perk sales, but it *predates* Pierre Boulle's *La Planète Des Singes* by damn near a full decade, and lays the groundwork for just about *everything* in the Boulle novel and the beloved film series that followed. Hence, I love it, and must include it here.

"The Gorilla World!" was written by Otto Binder, penciled by Carmine Infantino, and inked by Joe Giella. It is Binder's authorship we must focus upon here, given his history as a prolific writer for both sci-fi pulp fiction and for comic books, but it must be understood how comic book freelance script assignments were handled by the editors at National Periodicals/DC Comics in the 1950s and 1960s. Binder was indeed the author, but the concept for "The Gorilla World!" was most likely *assigned to* Binder by *Strange Adventures* editor (and long-time pioneer science-fiction fan and writer's agent) Julie Schwartz. Since the editors brainstormed all the covers back in those days (according to Julie, as related in countless interviews and in personal conversation with me back in 1986), the cover concept most likely would have been Julie's – so to speak. Given his encyclopedic knowledge of pulp science fiction and his having agented for many sci-fi authors, I find it unlikely (nigh on impossible, really) that Julie *wouldn't* have been aware of de Camp's and Miller's seminal novel, from its initial pulp debut. The classic DC/National Periodicals run of "gorilla covers"[11] had kicked off with *Strange Adventures* #8 (May 1951), and it didn't take long for Julie to either suggest an abridged spin on the de Camp/Miller novel for a cover story, or for freelance writer Binder to pitch the concept knowing Schwartz would jump on it.[12] Either way, it was a gem in the early run of *Strange Adventures*.

---

[11] Comic Book Resources' Brian Cronin featured 50 such covers in the 15 November 2015 edition of his "I Can't Cover What I Am" blog: http://goodcomics.comicbookresources.com/2014/11/15/i-cant-cover-what-i-am-is-that-a-gorilla-on-the-cover-i-must-have-it/.

[12] Alas, this story is not included in the DC Comics reprint editions of *Strange Adventures*, but you can read it online at http://savedfromthepaperdrive.blogspot.com/2014/11/the-gorilla-world.html. Comics scholar Bob Heer noted (in his comment on my original blog post about this comic book story), "No, unfortunately DC started their *Strange Adventures* b&w reprint with #54 (possibly picking the first code-approved issue as an arbitrary starting point), less than a year after the 'Gorilla World' story which doesn't seem to have ever been reprinted. Still a lot of gorilla stuff in that book, including 'The Gorilla Who Challenged the World,' 'Gorillas in Space,' and 'The Gorilla Conquest of Earth'..." Bob Heer, 12 July, 2012, posted on the comments thread at Myrant, 2 July, 2012, "Going Ape! Redux," archived at http://srbissette.com/planet-of-the-apes-precursors-2/.

The story's splash page instantly undermined the promise of the cover blurb ("What would you do if YOU were the only human being in – 'The Gorilla World!'"), by showing a well-dressed male/female couple surprised to find a military statue in a park of a gorilla general astride a horse. The first narrative page of the story lets us know this couple is "Albert Dawson and his wife Cora still missing, after a month..." as an investigator at the "Missing Persons Bureau" is startled by the sudden appearance on his desk of a mysterious talking book. The talking artifact essentially introduces the entire "Earth 1/Earth 2" premise central to the DC Comics Silver Age superhero comics of the 1960s (about which I'll say nothing more) and the same premise that later informed the whole of the J.J. Abrams/Alex Kurtzman/Roberto Orci TV series *Fringe* (2008-2013) – but in "The Gorilla World!" it's an evolved simian civilization dominating that second companion Earth:

> Attention! Open me! This is a message from a neighboring dimension to Earth! Our worlds exist side-by-side, but are invisible and intangible to each other! Sent via the fourth dimension pathway, this record will explain why two humans are missing from Earth – Albert and Cora Dawson! This talking book was sent by me, a scientist in the other dimension! I imagine you are astonished to see that I have the form of your Earthly gorilla! But you see, all our people are gorillas! Evolution here uplifted our species, not humans!

Having established all that on page 2 of the story, "The Gorilla World!" launches into its core mystery on its third page: why do Albert and Cora want to stay on the Gorilla World, caged as exhibits in a zoo? After a short historical chronology of the rise of the gorilla civilization, we see Albert's examination by the Science Council – Infantino's and Giella's art for page 5, panel 3, being almost identical to the issue's cover art, a trope of all Julie Schwartz DC comics (Julie always made sure whatever the comic book covers promised was repeated, *verbatim*, inside the promised story) – in the first visual media illustration of a concept central to the entire *Planet of the Apes* mythos. In another trope central to the *Planet of the Apes* narratives, the gorilla scientist feels responsible and sorry for the plight of the caged intelligent humans, leading to Albert's insistence that the gorilla not return the humans to their own world.

Why? It turns out, back on the human Earth, ol' Albert was "a freak on exhibit in a sideshow! A fake gorilla man!" Sick and tired of the lousy pay, impoverished lifestyle, and shoddy conditions of the couple's life back on Earth, they prefer imprisonment on the Gorilla Planet. Cora says, "With all this food and leisure, we never had it so good on our own world!"

Take *that,* 1951 middle-class America!

And that was, indeed, the end of the story...

Otto Binder was a prominent author in the first generation of 20th-Century science and science-fiction writers, co-writing sci-fi with his brother Earl Binder (under the moniker "Eando Binder") in the 1930s, including the justifiably famous Adam Link "I, Robot" stories (1939-1942, which inspired nine short stories that Isaac Asimov wrote from 1940 to 1950 that were published in novel form as *I, Robot,* against Asimov's wishes due to Binder's claim on the title). On his own, Binder subsequently carved out a remarkable career that also included more than 3,000 comic book scripts from 1938 to 1969. Binder's best-selling and most revered body of comics work remains his *Captain Marvel* and "Marvel family" stories for Fawcett throughout the 1940s, but he also scripted a great deal for National Periodicals / DC Comics throughout the 1950s and 1960s. Being prolific in the comics marketplace was a necessity, in part due to the low page rates (and lack of any benefits — including reprint fees or royalties of any kind — for comics creators) offered by the publisher. For more on Binder the man and writer, I refer the curious reader to Bill Schelly's excellent *Words of Wonder: The Life and Times of Otto Binder* (Hamster Press, 2003).[13]

Just ten issues later, *Strange Adventures* #55 offered "The Gorilla Who Challenged the World!" — sigh. Issue #55, out in 1955, the year of my birth. APE-ril of 1955, to be precise, meaning it was on the stands when I was born.

Many *Planet of the Apes* fans and scholars have long presumed the late, great Jack Kirby had lifted from *Planet of the Apes* when Kirby (as writer and penciler) spiced his 1970s comic book series *Kamandi: The Last Boy on Earth* (59 issues, 1972-1978) with post-apocalyptic anthropomorphized animal species, including simians. The Grand Comics Database describes *Kamandi* as "A post-nuclear war vision of the future, loosely based on *The Planet of the Apes,*" affirming the prejudices of many *Apes* fans and devotees.[14] While I presume it's unnecessary to provide an introduction to, or biography of, Jack Kirby — co-creator of some of America's most popular comics characters and concepts, including Captain America, the Fantastic Four, the Incredible Hulk, the Mighty

---

[13] Bill Schelly is, at the time of this writing, revising and expanding *Words of Wonder* for a new edition, to be published by North Atlantic Books in June 2016. I look forward to the new edition of *Words of Wonder: The Life and Times of Otto Binder.*
[14] http://www.comics.org/series/2028/

Thor, the Avengers, the Fourth World (the New Gods, the Forever People, Mister Miracle, etc.), the Demon, and so forth – it's *Kamandi* alone that most *Planet of the Apes* fans are aware of and fixate upon, and understandably so.

Kamandi #16 (April 1974) featured "The Animals Have Taken Over the World!," one of Kirby's liveliest spins on Boulle's *Planet of the Apes*, spiced with Mike Royer's and D. Bruce Berry's inks and Kirby's revelations of precisely *what* lay behind "the Great Disaster" that turned evolution on its ear. It's all spelled out in the diary of one Michael Grant, and involved a genetic stimulant named Cortexin, and I still remember first picking this up on the newsstand and reading and rereading the issue in my bedroom in Colbyville, Vt., the winter before I started college (at Johnson State College, in Johnson, Vt.).

Jack Kirby wasn't just riffing off *Planet of the Apes* by way of Gold Key's *The Mighty Samson* (co-created by Otto Binder, writer, and Frank Thorne, artist, edited by Wally Green; 32 issues, 1964-1982) when he created and launched *Kamandi: The Last Boy on Earth* at then-DC-publisher Carmine Infantino's request. Kirby was reviving and realizing a concept he'd played with years before Boulle's novel even existed.

Kirby had attempted to sell a *Kamandi* caveman-type strip in the late 1950s (sporting the name *Kamandi*, if memory serves), right around the time he drew the science-fiction story "The Last Enemy!" for Harvey Comics's *Alarming Tales* #1 (September, 1957).[15]

As with DC's "The Gorilla World!," Kirby was tapping that post-apocalyptic topsy-turvy conceit of bipedal, talking humanoid mammals unseating man's domination in the future a few years before Boulle published his novel. Unlike "The Gorilla World!," evolved simians were *not* among the humanoid mammalians featured in "The Last Enemy!" Bulldogs, foxes, bears, rodents, tigers: yes. Talking apes? No. The relevance to *Kamandi* is clear – there remains, in fact, an often one-to-one correlation between the civilized "manimals"

---

[15] According to the Grand Comics Database on other sources, Kirby both scripted and drew "The Last Enemy!" (see http://www.comics.org/issue/13800/), which also cites the probability of Kirby inking the story as well ("per Harry Mendryk") and notes the story being reprinted three times between 1959 and 1981, and again in 2010 by Titan Books in *The Simon and Kirby Library: Science Fiction*. You can read "The Last Enemy!" online at http://cartoonsnap.blogspot.com/2007/10/more-alarming-1950s-kirby-sci-fi-comics.html or at https://marswillsendnomore.wordpress.com/2012/09/24/alarming-tales-1-the-last-enemy-donnegans-daffy-chair/.

populating "The Last Enemy!" and key players in *Kamandi* – including the manner in which non-simian species are first introduced to Kamandi (and to the reader).

In "The Last Enemy!," the time-traveler human protagonist is shown on the splash page facing a bipedal bulldog military leader – legs locked firmly apart, arms folded behind his back, a cigarette (in tipped cigarette holder) jutting from his jaws and eyes fixed on the traveler – flanked by a flag-carrying uniformed bear and a rifle-wielding fox (or cat) behind this Winston Churchill-like canine commander. The first hyper-evolved mammalians whom the time-traveler encounters "five hundred years" in the future are a battlefield strewn with uniformed dead soldiers who are "tigers! Dozens of them – and wearing clothes!" His first conversation is with an evolved rat, leader of a rat army that takes our hero prisoner and interrogates him in their underground lair, revealing during the grilling their plans to build their own atomic weapons – with the help of the time-traveling scientist. He is rescued by gas-mask-wearing soldiers emerging from a vehicular drilling device, and awakens in a medical facility overseen by a canine doctor (with a black patch coloration over one eye and semi-floppy ears) and soldier fox and bear, all of whom snap to attention when the bulldog general enters the room. The dialogue exchange between the bulldog and the time-traveler brings the story to a rapid conclusion (read on).

Consider how closely Jack Kirby emulated "The Last Enemy!" in the October-November 1972 debut issue of *Kamandi, The Last Boy on Earth*. The first hyper-evolved sentient bidepal mammals Kamandi encounters are the armed, uniformed wolves that kill his grandfather while raiding their bunker, driving Kamandi from his former home forever; the first evolved mammals he stumbles across traveling the ruined New Jersey Turnpike (a sly direct reference to *Genus Homo*?) are an army of tigers riding horses, one of whom (the leader) Kamandi saves from the opposing Leopard army's sniper. It is as if Kirby was finally fully imagining and reveling in the battle that happened *before* the opening panels of "The Last Enemy!," leaving that battlefield littered with dead tiger-soldiers.

When Kamandi awakens in the tiger's prison (caged alongside howling, animalistic uncivilized humans), a bipedal bulldog prison guard hauls in a vat of gruel, and Kamandi soon sees with his own eyes that the tigers harbor and worship an atomic warhead (shades of *Beneath the Planet of the Apes*!). When Kamandi lashes out and tries to trigger the warhead, he is caught and captured by Doctor Canus – a slight variation on the dog-doctor in "The Last Enemy!"

Despite the lack of sentient apes, the first issue of *Kamandi, the Last Boy on Earth* (October-November 1972) clearly riffed on the ending of the 1968 *Planet of the Apes*. The same ruined statue featured prominently in the story's opening. Art by Jack Kirby. © Marvel Comics.

right down to having a black coloration over one eye. The cover art and opening sequence of *Kamandi* #2 (January 1973) features a scavenging party of armed bipedal hyper-evolved rats from beneath the Earth, and they are the villains of the entire second issue's action-packed storyline.

Sentient simians debuted with *Kamandi* #3 (February 1973), only after the *Kamandi* storyline and human characters (Kamandi's allies are a band of mutant super-humans with "cyclo-hearts" capable of transforming themselves into metallic super-beings when triggered) were well-established. Despite the fact that Kirby did keep his *Planet of the Apes* simian civilization and characters quite active throughout the run of *Kamandi*, they were only one species in a diverse menagerie of mutants and super-evolved mammalian lifeforms, building as much upon Kirby's own "The Last Enemy!" as Kirby did upon *Genus Homo, La Planète des Singes,* and the popular *Planet of the Apes* movie series (as it existed up to 1972 or 1973).

However, there were major differences between Kirby's self-standing 1957 "The Last Enemy!" and where he'd take the premise for *Kamandi* more than a decade later. There were no future-era human survivors interacting with the hyper-evolved mammals in the *Alarming Tales* story. The human species was extinct. The human protagonist was a time traveler who'd propelled himself half a millennium into Earth's future, to the year 2514 A.D., to find that the human species no longer existed. "Your kind left us many things – language – culture – weapons," a sophisticated, clothed, outsized bipedal rat tells him between puffs on a cigarette. "Something called an atomic war finished the humans!"

Unlike in *Genus Homo*, the villains here are hyper-evolved rodents. When the bulldog general confides in the time-traveling human how his own species once "fought them all – the foxes, bears, wolves... now, we are allies," he also reveals the common enemy of the united species remains the rodents. "They were the big competition. In the end, it would be the rodent against the entire animal kingdom!"

So much for de Camp's and Miller's beavers saving the day.

In the end, the human time-traveler chooses to leave, but only after delivering the formula for constructing an atomic weapon with the canine-led coalition. "Your place is among men... even if they are going to perish," he tells himself. "I wonder if another man would have given them the atom bomb? I think so! It's better that the world go to the dogs than a lot of scheming rats!"

A little over a decade later, an atomic weapon and Charlton Heston would arrive at a very different conclusion in the searing finale of *Beneath the Planet of the Apes* (1970).[16]

There is one more American comic book precursor to Boulle's 1963 novel – and, at this juncture, my own experience with the 1968 feature film adaptation of *Planet of the Apes* – that I must bring to your attention. In fact, it's the *first* visual story I thought of back in 1968 when I first watched the movie at Burlington's Strong Theater with my father, who had taken me to see it. I remember digging frantically through my comic books in search of the comic in which this story appeared, but alas, I could not find it – it was long gone, traded away, sold in a garage sale, or tossed out or lost. I did find, and hold onto, that coverless issue of *Strange Adventures* #45 I had, but the missing comic book story only acquired greater allure and mystique in my imagination as a result of being something I could not reread, revisit, and reassess.

I'd argue that "missing story" is yet another predecessor to *Planet of the Apes* – all the moreso for appearing in *The Twilight Zone* comic book, which featured Rod Serling's photo on the cover. Serling, of course, co-scripted *Planet of the Apes*, the movie. But I'm getting ahead of myself here. Let me back up a bit...

A January 2013 query about this dimly remembered comic on Facebook reacquainted me with this comic book story from my youth. Throughout the decades, I have often thought of, searched for, and even dreamed about this long-lost *Twilight Zone* comic book numerous times.

I asked on Facebook:

> OK, fellow Dell / Gold Key devotees: I have vivid childhood memories of a story in a very, very early *Twilight Zone* comic of an astronaut and his fellow astronauts transforming into apelike simian throwbacks once

---

[16] Note that the same year "The Last Enemy!" was published, Donald A. Wollheim's novel *Across Time* (1957, Ace Books) hit the paperback racks (under Wollheim's pen name "David Grinnell"). While some sources cite Wollheim's novel as another predecessor to *Planet of the Apes*, such is not the case, as a reading of the novel itself proves. Wollheim's tale involves an Air Force test pilot encountering alien beings from the far future, scattered over multiple galaxies, who are, in fact, all descended from Earth's human "seed." These include an evolutionary lineage which call themselves the Seroomi; despite their elongated extremities, the Seroomi are hardly hyper-evolved simians, and *Across Time* is not of the same breed as "The Last Enemy!" or "The Gorilla World!" For my money, the comic book stories rate as genuine roots in the *Planet of the Apes* family tree, whereas Wollheim's novel simply does not.

they've been on the moon or planet too long. My memory of the art, in hindsight, sure 'looks' like George Evans to me, in my mind's eye... but I've never, ever been able to find that comic or story again. Anyone?

Thankfully, John Wells responded within an hour or two of my Facebook appeal about this half-remembered comic book story, providing hard information and scans.

"The Ray of Phobos" appeared in *The Twilight Zone* #2 (Gold Key, February 1963; not *Dell Four Color Comics* #1288, which is Dell's *Twilight Zone* #2 to Dell Comics collectors), and I'm forever thankful to John for recovering it and sending it my way. I was eight years old when I read this story, and never laid eyes on it again until John made that possible. I've since purchased a hard copy of this comic book.[17]

"The Ray of Phobos" is an 11-page story that begins (as all *Twilight Zone* stories should and usually did) with host Rod Serling speaking to the reader: "Morning! The fierce sun beats down on the vast reaches of an endless desert..." Astronaut Matt Wayne awakens in said desert with no memory of where he is or how he got there, or even why he is wearing a spacesuit. Following his own footprints from where he fell and has awakened, Wayne finds a downed spaceship self-identified (via hull markings) as "Operation Trail Blazer: U.S. Expedition to Mars." As he enters the ship, his memory returns, but none of the equipment is working and there's no sign of his fellow crew members (Knight, Borkin, and Frazer), so he follows their tracks away from the wreckage, only to find their oxygen tanks discarded in the sand and "ape-like footprints" leading from the abandoned tanks. "I see it now! Those Martian creatures found Knight and the others and dragged them off!" Wayne concludes, only to find his progress following the ape-like tracks hampered by his own oxygen supply running out.

Succumbing to the initial stages of suffocation, the astronaut collapses near cave-like geological structures, terrified by the approach of monstrous ape-like forms wearing the helmets of the missing expedition members. Rescued by the "Martians," he is shocked when one explains, "Wayne! There's something you've got to understand... we're your friends!" Gasping for oxygen, one of the transformed astronauts hands Wayne a Martian rock, which puts him to sleep

---

[17] You can read the full *Twilight Zone* comic story at http://srbissette.com/before-the-planet-of-the-apes-comicbook-precursors-rediscovered/. It was reprinted by Western/Gold Key in *Mystery Comics Digest* #6 (August 1972) and in *The Twilight Zone* #R1245 (1982).

long enough for them to carry him back out into the desert, to expose him to the rays of the Martian moon Phobos. Exposure to the Phobos rays causes a change: Wayne is able to breathe the Martian atmosphere, and begins to change into a semi-simian form like his fellow astronauts. "Some scientists have always believed that Phobos was an artificial satellite launched by some ancient people," explains transformed astronaut Knight. "From what happened to us I believe they used that ray to adapt themselves to life here on Mars!"

Looking alarmingly like Ro-Man in Phil Tucker's *Robot Monster* (1953), the almost-fully-simian Wayne freaks out, yelling "No! No! I don't want to be a beast! No! I'd rather die!", and inexplicably wakes up back on Earth in a hospital bed surrounded by a doctor, a nurse, and military officials. In a "twist" that recalls *The Wizard of Oz* (1939) as much as it does *Dead of Night* (1945), it turns out Wayne is in hospital recovering from a mere test orbit flight, and has yet to join a planned expedition to Mars. He is then introduced to the fellow astronauts of Operation Trail-Blazer – Knight, Borkin, and Frazer, naturally – but upon deciding he has suffered nothing more than a nightmare, he finds something tucked beneath his pillow: "The red stone! The one they gave me when I couldn't breathe on Mars!"

According to the Grand Comic Database (GCD) and Martin O'Hearn, writer Leo Dorfman scripted this story.[18] I had no way of knowing that at the time, but I sure recognized the artist's handiwork, or at least the hand of the artist who inked the story. I had erroneously remembered the story looking like it might

---

[18] My thanks to Martin O'Hearn, who identified Dorfman as the author when he commented on my original blog post concerning this story; also see http://www.comics.org/issue/17514/. Martin wrote, "Paul S. Newman didn't write that much for the early *Twilight Zone* comic book. This story is by the one who did: Leo Dorfman. The adjective in the caption 'And in the next startling moment...' and the good number of captions using 'as' point to him; the same things distinguish his work in *Superman* at the same time. Dorfman was the sole writer on the first few years of the Gold Key *Ripley's Believe It or Not Ghost Stories*, and when he lost that assignment he just carried all his true-ghost notes to DC as the only writer on *Ghosts* in its early issues. As wholesome as Gold Key was, in some ways their books were just as strange-looking to a young DC reader as the Ditko stuff in Marvel's *Amazing Adult-Fantasy* – this issue stayed locked in my memories, too, although it was the cover story about the underground New Amsterdam ['The Lost Colony'] that reverberated." Martin O'Hearn, 24 February, 2013, posted on the comments thread at Myrant, 9 January, 2013, "Lost in Four-Color Space!," archived at http://srbissette.com/before-the-planet-of-the-apes-comicbook-precursors-rediscovered/.

have been one of George Evans' gigs for Dell Comics during this era – maybe even Evans and his pal Frank Frazetta, given my almost 50-year-old memories of the artwork, sight unseen since – but it's actually the work (in part) of Alberto Giolitti (14 November, 1923 – 15 April, 1993), the Italian-born comic book artist whose work I revered as a *Turok: Son of Stone* reader. GCD credits Giovanni Ticci with the pencils and Giolitti with the inks (with lettering by Ben Oda). And it's a Gold Key, not a Dell, comic book. Hence, I'd been digging in the wrong back-issues bins for decades![19]

The story is published in the issue of *Twilight Zone* cover-dated February 1963, meaning it was on newsstands and comic spinner racks closer to Christmas 1962 (cover dates refer to when a comic or magazine was to be *removed* from sale). It's interesting to note that the TV *Twilight Zone* episode "The Ray of Phobos" most resembles is "Death Ship," which was originally broadcast (gasp!) on 7 February, 1963! However, the Western / Gold Key editors and / or creative freelancers would have had no way to know about "Death Ship" prior to broadcast, really; it's more likely they could have read "Death Ship" author Richard Matheson's short story by the same title, initially published in *Fantastic Story Magazine* (March 1953). In Matheson's story and the very effective *Twilight Zone* adaptation, an exploratory spaceship crew discovers the wreckage of a downed spaceship eerily identical to their own vehicle. Entering the wreckage, they find their own bodies inside, and must decide whether to try and leave the planet (presumably causing the disaster that will claim their lives) or "cheat death" by staying where they are – but can they?

I daresay "The Ray of Phobos" is also an echo, of a kind, of the seminal Kurt Neumann science-fiction movie *Rocketship X-M* (1950). Forgotten today except by diehard science-fiction cinema afficianados, *Rocketship X-M* was rushed through production (reportedly shot in just 18 days) to beat the big production

---

[19] To make a long story short, 21st-Century comic book fans forget that the alliance between Western Publishing & Litho and Dell Comics was an incredibly successful one, until Western and Dell parted ways in 1962. From the 1940s into the early 1960s, Western/Dell boasted the highest newsstand sales of any American comics publisher; but in 1962, Western Publishing split from Dell Comics, to form their own imprint Gold Key Comics, and Western held on to its most valuable licensed comics titles, including *The Twilight Zone*. Both publishers suffered diminishing sales thereafter, and neither recovered the comic book market share they'd long enjoyed.

from producer George Pal (the seminal *Destination Moon*) into theaters – and did! It remains "that little movie that could" and that did, having oddly dated better then Pal's creaky melodramatic color opus.

I couldn't care less about the relative accuracy or inaccuracy of the science herein: when engine failure and a miscalculation results in the crew being knocked unconscious and *X-M* (Xpedition Moon) overshooting its lunar target, the ship detours to Mars and a still-imaginative passage on the Red Planet (first time California Death Valley locations filled in for same), where the remnants of a fallen civilization and radiation-scarred and blinded mutant tribes await. These tribal mutants look human, but move like more feral, primitive primates. When *Rocketship X-M* is viewed today with some awareness of the film's historical status, any misgivings give way to the almost intoxicating sensation of something being taken to completion the first time around for the big screen, simultaneously inventing and codifying what was, by 1950, already a formula for making a science-fiction movie. There were precedents, dating back to the 19th Century on through Fritz Lang's and Thea von Harbou's *Die Frau im Mond/The Woman in the Moon* (1929, from von Harbou's novel, among the oldest and rarest movie-tie-in novels in my own collection) and innumerable pulp science-fiction stories, novellas, and novels, but Kurt Neumann was doing it first for mainstream American motion pictures in the new decade, post-World War II.[20]

So: *Rocketship X-M* and this comic book story shared key elements. A Mars expedition, simian "throwbacks," Martian mutations, a message carried back to Earth, and some of the striking imagery – it all resonates, transmuted, in that fascinating way pop culture often does.

Ticci (pencils) and Giolitti (inks) also drew the other two primary stories in this issue of *The Twilight Zone* comic book, "The Lost Colonie" and "Journey into Jeopardy." Ticci's work is essentially unknown in the United States, since most fans who cared tended to only identify Giolitti as the artist. Ticci was born in Siena, Italy, and made his mark initially working on fumetti (Italian comics) for Rinaldi Dami's studio in 1956, later assisting Franco Bignotti on strips *Dick Darling* and *Kit Carson*. Ticci began his collaboration with Giolitti in 1960,

---

[20] For more on *Rocketship X-M*, see my article "SpiderBaby Cinema: To the Moon, Alice!" in *Weng's Chop* #5 (March 2014, Vol. 2, No. 1, pp. 169-176), available at http://www.amazon.com/gp/product/1497332060?keywords=Weng's%20Chop%20%235&qid=1450649483&ref_=sr_1_1&sr=8-1.

working with him on a number of adventure and western comics for Western/Dell (and, as of 1962, Western/Gold Key), including *The Twilight Zone, Turok: Son of Stone, Voyage to the Bottom of the Sea, Wells Fargo, Gunsmoke,* and *Paladin/Have Gun Will Travel.* Ticci and Giolitti also worked together on fumetti like the western *Un Ragazo nel Far-West* (1964+, for Bonelli).

But it's Giolitti's linework I remembered and loved most. The artist was born in Rome, where his family held (and still hold) one of the most famous of all cafés, Giolitti, where he reportedly worked for a time – if ever I make it to Rome, I'll be making my pilgrimage there, to pay my respects. Giolitti cut his teeth on fumettis in his home country, with his artwork appearing in *Il Vittorioso* before WW2, as well as work for Editorial Lainez and Columba of Buenos Aires after he moved to South America following the war. After subsequently moving to the United States, Giolitti started a decades-long body of brilliant comics work for Western Publishing and Dell, and I've held on to a few stray issues of Dell staples like *Indian Chief, Tonto, Cisco Kid*, and *Gunsmoke* – but it's Giolitti's *Turok: Son of Stone* that I loved and still love above all. Giolitti apparently drew most of the *Turok* run back in his native country (he gained American citizenship, but returned to Italy in the early 1960s, where he collaborated with Ticci). His association with Western trumped that with Dell – along with peers like Russ Manning, Dan Spiegel, Carl Barks, and Jesse Marsh, Giolitti's distinctive work continued under the new Gold Key Comics moniker.

I've held on to a lot of primo Giolitti gems from the 1960s, including a couple of the bound editions of his *Star Trek* run and a grand, glorious oversized 1968 *King Kong* adaptation. I started to lose interest in Giolitti's work when it became increasingly apparent that his studio was handling much of the duties (having founded the Rome-based Studio Giolitti before the end of the 1960s), and though I stuck with *Turok* into the 1970s, I'd become a half-hearted reader (once Jack Sparling took over, I was gone-o, baby, even as it got tougher to find Gold Key comics anywhere). I've read that Giolitti later finished a dream project of his, *Cinque Anni Dopo* (*Five Years Later*, 1986), but I've never laid eyes on a copy. He also returned to the western fumettis he loved, specifically *Tex Willer*, before his death. It would be nice to see those one day, but I suspect it's *Turok* I'll continue to love above all to my own dying day.

And I'll always have a soft spot for this particular *Twilight Zone* story, in which Ticci's pencils and Giolitti's inks lent the tale the distinctive "look" that stuck with me for oh, so long.

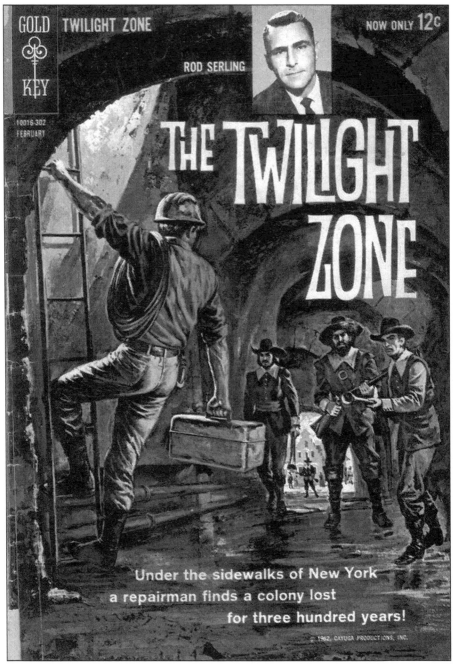

Gold Key's *Twilight Zone* #2 (Feb 1963) features "The Ray of Phobos," which includes astronauts being transformed into simian-like creatures, with pencils by Giovianni Ticci and line work by Alberto Giolitti.

IV. Ripples & Rip-offs: Monkeys See, Monkeys Do

"Godo, where are we going?"

– Pepe (Kazue Takita) in Saru No Gundan/Time of the Apes (1974, from the dubbed and edited Sandy Frank US version, 1987)

As noted earlier, many *Planet of the Apes* fans and scholars tend to cite Jack Kirby's comic book series *Kamandi, The Last Boy on Earth* as a rip-off of *Planet of the Apes*, but I've already countered that. If it's spinoffs, rip-offs, and ripple effects you want to trace, *Kamandi* remains the least off-putting of what followed in the wake of the 1968 *Planet of the Apes* becoming a box-office sensation around the globe.

Mind you, *Kamandi* emerged from a lively stew of *Planet of the Apes* four-color comic book successors, all eager to hook readers who might enjoy the comics due to associative links with the *Apes* franchise.

Prominent among those, of course, were the licensed, official *Planet of the Apes* comics. The Gold Key comic book adaptation of Ted Post's *Beneath the Planet of the Apes* (1970) was among my favorite Gold Key movie comics. I enjoyed it at the time of its publication (as I had the earlier Gold Key *Astroboy* and *Yellow Submarine* comics). Oddly enough, given the previously mentioned *Twilight Zone* comic book story with which I only recently reacquainted myself, Giolitti's studio did the artwork for *Beneath the Planet of the Apes*. Though I still have my copy of the comic book, I no longer have the insert poster which I'd tacked up on my bedroom wall the afternoon I bought the comic at Vincent's Pharmacy in Waterbury, Vt. This was the first authorized movie-based *Planet of the Apes* comic published – hence, its honorary status and position in this chronology.

Afterwards, there was of course the Marvel Comics series (a four-color comic book *and* a black-and-white magazine series), which I had little interest in at the time. However, my (late) friend Steve Perry loved the series, and I vividly recall his bringing to my attention time and time again some of the work published in the Marvel black-and-white magazine. The one image I cannot shake was drawn by Tom Sutton (for *Planet of the Apes* #12, September 1975, page 12) in which aristocratic apes assembled and seated themselves around an opulent table in a fireplace-let hall, the table groaning with food.[21]

There was, however, also a Hungarian *Planet of the Apes* comic adaptation with which I am quite enamored. Compliments of pop culture and Ray Harryhausen fan/archivist/scholar Péter Kollárik, I was alerted to this true rarity, an exquisite Hungarian comic book adaptation *A Majmok Bolygoja* (*Monkey Planet*) "by Hungary's best comic book artist, the late Ernő Zórád from 1980." Péter pointed out to me, upon initial contact, that the comic adaptation had "nothing to do with the movie: it is based on the French novel," Pierre Boulle's *La Planète Des Singes/Planet of the Apes* (1963).[22]

For more on the *Planet of the Apes* comics canon, see *The Sacred Scrolls: Comics on the Planet of the Apes*, edited by Rich Handley and Joseph F. Berenato (Sequart, 2015). There is a world of exploration – and, yes, exploitation – awaiting the curious reader there. Many of the comics may prove disappointing, but there is much rewarding reading there, too.

And then there's *Kamandi*…

No, it wasn't Jack Kirby's *Kamandi* that put me (and others) off at the time: it was the bizarre burst of cinematic shams, charades, and shameless snake-oil exploitation that left a bad taste in the mouth of any who fell for the likes of the following…

Why worry about comic books? The rip-offs associated with *Planet of the Apes* hit theater screens the same year that feature film was making box-office history.

High on the list of "What the hell?" *Planet of the Apes* knock-off cinematic confections was one curious title of undefinable origin – *Wild Wild Apes*, aka *Wild Is the Word for Wild Wild Apes* – evidenced solely by an old High Point, North Carolina, newspaper ad that appeared in December 1968: "Will Killer Apes Rule the World? In 2068 Who Will Rule – Men or Apes; The Strangest Adventure You've Ever Seen!"

Based on the last title listed in the ad, reprinted at the Temple of Schlock

---

[21] Special thanks to Tom Sutton, biographer and long-time comics author, and scholar Dana Marie Andra for sharing this image with me during the revision of this article, in time to properly cite the issue and page in which it appeared.

[22] Péter Kollárik subsequently and very kindly traded me a copy of this rare comic for a Ray Harryhausen rarity unavailable in his native country. For more on this comic adaptation, go to http://pota.goatley.com/hungarian.html, where overseer Hunter Goatley has posted two English translations of the Hungarian comic. Enjoy!

website,[23] I'd even argue this was the *first-ever* movie rip-off of *Planet of the Apes*: a retitling of a re-released action movie, luring unwary movie-goers in under false pretenses!

The ad graphics, lifted from multiple sources, demonstrate a puckish sense of humor about their shameless hucksterism ("Our President in 2068?"). Note the title lettering font, in which the word "Apes" (with the letters "e" and "s" graphically linked) matched that used in the 20th Century Fox *Planet of the Apes* film promotional artwork.[24] Front and center in the visuals was artist Frank McCarthy's stunning ad art for Cy Endfield's remarkable, forgotten *Sands of the Kalahari* (1965, below), and the credits visible in this ad seem to indicate that's precisely the film that was being double-billed with *Kingu Kongu Tai Gojira/King Kong vs. Godzilla* (1962/1963), though the shysters who cobbled this together tossed in elements from the exquisite MGM campaign for *I Criminali Della Galassia/Wild, Wild Planet* (1965, also below), a dash of Ursula Andress from Hammer's *She* (1965), and a Ray Harryhausen flying saucer from *Earth vs. the Flying Saucers* (1956) to sweeten the allure. Man, they must have had quite a pressbook collection in their files. I also love the *Hang 'Em High* (1968) showing slipped in for Christmas (FYI, *Apes* movie mavens, that was Ted Post's first theatrical director credit) – Christmas theater owners in North Carolina were eager to break out the mistletoe, but mind the rope burns![25]

Amando de Ossorio's *La Noche Del Terror Ciego/Tombs of the Blind Dead* (1971) was the lurid tale of the reanimated corpses of the infamous Knights Templar and their horses rising from their graves in Spain to sup upon the blood of the living. It was also, incredibly, re-released in some U.S. markets, in slightly edited form, as a *Planet of the Apes* "sequel." *Really.* This marketing lunacy was titled *Revenge from Planet Ape*, dating from 1976-'77, and evidence of its theatrical release popped up in Brownsville, San Antonio, Texas, and as far northeast as Biddleford, Maine(!).[26]"See Apes Rise from Their Graves to Destroy

[23] http://templeofschlock.blogspot.com/2010/01/wild-wild-apes-1968-huh.html

[24] As noted by "Chris," on 5 December, 2010, in his note to the comments thread at Myrant, 29 November, 2010, "Prime-Apes! My Fave Planet of the Apes Knockoffs," archived at http://srbissette.com/going-ape/

[25] This was a delicious discovery of the kingpins of the *Temple of Schlock* website, to whom all due glory must go: http://templeofschlock.blogspot.com/. Worship there regularly, as I do.

[26] See https://screen13.wordpress.com/2015/11/04/the-blind-dead-go-ape-revenge-from-planet-ape-at-screen-13s-last-stop-cinema/.

Man in a Battle that Survives Death!" read ballyhoo for the film, really hard-selling the phony *Planet of the Apes* "connection."

The definitive 2005 Blue Underground DVD release of *Tombs of the Blind Dead* included the new pre-title narration (claiming that the Blind Dead were long-dead *apes* resurrected to exact revenge on the human species that ravaged their society and destroyed their kind) and title for this stunning feat of hucksterism.[27] This only expanded my already almost unbelievable affection for de Ossorio's fantastic film *tenfold*. Now, *that's* showmanship!

While some have questioned whether this was a prank on the part of Blue Underground, such was not the case. I'd heard about this version from friends in the 1980s who claimed to have seen it at drive-ins, and surviving newspaper clip art provides further evidence of its theatrical life; the DVD footage with which Blue Underground spiced their DVD release was courtesy of collector Harry Guerro.

Devlin Thompson recalled his personal experience with this curious anomaly:[28]

> Sometime around 1978, I went to the Market Place Cinema in Anderson, SC (now a senior citizens' activity center) to see a movie listed on the marquee as "REVENGE PLANET APE." I had never been all that into the whole POTA phenomenon, but I figured I might like to see one in a theater, so I had my grandfather drop me off (he would sometimes come with me, but not in this instance... probably just as well). I was not amused at the bait-and-switch; I've never revisited it since to see how I'd feel about it on its own terms. It was also around that same time that I jumped at the chance to see a new Christopher Lee "Dracula" movie in a theater (at that point, as a ten-or-eleven-year-old, Lee was pretty much just a face in Famous Monsters to me), only to be confronted with the massive disappointment of Dracula and Son [the French Dracula Père et Fils, 1976].

Kiyo Sumi Fukazawa's and Atsuo Okunaka's *Saru No Gundan/Time of the Apes* (1974, 26 episodes; U.S. version: edited to 97 minutes by Sandy Frank, 1987) has burned a little hole in my brain and coiled itself in there like some fuzzy grub. I can't shake it; I love it. But it's terrible, truly, an opportunistic rip-off of *Planet of the Apes* mounted by the late great Eiji Tsuburaya's Tsuburaya Productions, the special effects and production studio that had scored mightily

---

[27] At the time of this writing, the clip is also viewable at
https://www.youtube.com/watch?v=IfVZdsllpdQ.
[28] Devlin Thompson, 4 December 2010, posted on the comments thread at Myrant, 29 November, 2010, "Prime-Apes! My Fave Planet of the Apes Knockoffs," archived at http://srbissette.com/going-ape/.

in the 1960s with *Urutora Kyū/Ultra Q* (2 January 2 to 3 July, 1966) and especially *Urutoraman/Ultraman* (10 July, 1966 to 9 April, 1967, 40 episodes), first of the smash-hit *tokusatsu* franchises.

But first, let us remember what little Johnny (Masaaki Kaji) exclaimed after being warned about possible cataclysmic earth tremors: "I don't care!"

Because, you see, I don't, either.

All we have had to go on for decades here in America is the Sandy Frank-edited-and-dubbed condensation feature, *Time of the Apes*. Therein, pre-teen siblings Johnny and Caroline (pig-tailed Hiroko Saito in a schoolgirl outfit) drop in to visit Johnny's Uncle Charlie in his amazing lab. While his shapely lab assistant Catherine (Reiko Tokunaga) gives them the tour and they're standing next to the cryogenic tubes, an earthquake hammers the facility – so they duck into the tubes (!) and falling debris hits the switch (!!) and they end up trapped on an alternate future Earth (!!!) where war-mongering apes dominate what's left of mankind. It turns out these future civilizations are all apparently under the iron thumb of UECOM, aka UCOMM, an evil supercomputer (which Catherine learns of via telepathic communication with a completely inexplicable flying saucer that appears amid the hubbub for no apparent reason).

The interminable escape / capture / escape / flee / capture antics prominently features actors in immobile facsimiles of John Chambers's Academy-Award-winning *Planet of the Apes* simian makeups zipping around in 1974 and 1860s Civil War garb, behind the wheels of obvious 1970s model Buicks and Jeeps, carrying and occasionally mock-firing M1 Carbines at the hapless human stooges. This drives Catherine, Johnny, and Caroline screaming into the tropical "Green Mountain," a "forbidden zone" to the simians, where they stumble upon a turtle-neck-wearing human hermit named Godo (Tetsuya Ushio), who pulls their sorry asses out of more chases and scrapes. They're also aided on occasion by the sympathetic but homely ape-lass Pepe (Kazue Takita) and the UFO commander (Wataru Omae), but it's all for naught. They end up thanklessly having to choose between remaining stuck thousands of years in the future, where apes rule and turtle-necked men hide in the jungle, or chance going further into the future.

Time of the Apes remains the best-known of all the *Planet of the Apes* knock-offs. Most folks caught this via the *Mystery Science Theater 3000* broadcasts (they mocked it twice: in 1989, and later in 1991: "Don't dub with your mouth full!"), when much fun was had at the expense of the electrical-whip-wielding ape lead villain, Police Chief Gebar (Baku Hatakeyama), since his name is pronounced "Gay Bar." I would pay dearly to see subtitled copies of the original 26 episodes; I first saw it via the 1987 Sandy Frank FHE (Family Home Entertainment) video release *Time of the Apes*, which is still how I prefer to screen it. Frank was the fellow behind the 1980s releases and re-releases (with new cuts/dubs) of the *Gamera* films; *Time of the Apes* hit video amid those FHE releases.

The *Mystery Science Theater* crew mocks *Time of the Apes*, a true *Planet of the Apes* rip-off.

And then, there is *Spectreman*...

Prominent among the tsumani of *Ultraman*-inspired *tokusatsu* spinoffs was producer Souji Ushio's *Supekutoruman/Spectreman* (1971-1972, 63 episodes). The series was also known (for its first 21 episodes) as *Uchû Enjin Gori/Space Apeman Gori* and *Uchû Enjin Gori tai Supekutoruman/Space Apeman Gori Vs. Spectreman* (episodes #22-39), which places its albino alien ape villain, Doctor Gori (Kiyoshi Kobayashi or Takanobu Toya; sources vary), in the spotlight and arguably makes this classic crazy series into an honorable *Planet of the Apes* knockoff extraordinaire. After being exiled from the peaceful simian Planet E, the mad, ultra-evolved simian scientist Gori and his boneheaded gorilla assistant Karas (named "Lla" in the original Japanese series) were the staple villains of

Spectreman. Gori appeared in every episode, emphasizing his every word via emphatic, almost robotic hand signals.

There was a tragic dimension to the absurdist villainy of Doctor Gori. Having failed in his bid to rule his home planet, Gori chose Earth as his new conquest due to its natural beauty and his outrage at mankind's waste, abuse, and pollution of the planet. Eager to seize the planet before the human race pollutes it into a wasteland, Gori chooses to mobilize and utilize the man-made pollution *against* mankind, causing endless environmental calamity, mutating and/or resurrecting countless oversized monsters to attack Earth, and fighting Spectreman every step of the way. Spectreman is the super-cyborg agent of faraway benevolent Nebula 71 Star, whose rulers fear Gori will only render the Earth completely uninhabitable before he's done. In the end (*"Sayounara Spectreman / Goodbye Spectreman,"* episode #63), Doctor Gori is defeated and Spectreman tries to talk him into redirecting his intelligence to aid mankind and Earth as a force of good. Utterly appalled and despondent, Gori commits suicide, choosing to terminate his existence rather than "serve" those whom he wishes to destroy.

As associate producer of the English-language version of the series, Mel Welles (*"Gravis Mushnick"* in Roger Corman's immortal 1960 classic *Little Shop of Horrors*) handled the dubbing of the American release, which was syndicated to TV markets in 1978 and on videocassette in the early 1980s in glorious paint oversized box-art. Welles made it all even funnier and more entertaining than it already was.[29] *Spectreman* enjoyed wide distribution into all Asian and almost all international markets, making it arguably the most visible and popular of all *Planet of the Apes* riffs. In any language, it remains crazy, compellingly berserk, loopy must-see, must-experience entertainment!

There are, no doubt, many, many other precursors and successors to the *Planet of the Apes* source novel and 20th Century Fox film and television franchises, but these are the ones I have stumbled upon in my own viewings, readings, and research. To me, these curios and oddities only enrich my enjoyment of the "official" canon, often suggesting paths untaken, concepts abandoned, and possible future directions. As I've already noted, there's no

---

[29] Sam McKinlay interviewed Mel Welles about his dubbing and reediting *Spectreman* for the American market in the fanzine *G-Fan* #58 (September-October 2002); it's still available at http://www.g-fan.com/html/gfan_index/index_58.php and is highly recommended and quite funny reading!

telling when a previously undiscovered root buried beneath the *Apes* family tree may sprout its own unexpected growth – as in the case of Manly Wade Wellman's pulp science-fiction story and *The Rise of the Planet of the Apes* – making one all the more attentive to the future of the licensed canon and creative lineage.

After all, we hapless, flawed, frail, "monkey-see-monkey-do" copycat humans are still in charge...

...for now.[30]

---

[30] This essay was considerably revised and expanded from a series of blog posts that led to my invitation to be part of this book; see Myrant on 29 November, 2010 ("Prime-Apes! My Fave Planet of the Apes Knockoffs," archived at http://srbissette.com/going-ape/); 19 December, 2010 ("Hungary for More Apes?," archived at http://srbissette.com/the-hungarian-planet-of-the-apes/); 21 December, 2010 ("Hungarian Apes in English?," archived at http://srbissette.com/apes-artists-smallpox-ho-ho-ho-hate-movies/); 2 July, 2012 ("Going Ape! Redux," archived at http://srbissette.com/planet-of-the-apes-precursors-2/); and 9 January, 2013 ("Lost in Four-Color Space!," archived at http://srbissette.com/before-the-planet-of-the-apes-comicbook-precursors-rediscovered/). The author especially wishes to publicly thank Matthew Peters for his hard work on rescuing the Myrant blog and digital files, which allowed for 11th-hour completion of this essay and its inclusion in this volume.

Ape Shall Never Spoof Ape: Skits, Parodies, and Piss-Takes

by Matthew J. Elliott

Some things are harder to spoof than others. *Airplane!*, a parody of many po-faced aviation disaster movies, and one in particular, works like a charm. *National Lampoon's Loaded Weapon 1*, which attempts to lampoon an already pretty ridiculous series of action movies starring one of Hollywood's most prominent and, of late, unemployable, anti-Semites... not so much. What's the reason? It's mostly a question of how close to absurdity the source material is. James Bond and Sherlock Holmes, for example, seem at first glance to be pretty much spoof-proof. Both characters could so very easily be ridiculous in their original form, so any sketches you might come across on YouTube are more wearisome than entertaining. And so it is with *Planet of the Apes*. A planet where apes evolved from men? You blew it up, damn you all to hell! Soylent Green is people!

That's not to say that Bond, Holmes, or ape (who, I'm reliably informed, shall never kill ape) are completely impossible to mock satisfactorily. Take a look at the *Austin Powers* movies – hard to believe after we were all hurt so badly by *The Love Guru*, but, yeah, they're still pretty funny. Or *Without a Clue*, a hilarious 1988 film in which brilliant but underrated detective Doctor John Watson (Ben Kingsley) hires drunken actor Reginald Kincaid (Michael Caine) to portray the fictional Sherlock Holmes. The key to these films' success is that they're not simply focusing on Bond or Holmes, but on an entirely fresh format into which elements of send-up can be inserted. OK, maybe Austin Powers isn't particularly original to anyone who's seen the cult 1960s TV show *Adam Adamant Lives!*, but that doesn't amount to many people, apart from me and Mike Myers' parents.

Roddy McDowall appeared on a 1974 episode of *The Carol Burnett Show* in full ape regalia, seemingly oblivious to the effect it had on the show's host.

During the first five years of the long-running *The Carol Burnett Show*, Roddy McDowall made a number of appearances, and it's only to be expected that at least one of them should have been in full ape make-up. In a 1974 episode, around the time the short-lived *Planet of the Apes* TV series was in production, Burnett introduces "One of Hollywood's nicest gentlemen and one of Hollywood's most familiar faces," only to be astonished when McDowall steps out in tuxedo and ape-head. Much of the humor comes from Burnett's discomfort at her guest's utter obliviousness to the fact that he happens to look like Cornelius. Or maybe Caesar. Or possibly Galen. To her relief, McDowall asks to be permitted to enact a scene from his favorite movie – which turns out to be *Cleopatra*, making his choice of apparel stranger still. After a brief duet, the two break character in order to show some home movie footage of the actor getting into his simian make-up.

It's all good fun, and a worthy addition to the history of what I can only assume must be a beloved piece of American television. A small confession here: to the best of my knowledge, *The Carol Burnett Show* was never screened in my home country of England. If I ever think about the series at all, I tend to view it as the place where Lyle Waggoner went to get out of the rain. To tell the truth, I have a hard time distinguishing between Carol Burnett and Lily Tomlin. I know, I know, it makes no sense. But be honest, as an American reading this, didn't you ever experience any difficulty in telling Bruce Forsythe and Bob Monkhouse apart?

A further ape spoof appeared during the second season of *The Sonny & Cher Comedy Hour* – it was during an age when you weren't considered a pop-music sensation unless you had a variety show that later generations would be unable to tolerate a single second on.[1] Apparently, a support group for those who masturbated to the sight of Cher in the role of Nova still meets on every alternate Wednesday.

A year earlier, during the shooting of *Battle for the Planet of the Apes*, Paul Williams also appeared in ape make-up to perform a number on *The Tonight Show Starring Johnny Carson*. At least, I'm, like, 80 percent certain he was in make-up. If you know Paul Williams at all, you'll understand my doubt. Let this serve as a poignant reminder that real-life songwriters don't look like Hugh Grant in *Music and Lyrics*. If they're very lucky, they look like Paul Williams.

I'd love to believe that the 1973 variety show *A Couple of Dons*, starring Don Adams and Don Rickles, was in some way inspired by the long-running British comedy show *The Two Ronnies* (Ronnie Barker and Ronnie Corbett), but frankly, I doubt it.[2] The all-too brief *Apes* sketch is barely worth recounting, and you'll understand why when I tell you that the punchline is "You're sitting on my bananas!" Seems like a lot of work to go to for such a piddling result. By the way, the special also features Charo, best known for playing Gloria opposite

---

[1] See *Donny and Marie* for further examples. And see any decent grammar guide for an explanation of how to avoid dangling participles.

[2] A similar vehicle intended for Messrs Cavett and Van Dyke failed to get off the ground, for some inexplicable reason.

Darren McGavin as Jay in the beloved '70s sitcom *Modern Family*. Or maybe that was just a dream I had – damn, that Ambien is good stuff.

The pilot for *The Muppet Show*, *Sex and Violence*, aired on 19 March 1975.[3] The Muppets themselves were in a state of flux at this point in their history, gradually transforming from the frankly terrifying creatures that held up every early episode of *Saturday Night Live* to the cuddlier personae we're familiar with today. This, and the absence of even canned laughter, makes the sketch "Return to Beneath the Planet of the Pigs" a very chill affair. Introduced by a Michael Medved-like Muppet (and, let's be honest, Michael Medved is very much like a Muppet in real life, so it's not that much of a stretch), the sketch covers the early portion of the Chuck Heston movie, but with pigs instead of apes. And that's pretty much it. Apes=pigs, no jokes required or supplied. The Muppets are national treasures nowadays, so it'd be heresy to say that "Return to Beneath the Planet of the Pigs" is slightly less entertaining than *A Couple of Dons*, but I think you get the point I'm trying to make.

A part of me will always love Brazilians.[4] The 1976 film *O Trapalhao no Planalto dos Macacos* (*A Tramp on the Plateau of the Apes*), made by Brazil's premier comedy troupe The Tramps[5], does everything possible to test that fondness almost to the point of destruction. It certainly shows how very different the concept of humor can be from country to country.

The film's 84-minute running time – which is about 82 minutes longer than my attention span will allow for – contains more slapstick than even the Shemp-era stooges would consider dignified. The plot, such as it is, concerns a couple of amiable bunglers (who probably have names, but I somehow managed not to catch them) being pursued by an equally incompetent police officer who believes them to be jewel thieves. Actually, maybe they *are* jewel thieves, and that particularly subtle element of the screenplay passed me by.

After a fight involving dozens of crates of eggs, the Tramps and their would-be captor wind up taking a hot-air balloon to the Plateau of the Apes. It might surprise you to learn that the beings they encounter don't look any more

---

[3] Go ahead, Google "Muppets" and "sex and violence," I dare you. I've been dealing with calls from the FBI and the estate of Jim Henson all week.

[4] We're playing "make up your own punchline" all day at *Bright Lights, Ape City*. Why not get the whole family together and play along?

[5] The last time I had any dealings with a tramp, he asked me for some money for a cup of tea. Despite my waiting for more than half an hour, he never came back with the tea. To this day, I suspect he drank it himself.

convincing than the costumes you might procure in the average fancy dress shop, but, hey – comedy, am I right? The Tramps eventually get their balloon re-inflated and head back to Brazil, taking with them the Nova-equivalent they discovered among the mute humans, so the expedition wasn't a total loss. For them, I mean. Having seen the entirety of *O Trapalhao no Planalto dos Macacos*, I can say with complete honesty that I've lost all patience for anything Brazilian that doesn't involve beach volleyball, a sport for which I will cheerfully be up at the crack of dawn.

O Trapalhao no Planalto dos Macacos presented a Brazilian *Apes* spoof that has sapped the fun out of almost everything Brazilian.

By the '80s and '90s, *Planet of the Apes* and its sequels were no longer simply a gradually less-profitable 20th Century Fox franchise – they were the stuff of legend. Kids who'd grown up watching the movies on TV were now making movies and shows of their own. And now kids have grown up watching *those* movies and shows. "Sunrise, sunset..."

A 1999 Serta Mattress commercial suggested that, upon purchasing one of their fine products, you might find yourself spending time with a former sweetheart and Cornelius the chimpanzee. This remarkably bold assumption on the part of Serta fails to take into consideration the likelihood that, of the entire cast of *Planet of the Apes*, Maurice Evans undoubtedly seems the cuddliest.[6] Yes, if I was going to spoon with any of Samantha's relatives from *Bewitched*, he'd definitely be my first choice.[7] Another commercial for the same mattresses promises you multiple Mickey Rooneys – which, for someone who sat through his DVD commentary for the *Twilight Zone* episode "Last Night of a Jockey," sounds like the worst dream I could possibly imagine, and I regularly consume pickles and a pint of Ben & Jerry's before retiring to bed.

The Simpsons has, at the time of writing, been on the air for something close to 200 years, and no longer seems like the ground-breaking piece of animation it once was. But from almost the start, Matt Groening's jaundiced creations were obsessed with the *Apes* movies. Season two's "Bart's Girlfriend" sees the parents of Springfield capture their children in nets, all the while accompanied by a Jerry Goldsmith-style score, before forcing them to attend church. "Rosebud," in season five, concludes with a vision of the future in which apes are our masters (a scenario envisioned by Homer in "I Married Marge") and both Monty Burns and Waylon Smithers have been robotized. It's not until he's about to be become the world's first blue-collar astronaut, in "Deep Space Homer," that everyone's favorite Angry Dad finally realizes that our own world and "that dreaded planet of the apes" are one and the same. Homer's always had a problem differentiating between fiction and real life, which is probably why, in "The Seven Beer Snitch," he considers *The Towering Inferno* to be a "prophetic vision" instead of the culmination of the Paul Newman / Steve McQueen rivalry put on film with some stuff about O. J. Simpson and a burning building going on in the background.

The Simpsons' cartoon-within-a-cartoon, *Itchy and Scratchy* – a sort of *Tom and Jerry* for sociopaths – takes its own swipe at the *Apes* movies, and the first sequel in particular, in "Planet of the Aches," which sees Itchy (the mouse – I think) bricking up Scratchy (the cat – I think), who is freed three thousand years in the future by apparently benevolent but big-brained rodents, who more closely resemble the Talosians from the Jeffrey Hunter *Star Trek* pilot "The Cage" than they do the mutants of *Beneath the Planet of the Apes*. Bloodshed then ensues, as it always does in Itchy and Scratchy Land.

The Simpsons' fascination with *Planet of the Apes* pretty much reached its climax in the 1996 episode "A Fish Called Selma." Has-been actor Troy McClure

---

[6] No, wait, I mean Nova. Is it too late to change my answer?
[7] Don't go there.

(who you may remember from such films as *They Came to Burgle Carnegie Hall*, *The Leakiest Boat on the Ganges*, *Hitler Doesn't Live Here Anymore*, and *Look Who's Still Oinking*) lands the lead role in the stage production *Stop the Planet of the Apes, I Want to Get Off*, a particularly brilliant musical by Alf Clausen and Jack Barth, which not only incorporates a parody of one-hit wonder Falco's "Rock Me, Amadeus" (as "Help Me, Doctor Zaius"), but also features the lyric "I hate every ape I see, from chimpan-a to chimpan-z, No, you'll never make a monkey out of me." It's kind of astounding that some version of that line doesn't actually appear in the original movie. All of this, along with the incredible voice of the late Phil Hartman as Troy, makes *Stop the Planet of the Apes, I Want to Get Off* the parody *ne plus ultra*. After this milestone, the show pretty much left it to *Family Guy* to hammer movie references so far into the ground that they actually penetrated the Earth's molten core.

The Simpsons' not-quite-spinoff *The Critic* gives the briefest of nods to *Apes* with "Planet of the Dogs." Think "Return to Beneath the Planet of the Pigs," but with dogs instead of pigs instead of apes. Oh, and one of the best Charlton Heston impersonations you're likely to hear anywhere.

Of course, if you're going to be really serious about your lack of seriousness, you're going to want to get *the* guy in your parody. Which is why, when Charlton Heston hosted *Saturday Night Live* in 1993, his monologue addressed the topic of what was, by now, one of his most iconic roles.[8] In the cold opening, Chuck dozes off in his dressing-room while recording a log not unlike the one he dictates at the top of the movie. He reawakens in the year 3978, where the studio is now run by apes, who have rounded up the human cast and cut out Phil Hartman's brain. Chris Farley's brain, it seems, is intact, though had he been lobotomized, it might go some way toward explaining *Beverly Hills Ninja*.

After the titles, Heston is brought onstage by two apes, to the musical accompaniment of a band made up of apes, and to address an audience of apes. He fields a number of questions from his simian audience, and while you would expect most of them to be along the lines of "Seriously, it's a wig, right?" they're all about the fact that he's apparently some sort of mutant, which might have been funnier if the writers hadn't been afraid that someone watching might not get the set-up and written dialogue for Heston making it patently clear, before the sketch began, that he was not, repeat, *not* a mutant.

---

[8] Hint: Not Jason Colby.

It's every bit as awkward as if Bob Newhart had begun his classic Driving Instructor routine by saying "Before I get started, I need you to get this into your heads. Every time I mention the name 'Mrs Webb,' I want you to think 'bad driver,' OK? Got that? Mrs Webb: bad driver. Annnnd.... begin." Nor does Heston's heart really appear to be in it. Incidentally, it turns out Norm MacDonald makes a better ape than he does a Colonel Sanders. Who knew?[9]

The 1987 Mel Brooks movie *Spaceballs* serves, in part, as a *Star Wars* send-up, but also reminds us all how much funnier *Blazing Saddles* was, despite the fact that even that isn't as funny as we remember it being. The movie's equivalent of the Death Star is the Mega Maid – a gigantic female wielding a vacuum cleaner – yes, I know I'm supposed to be writing about *Planet of the Apes*, but bear with me; I'm going somewhere with this. At the story's climax, the head and one arm of the Mega Maid become detached from the craft's main body and eventually crash on the shoreline of an unnamed world, in such a position that they look almost exactly like a certain statue in the final scene of a well-regarded science-fiction film. Two snooty apes ride up on horseback and observe villainous Dark Helmet (Rick Moranis) and his henchmen emerging from Lady Liberty's nose. "Oh, shit – there goes the planet," one proclaims.

The destruction of Mega Maid at the end of *Spaceballs* recreated the famous ending to *Planet of the Apes.*

---

[9] How that man managed to find the time to make delicious fried chicken *and* manage Elvis, I'll never know.

Kevin Smith's 2001 effort *Jay and Silent Bob Strike Back* features a brief fantasy sequence set on a world where apes evolve from men, if one can imagine such a thing. The notable thing about this one is that it involves several actual apes, as well as the costumed variety. I'm afraid I'm not Kevin Smith's target audience, unfortunately; the last time I had the sense of humor of a 14-year-old was when I was 14. The good news is that *Jay and Silent Bob* is full of movie industry in-jokes, so if you Google them to find out what they mean, you'll feel like *you* work in the movies, too!

In case you were expecting to find mention of James Franco's 2005 short *The Ape*, in which a frustrated writer shares an apartment with, well, an ape, then you're out of luck. Except for the fact that I mentioned it just now. But I'm afraid it doesn't count, since it was made six years before he was cast in *Rise of the Planet of the Apes*. That's not to say that we won't all learn, in time, that Franco's entire career isn't some elaborate spoof. I fully expect that to be the case, in fact; it just seems like the punch-line's a long time coming.

Another parody of *Rise*, this one from the makers of *Mad*, the animated TV version of a celebrated magazine (hint: not *Vanity Fair*), might serve as a good example of the oft-used criticism "too soon." Unexpectedly, however, this opinion has nothing to do with taste or respect for the deceased, but because it was literally done too soon. Broadcast in 2011, it starts out as a straight spoof, with photos of Franco and the other movie actors pasted onto cartoon figures in a *South Park*-style. Once Caesar moves into the zoo, he finds himself rubbing shoulders with other famous talking primates, including *Dora the Explorer*'s pal Boots, and the Great Grape Ape.

To their mutual astonishment, their captor turns out not to be the albino kid from the *Harry Potter* movies, but rather Kevin James, whose movie *Zookeeper* was still a fresh horror in the minds of the American viewing public. The assistance James provides to the apes causes them to eventually conquer humanity, leading to the obligatory discovery of Lady Liberty on the shoreline. It's somewhat redundant, however, when one bears in mind that Kevin James, acting on the instructions of Adam Sandler, will undoubtedly be the cause of the downfall of our civilization, and probably sooner rather than later.

In that same episode, we get the "too soon" component of your evening's entertainment, with Caesar, Donkey Kong, and Mojo Jojo from *The Powerpuff Girls* competing in *The Celebrity Ape-Prentice*, hosted by a knuckle-dragging Donald Trump... oh, yeah, and he's also an ape. Obviously, the program-makers weren't aware of the trouble Bill Maher got into likening America's most repeatedly bankrupt businessman (morally, I mean) to an orangutan, but it's noteworthy that Trump makes entirely the wrong decision in appointing Caesar to the construction job for which Donkey Kong is obviously best-suited. But just think how much more material could be added to this scenario five years later:

> You know, when NASA sends its astronauts from thousands of years in the past, they're not sending their best – some of them have lobotomies, some of them played Longstreet, and some, I assume, are good people. We should build a wall around the Forbidden Zone and make the mutants pay for it. I saw thousands of them on rooftops cheering when the Doomsday Bomb went off. Not good.

It pretty much writes itself.

If I have one criticism, it's that both segments use the same gag about Caesar yelling "Noooo!" but I'm sure that's strictly a one-off. When have the people behind *Mad* ever run a joke into the ground? "Blechhh" to that accusation, I say.

Not all spoofs are intentional. If one were feeling generous, it might be said that the 1974 Japanese television series *Saru No Gundan* bears a striking but wholly coincidental resemblance to the *Planet of the Apes* saga. A less generous person might call it a rip-off.[10] The story of a female scientist and two kids who accidentally place themselves into suspended animation chambers (it could happen) in order to avoid what's described as an earthquake, but is depicted onscreen as a volcanic eruption, only really became interesting when the series fell into the hands of American TV producer Sandy Frank.

Frank not only gave the world *Name That Tune* and *The Bill Cosby Show*,[11] but also purchased and dubbed a great many Japanese productions, including the fondly remembered animated series *Battle of the Planets* (originally called *Science Ninja Team Gatchaman*) and *Saru No Gundan*, which was edited into feature form – using mostly the first and final episodes – and retitled *Time of the Apes*. In the dubbed version, the kids are rather improbably named Johnny and Caroline. Together with their designated adult Catherine, they awaken in a militant simian world run by the foppish ape Geba (pronounced "Gaybar"). Yes, Gaybar, an ape who is just missing a wide-brimmed hat with a feather in it to

---

[10] I am not, however, that less generous person. I am a hard-working writer with a mortgage to pay, a wife and child to support, and no time to become involved in drawn-out legal proceedings. That is why it is my opinion that *Saru No Gundan* is an entirely original work.

[11] A series of which I have only vague memories; I think I may have dozed off while watching it. Oddly, when I came to, my underpants were on backwards.

pass for Doctor Zaius, super-pimp. There's also an eyepatch-wearing ape who, inconceivably, sounds like Wallace Shawn. Where he fits into the plot, I'm not entirely sure. This is the problem with a production cut together from 26 separate episodes. Eventually, the three humans are sent back to their proper place in time. Thankfully, the eruption turned the suspended animation chambers into time machines. It could happen.

So far, so – well, I'm not sure you'd actually call it "good," but in truth, the ape masks are pretty credible, and show a decent amount of variety, but very little lip movement, although does that really matter when everyone's dubbed?[12] *Time of the Apes* only really became of interest to spoof enthusiasts in 1988, when a group of Minneapolis comedians devised a show called *Mystery Science Theater 3000 (MST3K for short)* for local UHF TV station KTMA. The format of the series – not dissimilar to the 1972 sci-fi film *Silent Running*, it must be said – involved a lone human trapped on a spaceship with no means of escape, and only two robots for company. As part of a fiendish experiment, these three are forced to watch some of the worst movies in the world, and manage to retain their sanity through the judicious use of wisecracks ("riffs" to the *cognoscenti*) at the expense of whatever cinematic punishment they happened to be undergoing at the time.

The films at this point in *MST3K*'s existence consisted of whatever KTMA happened to have in their vaults at the time. In April 1989, that included *Time of the Apes*. When the show moved to Comedy Central, the list of available material widened considerably. Nevertheless, they decided to take another crack at *Time of the Apes* during their third season.[13] Given that head writer and eventual host Michael J. Nelson described it as "the most punishing movie we had written to that point," one might well wonder why. There are surprisingly few references to *Planet of the Apes* in the riffing of *Time*. Most of the jokes are at the expense of Sandy Frank himself, who was allegedly less than amused by this treatment. There's also a joke about something called *Doctor Who*, whatever in hell that is.[14]

---

[12] No, really, I'm asking.

[13] The show's makers don't consider their year at KTMA to count as a season, but IMDb does. I'm going with the makers on this one.

[14] To discover whatever in hell that is, purchase a copy of *Lost in Time and Space: An Unofficial Guide to the Uncharted Journeys of Doctor Who* (http://www.hassleinbooks.com/pages/book_lostWho.php) by Matthew J Elliott, whoever in hell he is.

It wasn't until *MST3K* switched to the Sci-Fi Channel for its eighth season that the makers really went to town on their love of all things *Ape*. Mike Nelson[15] and his two robot buddies are hurled forward through time to the year 2525, when man is no longer still alive, and nor did woman survive. The world is now controlled by apes who, despite their academic qualifications, all have cute circus names like Bobo and Peanut. A few episodes down the line, the apes are visited by their neighbors, a group of cheerful human mutants, who happen to have brought their beloved thermonuclear bomb along with them. The celebrations don't last, and neither does the Earth, although Professor Bobo (Kevin Murphy) manages to escape in the company of Mike's tormentor, the evil Pearl Forrester, played by Mary Jo Pehl. Bobo becomes progressively more stupid as the years pass, until he eventually accepts a position at a zoo, imagining he's landed a top job – kind of like how Glenn Beck went from Fox News to TheBlaze.

Mystery Science Theater 3000 went off the air in 1999, but its legacy continues online in the form of RiffTrax.com, where, in addition to more badly bumbled B-movies, fans can download comedy commentaries for films they might already have in their DVD collections. A few new humorists were added to the roster, including one Englishman, Matthew J Elliott,[16] who in 2009 recorded a track for the original *Apes* movie. This Elliott person seems to be utterly convinced that he can do a perfect Charlton Heston impersonation, when in fact he can't hope to match the "Planet of the Dogs" guy, and actually sounds more like Skipper the penguin from *Madagascar*, a franchise that has referenced the saga several times, to the bemusement of its young viewers (the original *Madagascar* features Alex the lion exclaiming "Darn you all to heck!"). All things considered, if you can get past Elliott's accent, the *Planet of the Apes* riff isn't too bad, I guess, but it certainly can't compare with the track recorded for the more-than-passable reboot *Rise of the Planet of the Apes* by the original *MST3K* cast, one that includes an incredibly torturous and yet brilliant pun relating to co-star John Lithgow's past as a star of *Third Rock from the Sun*.

There are very few pornographic interpretations of *Planet of the Apes*, and for good reason: viewers have always been terrified of witnessing any human-on-monkey action. This has long been true of mainstream cinema, which is why a human-ape hybrid never made it beyond the test footage stage of *Beneath*

---

[15] Not the one from *Sea Hunt*.
[16] No, me neither.

the Planet of the Apes, and why audiences considered Max, Mon Amour less a searing comedy of social and sexual manners in 1980s Paris and more a film in which Charlotte Rampling fucks an actual chimp.

Viewers of porn are, of course, famously discerning, so it's entirely understandable that this would be uppermost in their thoughts as they type their preferences into a search engine with their good hand. Seduction Cinema's 2002 effort, Play-Mate of the Apes, concerns a trio of female asstronauts (yes, you read that right), who are revived from suspended animation only to find themselves unexpectedly horny. Actually, one of the asstronauts is called Misty Mundae, so maybe it's entirely expected.

During their love-making session, one of them accidentally pushes a button[17] which causes them to crash into a lake on the planet of – well, you get the idea by now. There are a few female humans with whom they – well, you get the idea by now, and several apes, including a British-accented General Laid (a subtle take-off of Tim Roth's General Thade – it's there if you look for it). Oh, and there's a pink chimpanzee called Doctor Kweera. I think that about covers it. The enthusiastic onanist will be thankful to learn that there's no bumping uglies between apes and asstronauts, although the blonde chimp, Doctor Cornholeous, does seem to view it as an option. Ultimately, though, the apes are just window-dressing, as are plot and dialogue – or, as they're known in the industry, the parts everyone fast-forwards past.

It's been brought to my attention[18] that the internet can be used for more than just porn. New Apes movies and new media have coincided, meaning that the good people at Screen Junkies have been afforded the opportunity to attempt to dispel the lingering taint of Tim Burton's 2001 remake.[19] Their "Honest Trailer" for Planet of the Apes describes the film as "the $100 million version of Mark Wahlberg Talks to Animals" – a reference to the famous and bizarre sketch featuring Andy Samberg's dead-on impersonation – and also notes the alleged actor's unmatched ability to stare at things.[20] The trailer also claims that the movie includes the creepiest kiss ever – proof only that its

---

[17] Not a euphemism.

[18] By the present Mrs. Elliott, who walked in on me unexpectedly. We've all been there, am I right, guys?

[19] Taint. Heh-heh.

[20] Including, in April 1988, the possibility of an attempted murder conviction following his brutal attack on two Vietnamese men. Seriously. Google it. Say hi to your mother for me.

makers obviously have not watched Julie Andrews and Walter Matthau in *Little Miss Marker*.

In David Stodolny's brilliantly animated alternative ending for *Dawn of the Planet of the Apes* – actually, I'm just going to stop right there for a moment, as there's something I really need to get off my chest. Doesn't it seem to you like the last two movies got their titles mixed up? Surely, the first film represents their dawn, and the second is the one where they rise? I can't be the only one thinking this. Anyway, the alternative ending has the human Malcolm totally misreading the signals of his one-on-one moment with Caesar. Turns out that while apes *do* swing, they don't necessarily swing *that way*.

The guys at CinemaSins have attempted to find every single flaw in the last three *Apes* movies because – good or bad – there's no such thing as a faultless motion picture.[21] Their typically quickfire "Things! Excitement! Horses! Physics!" just about sums up the Tim Burton effort. The CinemaSins for *Rise of the Planet of the Apes* draws our attention to the improbability of a) James Franco keeping a chimp in his home for three years without anyone noticing, and b) James Franco dating Freida Pinto for five years without at least buying her a damn ring. It's also a fair point that, with its final sequence depicting a disease spreading through the human population of the Earth, a better title might have been *Rise of the Twelve Monkeys*.[22] It's almost hard to believe there would be any sins to find in *Dawn*, but I did say there was no such thing as a faultless motion picture, didn't I?[23] It's a fair point, however, that the apes seem remarkably comfortable with rifles and other weapons. I guess the only deterrent for a bad human with a gun is a good ape with a gun.

Will there be more parodies to come? As long as *Planet of the Apes* remains a thing, almost certainly. And as more *Apes* variations are produced (and as there are more formats in which they might be lampooned), there's no reason to imagine an end to the tomfoolery. It's a madhouse – a madhouse, I tell ya.

---

[21] Although Wim Wenders' *Hammett* comes close. And the first *Timecop*.

[22] Or, just maybe, *Dawn of the Planet of the Apes*! I'm sorry, it just bugs me, that's all.

[23] Except for Bob Clark's *Murder by Decree*. Or maybe *The Karate Dog*, by the same director.

About the Contributors

Dave Ballard is a Londoner with an accent to rival that of Dick Van Dyke's Bert from *Mary Poppins*. He is a graphic artist by trade, but his "real job" is as a co-editor of British fanzine *Simian Scrolls: The U.K. Apezine*. Dave is the author of several *Planet of the Apes* fan-fiction tales, including the audio drama *Values* and the online comic strip *Beware the Beast*. He lives close to Wimbledon with the love of his life, Caroline, his son Chris and two jet-black rescue cats. Dave's lifelong love of *POTA* began at age seven, when his elder brother brought home some packs of the original movie trading cards. Dave recalls seeing them spread across the dining-room table and finding the images of semi-naked humans strung up like animals disturbing... but he kept going back to view them again and again. Another image that seared itself into his young brain was that of a dart-shaped spacecraft sitting in vivid blue waters, surrounded by vivid red rocks under an impossibly blue sky. In 2012, he realized his lifelong ambition to swim in the waters of Padre Bay, Lake Powell, right about where Taylor's spacecraft sank. In 2016, he plans to visit Malibu State Park and bring home a chunk of Ape City.

Corinna Bechko has been writing comics since her horror graphic novel *Heathentown* was published by Image/Shadowline in 2009. She has worked for numerous comics publishers, including Marvel, DC, BOOM! Studios, and Dark Horse, on titles that include co-creating *Invisible Republic* for Image Comics and co-writing *Planet of the Apes*, *Star Wars: Legacy Volume II*, and *Savage Hulk*, as well as writing *Aliens/Vampirella* and *Miss Fury* for Dynamite. She is a zoologist by training and has worked closely with nonverbal orangutans and chimpanzees.

Joseph F. Berenato obtained a B.A. in English and spent four years as the entertainment editor of *The Hammonton Gazette* before returning to his roots at his family's blueberry farm in Hammonton, NJ. In 2014, Joe conceived, edited, and contributed to *New Life and New Civilizations: Exploring Star Trek Comics*. In addition to *The Sacred Scrolls: Comics on the Planet of the Apes*, he co-edited two *Star Wars* volumes for Sequart with Rich Handley, with a third in the works. Joe wrote the introduction for IDW Publishing's *Star Trek: Gold Key Archives Volume 3* as well as retrospective essays for that company's *Star Trek #50* and their forthcoming *Gold Key 100-Page Spectacular.* He also contributed to ATB Publishing's *Star Trek* anthology *Outside In Boldly Goes*. He holds a Master of Arts in Writing from Rowan University, and is adjunct professor with Atlantic Cape Community College in Mays Landing, NJ, where he teaches freshman composition and serves as advisor for the school's newspaper, the *Atlantic Cape Review*. You can find Joe at jfberenato.wordpress.com and on Twitter at @JFBerenato.

Stephen R. Bissette, a pioneer graduate of the Joe Kubert School, teaches at the Center for Cartoon Studies. Renowned for his work on *Swamp Thing*, *Taboo* (launching *From Hell* and *Lost Girls*), *1963*, and *S.R. Bissette's Tyrant*, and for co-creating John Constantine, he created the world's second '24-Hour Comic' (invented by Scott McCloud for Bissette). Steve writes, illustrates, and co-authors many books, including illustrating *The Vermont Monster Guide* (2009), writing *Teen Angels & New Mutants* (2011/2016), fiction for *The New Dead* (2010), and *Mister October* (2013), etc. He regularly writes for *Monster!* and *Weng's Chop*, and is currently completing *S.R. Bissette's How to Make a Monster.*

Ian Brill is a writer and editor. At BOOM! Studios, he edited the highly regarded licensed comics *28 Days Later*, *Planet of the Apes*, *Big Trouble in Little China*, *Escape from New York*, and *CBGB*, which was nominated for a Harvey Award for Best Anthology. Ian has written for *Zombie Tales* at BOOM! Studios, as well as various *Simpsons* comics for Bongo Comics, and has published his own original horror-adventure comic *Dracula World Order*.

Pat Carbajal, a cover and interior illustrator for Hasslein Books, started as a political cartoonist for national newspapers in Argentina, then created realistic portraits for financial newspaper *Ambito Financiero*. He started producing art for the U.S. market in 2007, with covers for Adamant Entertainment's *Tales of*

Fu Man Chu and *Foe Factory: Modern*. In 2009, Pat painted the cover of Bluewater Productions' *Female Force: Sarah Palin*, followed by biographical comics on Barack Obama, George W. Bush, Bill Clinton, Ronald Reagan, Richard Nixon, Al Gore, Ted Kennedy, and Colin Powell, in the *Political Power* series. Rock stars were next, including Bob Dylan, Jim Morrison, and Jimi Hendrix, in *Rock and Roll Comics: The Sixties*, as well as Ozzy Osborne, AC/DC, and Guns n' Roses, in *Rock and Roll Comics: Rock Heroes*. The first graphic novel illustrated by Pat was Bluewater's *Allan Quatermain*, written by Clay and Susan Griffith. Together with the Griffiths, he created "The Raven" for Bluewater's horror comic, *Vincent Price Presents*, in which he debuted as a writer.

Joseph Dilworth, Jr., was born at a very young age in a small hospital the day before episode six of the *Doctor Who* serial "The War Games" aired. He's been hooked ever since. A lifelong writer, he served for six years as the founder, editor, and lead writer of Pop Culture Zoo. At PCZ, Joe wrote numerous reviews, conducted many highly acclaimed interviews, and offered fair and balanced opinions about numerous topics. He is currently a co-host of The Flickcast's weekly podcast and a staff editor at Hasslein Books, and he writes a regular column about TV for *Long Island Pulse Magazine*. He firmly believes that *Doctor Who* is the greatest show ever created, period, and *Cinema Paradiso* is his favorite film. Joe resides in the Pacific Northwest, where he spends time with his family, brews beer, writes, reads, and expresses his opinion to whoever will listen. Just be warned: He has little regard for the laws of space and time.

Matthew J Elliott is the author of *Lost in Time and Space: An Unofficial Guide to the Uncharted Journeys of Doctor Who* (2014), *Sherlock Holmes on the Air* (2012), *Sherlock Holmes in Pursuit* (2013), *The Immortals: An Unauthorized Guide to Sherlock and Elementary* (2013), and *The Throne Eternal* (2014). His articles, fiction, and reviews have appeared in the magazines *Scarlet Street*, *Total DVD*, *SHERLOCK*, and *Sherlock Holmes Mystery Magazine*, as well as the collections *The Game's Afoot*, *Curious Incidents 2*, *Gaslight Grimoire*, and *The Mammoth Book of Best British Crime 8*. Matthew has scripted more than 260 radio plays, including episodes of *Doctor Who*, *The Twilight Zone*, *The New Adventures of Mickey Spillane's Mike Hammer*, *Fangoria's Dreadtime Stories*, and award-winning adaptations of *The Hound of the Baskervilles* and *The War of the Worlds*. He is a writer and performer on RiffTrax.com, the online comedy experience from the creators of cult sci-fi TV series *Mystery Science Theater 3000* (MST3K to the initiated) and has also written a few comic books.

David Gerrold's work is famous around the world. His novels and stories have been translated into more than a dozen languages, and his TV scripts are estimated to have been seen by more than a billion viewers. Gerrold's prolific output includes stage shows, teleplays, film scripts, educational films, computer software, comic books, more than 50 novels and anthologies, and hundreds of articles, columns, and short stories. He has worked on a dozen different TV series, including *Star Trek*, *Land of the Lost*, *The Twilight Zone*, *Star Trek: The Next Generation*, *Babylon 5*, and *Sliders*, and is the author of *Star Trek*'s most popular episode, "The Trouble With Tribbles." Many of Gerrold's novels are classics of the science-fiction genre, including *The Man Who Folded Himself*, the ultimate time travel story, and *When HARLIE Was One*, considered one of the most thoughtful tales of artificial intelligence ever written. His stunning novels on ecological invasion, *A Matter for Men*, *A Day For Damnation*, *A Rage for Revenge*, and *A Season for Slaughter*, have all been best-sellers with a devoted fan following. His young adult series *The Dingilliad* traces the healing journey of a troubled family from Earth to a far-flung colony on another world. His *Star Wolf* series of novels, about the psychological nature of interstellar war, are in development as a television series. A ten-time Hugo and Nebula Award nominee, Gerrold is also a recipient of the Skylark Award for Excellence in Imaginative Fiction, the Bram Stoker Award for Superior Achievement in Horror, and the Forrest J. Ackerman Lifetime Achievement Award. In 1995, he shared the adventure of how he adopted his son in *The Martian Child*, a semi-autobiographical tale of a science-fiction writer who adopts a little boy, only to discover he might be a Martian. *The Martian Child* won the science-fiction triple crown – the Hugo, the Nebula, and the Locus Poll – and was the basis for the 2007 film *Martian Child*, starring John Cusack and Amanda Peet. Gerrold's greatest writing strengths are his readable prose, his easy wit, his facility with action, the accuracy of his science, and the passions of his characters. An accomplished lecturer and world traveler, he has made appearances all over the United States, England, Europe, Canada, Australia, and New Zealand. His easygoing manner and disarming humor have made him a perennial favorite with audiences. Gerrold will be a Guest of Honor at the 2015 World Science Fiction Convention. He is currently completing *A Method for Madness*, the fifth book in *The War Against the Chtorr* series.

Robert Greenberger is a writer, editor, and teacher. He began his career working at Starlog Press before joining DC Comics in 1984. He has since worked for Gist Communications, Marvel Comics, and *Weekly World News* in various editorial and management capacities. He is also a freelance writer with a wide range of genres and audiences, from media tie-in fiction to young-adult nonfiction. Robert's novelization of *Hellboy II: The Golden Army* won the 2009 Scribe Award. He cofounded the digital imprint Crazy 8 Press and continues to write. He reviews for ComicMix and has a twice-monthly column at Westfield Comics. Currently, he teaches English, creative writing, and journalism in Maryland, where he lives with his wife Deb and dog Ginger.

Edward Gross is a veteran entertainment journalist who has been on the editorial staff of a wide variety of magazines, among them *Geek, Movie Magic, Cinescape, Starlog, SFX, Life Story, CFQ*, and *Sci Fi Now*. He has authored or co-authored numerous nonfiction books, such as *Planet of the Apes Revisited, Rocky: The Complete Guide, Above & Below: A 25th Anniversary Beauty and the Beast Companion*, and summer 2016's two-volume *Fifty-Year Mission: The Complete Uncensored, Unauthorized Oral History of Star Trek*. Currently, Ed serves as the executive editor of *Empire* magazine's website, empireonline.com/us.

Rich Handley is the author or co-author of *Planet of the Apes: Tales from the Forbidden Zone, Watching Time: The Watchmen Chronology, Timeline of the Planet of the Apes, Lexicon of the Planet of the Apes, Back in Time: The Back to the Future Chronology*, and *A Matter of Time: The Back to the Future Lexicon*. Rich has co-edited five Sequart essay anthologies about *Planet of the Apes* and *Star Wars*, and has contributed essays to IDW's *Star Trek* and *Star Wars* comic-strip reprint hardcovers; Eaglemoss's *Star Trek: The Graphic Novel Collection*; BOOM! Studios' *Planet of the Apes Archive* series; Sequart's *New Life and New Civilizations: Exploring Star Trek Comics* and *The Cyberpunk Nexus: Exploring the Blade Runner Universe*; and ATB Publishing's *Outside In Boldly Goes*. In addition, he has contributed to many magazines and websites, including StarTrek.com, StarWars.com, HeroCollector.com, BlastoffComics.com, 13thDimension.com, *Star Trek Communicator, Star Trek Magazine, Movie Magic, Dungeon/Polyhedron, Cinefantastique, Cinescape*, and Lucasfilm's various *Star Wars* licensees. He is also the editor of Hasslein Books (hassleinbooks.com).

Zaki Hasan was born and raised in Chicago—with a decade-long detour in Saudi Arabia—before settling in the San Francisco Bay Area. He is a professor of communication and media studies, and a co-founder of Mr. Boy Productions, an L.A.-based independent film and video company. A lifelong *Planet of the Apes* fan, Zaki self-published an *Apes*-themed fanzine called *The Sacred Scrolls* in the mid-1990s, while he was still in high school. He is currently a co-host of the

MovieFilm Podcast and a co-author of Quirk Books' *Geek Wisdom: The Sacred Teachings of Nerd Culture*, and his work has been featured in *Q-News*, *Illume*, and *The Huffington Post*. In addition, he has appeared as a panelist on Al Jazeera America's *The Stream*, and is a contributing editor at Altmuslimah.com. Since 2004, his blog, *Zaki's Corner*, has been his one-stop forum for musings on news, media, politics, and pop culture.

Jim Johnson, a reviewer for Comic Book Resources, has been working mostly within the comic industry for nearly 20 years as a writer, columnist, critic, and reporter for any publisher or website that will have him. Before discovering comics as a teen, he discovered *Planet of the Apes*, then spent many of his formative years hiding under the covers fearing a worldwide simian takeover. Jim lives in suburban Detroit and spends a lot of time in his man cave, which becomes the Forbidden Zone while he is writing, or watching football, or binge-reading. He leaves more footprints than a gorilla army on social media, where he can be found swinging about at www.facebook.com/QuiGonJimm, www.twitter.com/QuiGonJimm, and www.linkedin.com/in/QuiGonJimm.

Neil Moxham is currently working in the Film Archive of the Irish Film Institute and is studying for a BA in Humanities in Dublin. Neil has been a science-fiction fan for many, many years, with a particular interest in the early origins of the genre. An administrator of the Sacred Scrolls *Planet of the Apes* wiki (planetoftheapes.wikia.com) since 2008, he also writes for a number of websites on subjects ranging from rock music to genealogy.

Steven Jacques Roby is a librarian in Ottawa, Canada. A longtime science-fiction fan, he maintained the first extensive *Star Trek* books website, the Complete Starfleet Library, and has contributed to the official *Star Trek* magazine and Robert Greenberger's *Star Trek: The Complete Unauthorized History*. Steve has been a *Planet of the Apes* fan since seeing *Conquest of the Planet of the Apes* in the early '70s. He occasionally blogs and reviews stuff at thefifteenth.wordpress.com. Steve didn't marry his wife, Laura Thomas, only because she had a cat named Phaser, but it was a good sign.

John Roche suspects that his first exposure to *Planet of the Apes* was actually a U.K. television advert for the launch of the Marvel *Apes* weekly in 1974, featuring Bob Larkin's glorious cover to the second issue of the U.S. magazine. John was, therefore, utterly powerless in Fate's decision to immediately render him a lifelong *Apes*, Marvel, and Larkin fan. John's imagination was ignited by the *Planet of the Apes* TV series in 1974, and by the wonderful bounty of trading cards, novels, and action figures that blazed the trail for other franchises. John lives in Wales, U.K., with his very own Welsh Dragon of a wife, Gill, and a ridiculous amount of *Apes* and Marvel memorabilia. He is a co-editor of *Simian Scrolls: The U.K. Apezine*. John still recalls a bitter, tragic day in 1977 when, having read the final page of "Future History Chronicles V" in *Mighty World of Marvel* #246, he realized it was "over." Little did that sad young boy dream that, one day, decades later, *Apes* would be topping the box office again, new *Apes* merchandise would be plentiful, and he would enjoy the privilege of being part of this wonderful book. "APES RULE!!!"

Paul Simpson is the author of more than two dozen books on topics ranging from James Bond and *Doctor Who* to prison breaks, air disasters, and *The Sound of Music*. He edited *DreamWatch* magazine for five years, as well as the official *Star Trek Magazine* for a similar period, and is currently the managing editor of the genre website *Sci-Fi Bulletin* (scifibulletin.com). Paul has also been a conductor, composer, and arranger for most of his life, and is currently conducting two choirs and regularly playing organ at various churches.

Dayton Ward is a *New York Times* bestselling author or co-author of numerous novels and short stories, including a whole bunch of stuff set in the *Star Trek* universe, and often works with friend and co-writer Kevin Dilmore. He has also written (or co-written) for *Star Trek Communicator, Star Trek Magazine, Syfy.com*, StarTrek.com, and *Tor.com*, and is a monthly contributor to the Novel Spaces writers blog (novelspaces.blogspot.com). Dayton is known to wax nostalgic about all manner of geek and sundry topics over on his own blog, *The Fog of Ward* (www.daytonward.com).

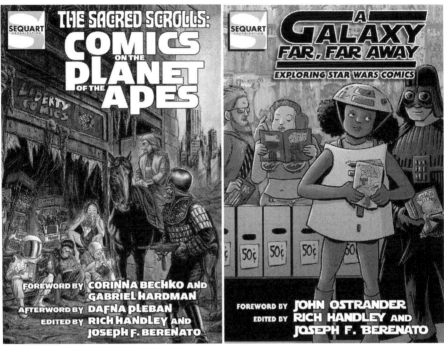

THE SACRED SCROLLS: COMICS ON THE PLANET OF THE APES

A GALAXY FAR, FAR AWAY: EXPLORING STAR WARS COMICS

A LONG TIME AGO: EXPLORING THE STAR WARS CINEMATIC UNIVERSE

NEW LIFE AND NEW CIVILIZATIONS: EXPLORING STAR TREK COMICS

GOTHAM CITY 14 MILES: 14 ESSAYS ON WHY THE 1960S BATMAN TV SERIES MATTERS

BOOKS ON GRANT MORRISON:

GRANT MORRISON: THE EARLY YEARS

OUR SENTENCE IS UP: SEEING GRANT MORRISON'S *THE INVISIBLES*

CURING THE POSTMODERN BLUES: READING GRANT MORRISON AND CHRIS WESTON'S *THE FILTH* IN THE 21ST CENTURY

THE ANATOMY OF ZUR-EN-ARRH: UNDERSTANDING GRANT MORRISON'S BATMAN

BOOKS ON WARREN ELLIS:

SHOT IN THE FACE: A SAVAGE JOURNEY TO THE HEART OF *TRANSMETROPOLITAN*

KEEPING THE WORLD STRANGE: A *PLANETARY* GUIDE

VOYAGE IN NOISE: WARREN ELLIS AND THE DEMISE OF WESTERN CIVILIZATION

WARREN ELLIS: THE CAPTURED GHOSTS INTERVIEWS

OTHER BOOKS:

THE BRITISH INVASION: ALAN MOORE, NEIL GAIMAN, GRANT MORRISON, AND THE INVENTION OF THE MODERN COMIC BOOK WRITER

THE WEIRDEST SCI-FI COMIC EVER MADE: UNDERSTANDING JACK KIRBY'S *2001: A SPACE ODYSSEY*

HUMANS AND PARAGONS: ESSAYS ON SUPER-HERO JUSTICE

CLASSICS ON INFINITE EARTHS: THE JUSTICE LEAGUE AND DC CROSSOVER CANON

THE DEVIL IS IN THE DETAILS: EXAMINING MATT MURDOCK AND DAREDEVIL

TEENAGERS FROM THE FUTURE: ESSAYS ON THE LEGION OF SUPER-HEROES

MINUTES TO MIDNIGHT: TWELVE ESSAYS ON *WATCHMEN*

AND THE UNIVERSE SO BIG: UNDERSTANDING *BATMAN: THE KILLING JOKE*

IMPROVING THE FOUNDATIONS: *BATMAN BEGINS* FROM COMICS TO SCREEN

WHEN MANGA CAME TO AMERICA: SUPER-HERO REVISIONISM IN *MAI, THE PSYCHIC GIRL*

THE FUTURE OF COMICS, THE FUTURE OF MEN: MATT FRACTION'S *CASANOVA*

THE BEST THERE IS AT WHAT HE DOES: EXAMINING CHRIS CLAREMONT'S X-MEN

MUTANT CINEMA: THE X-MEN TRILOGY FROM COMICS TO SCREEN

MOVING PANELS: TRANSLATING COMICS TO FILM

DOCUMENTARY FILMS:

DIAGRAM FOR DELINQUENTS

SHE MAKES COMICS

THE IMAGE REVOLUTION

NEIL GAIMAN: DREAM DANGEROUSLY

GRANT MORRISON: TALKING WITH GODS

WARREN ELLIS: CAPTURED GHOSTS

COMICS IN FOCUS: CHRIS CLAREMONT'S X-MEN

For more information and for exclusive content, visit Sequart.org.

Printed in Great Britain
by Amazon

35579819R00182